D1614717

Race, Gender, and Political Representation

Race, Gender, and Political Representation

Toward a More Intersectional Approach

BETH REINGOLD, KERRY L. HAYNIE,
AND KIRSTEN WIDNER

OXFORD
UNIVERSITY PRESS

OXFORD
UNIVERSITY PRESS

Oxford University Press is a department of the University of Oxford. It furthers
the University's objective of excellence in research, scholarship, and education
by publishing worldwide. Oxford is a registered trade mark of Oxford University
Press in the UK and certain other countries.

Published in the United States of America by Oxford University Press
198 Madison Avenue, New York, NY 10016, United States of America.

Library of Congress Cataloging-in-Publication Data
Names: Reingold, Beth, author. | Haynie, Kerry Lee, author. | Widner, Kirsten, author.
Title: Race, gender, and political representation : toward a more
intersectional approach / Beth Reingold, Kerry L. Haynie, Kirsten Widner.
Description: New York, NY : Oxford University Press, [2021] |
Includes bibliographical references and index.
Identifiers: LCCN 2020021968 (print) | LCCN 2020021969 (ebook) |
ISBN 9780197502174 (hardback) | ISBN 9780197502198 (epub)
Subjects: LCSH: Political participation—United States. |
Representative government and representation—United States. |
Minorities—Political activity—United States. |
Women—Political activity—United States. | Identity politics—United States. |
Intersectionality (Sociology)—United States.
Classification: LCC JK1764 .R445 2021 (print) | LCC JK1764 (ebook) |
DDC 328.73/073408—dc23
LC record available at https://lccn.loc.gov/2020021968
LC ebook record available at https://lccn.loc.gov/2020021969

3 5 7 9 8 6 4 2

Printed by Integrated Books International, United States of America

Contents

Acknowledgments

This book has been in the works for a long time and we are fortunate to have had the support of a great many students, colleagues, and family members along the way. We are immensely grateful for all of their work, feedback, encouragement, patience, and faith. We take this opportunity to acknowledge the tremendous value of their contributions by detailing them as best we can.

We have had the privilege of working with three individuals as co-authors of articles and papers that built the foundation upon which this book rests. Kathleen Bratton was instrumental in getting the project off the ground as we applied for funding, built our biographical database, and began presenting and publishing some of the project's earliest results. Kate also helped design and implement the original protocol for hand-coding bills and contributed a few crucial state-years of bill data. Adrienne Smith was among our first cohort of bill content coders and quickly assumed a great many other responsibilities as co-author of the *American Journal of Political Science* 2012 article that forms the basis of Chapter 6. Adrienne was involved in almost every aspect of that project and contributed at every stage; she deserves full credit for all aspects of data collection and analysis—scholarly feats of remarkable quality and quantity. Finally, Rachel Harmon performed with great skill the bulk of the extensive work necessary for developing, testing, and implementing the keyword dictionaries used to expand the database of bills sponsored. Her work made that expansion feasible and laid the groundwork for Chapters 3 and 4.

We wish to thank all the graduate students (and a couple of undergraduates) who painstakingly hand-coded the subject-matter, sponsors, committee referrals, and final dispositions of tens of thousands of bills, including Gloria Ayee, Moya Bailey, Jessica Carew, Alysia Davis, Jessica Harrell, Clara Boulianne Lagace, Alyssa Levy, Whitney Peoples, Brittany Perry, Candice Watts Smith, Stefanie Speanburg, Hyeseung Suh, Danica Tisdale, Ashlee Tran, Leigh Ann Webster, Elizabeth Wiener, and Claire Wofford. Special thanks go to those in the first cohort who helped us develop the coding protocols and convinced us through their conscientious efforts of the infeasibility of a suitably valid and reliable measure of bill ideology. Special thanks also go to Jessica Harrell, who coded far more bills than anyone else and did so with great accuracy, reliability, and efficiency.

Many other undergraduate and graduate students at Emory and Duke contributed significantly to this project. Margaret Beck-Coon, Valerie Delp, Vlad Golgotiu, Arielle Gordon, Nadya Hajj, Jesse Hamner, Barry Hashimoto, Alden Mahler, Susan McMillan, Paula Mukherjee, Baekkwan Park, Margit Peters, Andrew Pierce, Paige Schneider, Katy Stiger, and Keerthika Subramanian helped build our biographical database, identifying and recording the racial/ethnic identities of an even larger sample of state legislators than is included here. Nancy Arrington, Emily Calvert, Ly Ngoc Le, and Yaesul Park assisted with our first attempts to analyze race-gender patterns of bill sponsorship. Rebecca Berge and Carleen Graham assisted with early versions of Chapter 2. Along with Rachel Harmon, Amanda Anderson, Corinne Collard, John Day, Dian Dian, Hannah Fleischmann, Taryn Jordan, Marcella Morris, Timothy Perkins, Kelsey Sattler, Becky Shepard, Devon Thurman, and Maggie Wells enabled us to expand the bill database by testing and implementing the keyword search terms; screening the results; and recording sponsors and committee referrals for the thousands of bills ultimately included. Rachel Harmon, Taryn Jordan, Ryan Kendall, Jamie Svatora, and Elizabeth Wiener assisted with other data-gathering efforts key to our final analyses of bill sponsorship. Amanda Anderson, Dian Dian, and Devon Thurmon provided additional bibliographic assistance; and Becky Shepard searched high and low for relevant media coverage of key figures (especially women of color) and events in the politics of race, gender, and representation in the United States.

Much of this research assistance was made possible by generous funding from the National Science Foundation (SES-0618368, Kathleen A. Bratton, Kerry L. Haynie, and Beth Reingold, Principal Investigators); the Provost's Strategic Fund, the University Research Committee, and the Departments of Political Science and Women's, Gender, and Sexuality Studies at Emory University; and the Arts and Sciences Research Grant Program and the Department of Political Science at Duke University. We also received valuable support from the Hoover Institution's National Fellows Program.

Our thinking, writing, and methods have benefited greatly from the generous feedback and advice we received from our colleagues. We thank our department colleagues for all of their support, including their participation in various brown-bag presentations, workshops, and research seminars. Scott de Marchi, Adam Glynn, Drew Linzer, Greg Martin, Paula McClain,

Michael Munger, and David Siegel have been especially generous with their time and expertise. A number of conference panel discussants have lent us their support and insight, including Jessica Lavariega Monforti, Neil Malhotra, Holona LeAnne Ochs, Tracy Osborn, and Evelyn Simien. We are grateful to Maria Escobar-Lemmon and Michelle Taylor-Robinson for organizing and inviting us to participate in their conference on Identity, Gender and Representation and for giving us the opportunity to circulate and publish some of our earliest work on bill sponsorship.

Kirsten acknowledges the ladies of Goals, including Nancy Arrington, Stephanie Dean Kearce, Bethany Morrison, Anna Gunderson, Laura Huber, Dani Villa, Maggie MacDonald, Lizzy Wiener, and Devon Thurman. They have helped keep me focused through goal-setting and accountability, given me new ways to think about my work through their great questions and feedback, and helped keep me sane with their humor and support.

Our deepest appreciation goes to our families. From Kirsten to my husband Kevin Brown for supporting me in all my endeavors, academic and otherwise; and to my son Alex Locke, who fills me with love and purpose. From Kerry to Mina for her constant support and for being a valuable sounding board; and to Olivia for understanding the time demands that come with an academic career. From Beth to Tom for being my strength and salvation; and to Ellie and Halia for being (becoming) the colorful women who inspire me most.

1

Introduction

With record numbers of women running for and winning public office, the 2018 US midterm elections were dubbed by many as the second "Year of the Woman." Not since the first Year of the Woman in 1992 have we seen comparable jumps in women's candidacies and officeholding, across the nation and within most states (Dittmar 2019). There are other remarkable parallels between the 1992 and 2018 elections: the vast majority of these women ran as Democrats, spurred in part by outrage against male-dominated politics and its unwillingness to grapple with women's issues such as sexual harassment and violence against women.[1] Equally remarkable but less often acknowledged was the role of women of color. As in the first Year of the Woman, women of color were the driving force behind these 2018 gains—as both candidates and voters.[2]

Indeed, women of color candidates have for decades been the driving force behind the electoral gains of Democratic women, African Americans, Latinxs, and Asian Americans alike (Carroll and Sanbonmatsu 2013; Hardy-Fanta et al. 2016; Reingold 2014; Shah, Scott, and Juenke 2019; Smooth 2006b). In the years in between 1992 and 2018, women of color gained public office at faster rates than either White women or men of color. As a result, women are and have been a larger proportion of minority officeholders than of White officeholders. At the same time, however, women of color remain the most under-represented in comparison to their proportion of the overall population (Hardy-Fanta et al. 2016, 61–63). Even in the aftermath of the record-breaking 2018 elections, women of color, who made up 20.1% of the total US population, claimed only 8.8% of seats in Congress and 7.4% of seats

---

[1] Li Zhou, "The Striking Parallels between 1992's 'Year of the Woman' and 2018, Explained by a Historian," *Vox* (2 November 2018): https://www.vox.com/2018/11/2/17983746/year-of-the-woman-1992. Alex Seitz-Wald, "Meet the Women Candidates Taking #MeToo to the Ballot Box," *NBC News* (24 July 2018): https://www.nbcnews.com/politics/elections/meet-women-candidates-taking-metoo-ballot-box-n894106

[2] Aimee Allison, "Women of Color Are Making Election History in 2018," *Teen Vogue* (24 May 2018): https://www.teenvogue.com/story/women-of-color-making-election-history-2018/. Taeku Lee and EunSook Lee, "Why Trump Fears Women of Color: The Right Recognized Their Political Power. The Left Takes Them for Granted," *New York Times* (13 August 2019).

Race, Gender, and Political Representation. Beth Reingold, Kerry L. Haynie, and Kirsten Widner, Oxford University Press (2021). © Oxford University Press. DOI: 10.1093/oso/9780197502174.001.0001.

in state legislatures (Dittmar 2019, 7 and 19).[3] Shah, Scott, and Juenke (2019, 438–39) call this "the paradox of women of color candidates—they are seen as making the most progress of gendered and racial minorities, but their numbers are still very small." (See also, Hardy-Fanta et al. 2016.)

In conceding her bid for the US Senate in Maryland's 2016 Democratic primary, Representative Donna Edwards took the Democratic Party to task for its lack of "diversity and inclusion."[4] The party, she warned, "will not survive the 21st century with the votes of people of color without the real leadership of people of color, especially black women, at every level. This," she emphasized, "is about decision-making and agenda-setting, not about filling out the stage as a demonstration of inclusion."[5] To "call the question on diversity and inclusion" and explain what is at stake, Edwards then asked:

> Can we pass equal pay laws and give women control of their own health-care decisions when women represent just 20 percent of Congress? When just 8 percent of Congress is Hispanic, is it no wonder that even the most "balanced" and "fair" immigration bills include stratospheric increases in border security and funding for deportations? With only 9 African-American senators in the nearly 240-year history of our country, and just one black woman (Sen. Carol Moseley Braun over two decades ago), will we tackle successfully the issues of education equity, criminal justice reform, and the chronic lack of investment in communities of color? Even if the answer is "yes," why can't we as women, as people of color, as middle-class people, speak for ourselves?

[3] Women of color as a percentage of the total population is based on the most recent (July 2018) estimates from the US Census Bureau, "Annual Estimates of the Resident Population by Sex, Race, and Hispanic Origin for the United States, States, and Counties: April 1, 2010 to July 1, 2018," Table PEPSR6H: https://factfinder.census.gov/faces/nav/jsf/pages/guided_search.xhtml (last accessed 3 February 2020). For these calculations, "women of color" are all women not noted by the Census Bureau as "white alone, non-Hispanic."

[4] Donna Edwards, "The Problem Keeping America from Being the Democracy It Should Be," *Cosmopolitan* (24 May 2016): https://www.cosmopolitan.com/politics/news/a58888/donna-edwards-diversity/.

[5] Ayanna Pressley made a similar argument in her 2018 campaign to become the first Black woman in the Massachusetts congressional delegation: "I'm not going to pretend that representation doesn't matter. But it doesn't matter about how inclusive and representative we are. It matters because it informs the issues that are spotlighted and emphasized, and it leads to more innovative and enduring solutions. That's why it matters." P. R. Lockhart, "In 2018, Black Women like Ayanna Pressley Are Fighting for Political Power—and Winning," *Vox* (5 September 2018): https://www.vox.com/policy-and-politics/2018/9/5/17823582/ayanna-pressley-massachusetts-black-women-voters-2018-midterm-elections.

Aimee Allison, founder of She the People and a leading force in recruiting and electing women of color candidates, promises that their political leadership "could transform the political landscape for generations to come."[6] But what that transformation looks like is often unarticulated. What do women of color say and do as representatives? For whom do they speak and act?

Like Representative Edwards, political scientists know how women, Latinxs, and African Americans in public office can make a difference for women and communities of color, thanks to decades of rigorous, corroborating research. And like Edwards and Aimee Allison, we remain unclear as to what the leadership of women of color might offer. We have devoted much less attention to the behavior and impact of women of color elected to public office than we have to differences based on race *or* gender; and what little research there is provides seemingly contradictory insights. Black women sponsor fewer women's interest bills than do White women and fewer Black interest bills than do Black men (Bratton and Haynie 1999); but they are more likely to sponsor at least one of each type of group interest bill (Bratton, Haynie, and Reingold 2006). Women of color, men of color, and White (Democratic) women share many of the same policy priorities (Barrett 1995; Fraga et al. 2008; Hardy-Fanta et al. 2016, 324–25); but women of color are more united in their progressive policymaking commitments (Barrett 1995; Orey et al. 2006). Black women legislators are united on some issues, acting forcefully on behalf of women of color; but they are by no means a monolithic group. On other issues, they are divided by generational, religious, and class differences, among others (Brown 2014b). Women of color are uniquely attentive to the needs and interests of those who, like them, are multiply disadvantaged (Brown and Gershon 2016; Hawkesworth 2003) and they are uniquely positioned to build the diverse coalitions necessary for effecting policy change on their behalf (Bejarano 2013; Fraga et al. 2008). Yet they are often marginalized, silenced, and disempowered as women of color working within White-male dominated legislative institutions (Hawkesworth 2003; Smooth 2008).

Between the first and second Year of the Woman, politicians and political scientists (among other political actors and observers) have had a lot to say about the representation of women and minorities in US politics, but have paid less attention to the election and impact of women of color. Too often,

---

[6] Aimee Allison, "Women of Color Are Making Election History in 2018," *Teen Vogue* (24 May 2018): https://www.teenvogue.com/story/women-of-color-making-election-history-2018.

the questions, puzzles, contradictions, and paradoxes surrounding women of color as representatives go unrecognized and unaddressed. The problem, we argue, is not that there are simply too few women of color to study. The deeper problem is in how we think about gender, race, and representation.[7] In the predominant "single-axis" studies of representation that group all women together, or all African Americans, or all Latinxs, women of color are relatively invisible (Crenshaw 1989; Hull, Bell Scott, and Smith 1982). Instead of investigating what conditions are ripe for "women's" representation or for "minority" representation, rather than ponder whether "women" and "minorities" in office are more likely to advocate on behalf of other women and minorities, respectively, we must ask: *How do gender and race interact to affect the election, behavior, and impact of all individuals—raced women and gendered minorities alike?* This is the key question that motivates this study of *Race, Gender, and Political Representation.* Only by addressing this question can we learn how women of color fit into the picture—*and* also get a more accurate portrait of how men of color, White women, and White men are situated within it. Indeed, we may get a different picture altogether.

Race, Gender, and Political Representation

Over the past three decades, political science research has uncovered substantial evidence that gender and race influence political representation in the United States. Historically, a variety of institutionalized gender and racial biases have worked not only to limit the number of women and minorities running for office, but also to channel and confine their opportunities to certain "women-friendly" or majority-minority jurisdictions (Arceneaux 2001; Darcy, Welch, and Clark 1994; Davidson and Grofman 1994; Lublin 1997; Lublin et al. 2009; Palmer and Simon 2012; Preuhs and Juenke 2011; Sanbonmatsu 2006). Once in public office, women are generally more likely than men to focus their representational activity on interests or issues particularly relevant to women; similarly, African American representatives are more likely to focus on interests relevant to African Americans and Latinx legislators are more likely to do the same on behalf of Latinx interests

---

[7] Here and throughout the book, we use the terminology of race to include processes of racialization that structure and constrain the lives of certain "ethnic" groups in the US, particularly Latinxs, as well as groups like African Americans who are widely recognized and officially designated as a "racial" minority (Cornell and Hartmann 2004; Omi and Winant 1994).

(Bratton and Haynie 1999; Canon 1999; Casellas 2011; Griffin and Newman 2008; Grose 2011; Haynie 2001; Minta 2011; Osborn 2012; Reingold 2000; Rouse 2013; Swers 2002, 2013; Thomas 1994; Wilson 2017). Yet little research has examined whether and how race *and* gender together simultaneously influence who our elected officials are ("descriptive representation") and what they do in office ("substantive representation") (Pitkin 1967).

When studying race, gender, and representation, political scientists have often assumed that there are no gender differences among minority representatives, and no racial differences among female representatives. More often than not, attention has been paid only to what factors influence the descriptive and substantive representation of women *or* to what factors influence the descriptive and substantive representation of African Americans and/or Latinxs. Such one-at-a-time, "single-axis" approaches (Crenshaw 1989) to the study of representation are clearly overly simplistic; as Hawkesworth (2003) and others implore, we need to think about and study representation as not only raced, and not only gendered, but "raced-gendered" (Brown 2014b; Fraga et al. 2008; Hardy-Fanta et al. 2016; Reingold 2008; Smooth 2006b, 2011).

Race, Gender, and Political Representation takes up that call and examines *how* and to what extent political representation is simultaneously gendered and raced—in the context of late 20th- and early 21st-century US state legislatures. State legislatures have long been a natural focus for the study of race, gender, and representation, given that they offer large numbers of diverse lawmakers working within and across many comparable governing institutions and political contexts. We take full advantage of these empirical resources to examine the race-gender complexities of descriptive and substantive representation across a large number and variety of individual lawmakers and state settings.

When possible, we examine representational outcomes across 49 states (all but Nebraska with its unicameral and nonpartisan legislature). To see how race-gender identity shapes representational activity, we focus on a sample of 15 state houses purposefully chosen to provide maximum variation in legislator identity, party control, ideology, and region.[8] This sample includes many of the most racially diverse state houses as well as some of the most

---

[8] The 15 states are Arizona, California, Florida, Maryland, Minnesota, Mississippi, North Dakota, New Jersey, New Mexico, Nevada, Ohio, South Carolina, Tennessee, Texas, and Utah. See Appendix Table A.1 for detailed information on the gender and racial/ethnic composition of these state houses, as well as the distribution of party control and ideology.

homogeneous ones; it also spans the full range of gender diversity. We are thus able to maximize the number of female and/or minority legislators we study without restricting our analysis to only the most diverse institutions. A few of the most diverse state houses (California, New Jersey, and Texas) prove particularly useful for our in-depth exploration into the race-gender possibilities within legislators' policy proposals. For it is within and across these three state houses that we find Black, Latinx, and White women and men who are similarly situated in majority-minority districts and thus more likely than others to engage in policy leadership at the intersections of race and gender.

The time frame of our analysis—focusing on the years 1997 and 2005 in particular—is also purposefully chosen. Coming in the aftermath of the first Year of the Woman but before the Great Recession, this period provides the best possible historical precedent for understanding and predicting the impact of the second Year of the Woman. We are able to examine the dynamics of identity and political representation following an unprecedented increase in race-gender diversity among elected officials and during a period of relatively stable economic growth—conditions similar to those immediately following the 2018 elections. Coming before and after the decennial redistricting process, which alters district boundaries and increases officeholding turnover, 1997 and 2005 also enable us to further maximize the number and variety of individual legislators and the constituencies that elect them. Finally, the 1990s and 2000s have been the focal point of a great deal of foundational women-and-politics and race-and-ethnic politics research on issues of representation in the United States. Our chosen time frame then allows us to re-visit and re-evaluate the dominant single-axis scholarship more directly and effectively than if we were to look only at more recent years. For all these reasons, 1997 and 2005 are particularly opportune for studying the intersections of race, gender, and representation in US state legislatures.

Following the 1992 Year of the Woman boost, which also corresponded with significant increases in the number of majority-minority districts, levels of descriptive representation for women and people of color in state legislatures remained fairly stable—and low, compared to the overall population. From 1997 to 2005, the proportion of state legislative seats held by women increased by only a percentage point: from 21.6% to 22.7%.[9]

---

[9] Information obtained from the Center for American Women and Politics (CAWP), Eagleton Institute of Politics, Rutgers University: https://cawp.rutgers.edu/sites/default/files/resources/stleg2005.pdf.

Similarly, the share of state legislative seats held by African Americans hovered around 8% (7.6% in 1997 to 8.3% 2005).[10] The numbers of Latinxs elected to state legislatures saw a modest (33%) increase from 2.4% in 1997 to 3.1% in 2005.[11] Asian Americans and Native Americans each held no more than 1% of state legislative seats during these years.[12] Women of color (Black, Latina, Asian American, and Native American) increased their share of state legislative seats (by 31%), going from 3.4% in 1997 to 4.5% in 2005.[13] By all accounts, most of the women and the vast majority of people of color elected to state legislatures during this time were Democrats. In the 2005 state houses we examine in Chapter 2, most (59%) of the White men were Republicans, but only 44% of White women, 35% of Asian American women, 34% of Native American men, 25% of Native American women, 17% of Latinos, 13% of Latinas, 9% of Asian American men, and 1% of Black men and women served as Republicans.[14] Given these highly skewed distributions, our analysis pays close attention to partisan differences within and between race-gender groups of legislators, being careful not to over-simplify or over-generalize about race, gender, and representation across party lines.

In this book, our attention to "race" is centered on the descriptive and substantive representation of African American and Latinx women and men who comprised the overwhelming majority of legislators of color during this time period (recognizing that White legislators are raced as well). In part, this is because our reliance on quantitative analysis does not accommodate comparative analysis of the very small numbers of Asian American or Native American women and men—most of whom are clustered in a very small number of states. We are also constrained by the lack of research available on the political representation of racial/ethnic groups other than Blacks and Latinxs, especially during the 1990s (Hardy-Fanta et al. 2016). For example,

[10] Figures provided to the authors by the Joint Center for Political and Economic Studies, annual Rosters of Black Elected Officials.

[11] Information for 1997 obtained from the annual directory of the National Association of Latino Elected and Appointed Officials (NALEO); data for 2005 provided by the National Latino Legislative Database Project (Ramirez 2006).

[12] Information on Asian Americans and Native Americans in state legislatures is relatively sparse, especially in the 1990s. Our figures for Asian Americans are based on 1996 and 2005–6 editions of the *National Asian Pacific American Political Almanac* (published by UCLA's Asian American Studies Center) and 1999 and 2005 lists of Native American state legislators provided by the National Council of State Legislatures' (NCSL's) State-Tribal Institute (personal communication, April 27, 2009).

[13] Information obtained from CAWP Fact Sheet archive (https://cawp.rutgers.edu/fact-sheet-archive-women-state-legislatures) and personal communications.

[14] Republican state representatives of color were (in 2005) spread across 21 different states, with large clusters of Latinos in Florida and Native American men in Oklahoma.

there is little research with which we can engage questions about how scholars have defined and measured the substantive representation of Asian American or Native American group interests. Even given these limitations, ours is one of a growing number of studies of race and representation that include both African Americans and Latinxs (e.g., Griffin and Newman 2008; Lublin 1997; Minta 2011), and one of few studies of race and gender to do so (e.g., Hardy-Fanta et al. 2016; Hawkesworth 2003; Scola 2014).

We include Latinxs under the rubric of "race" recognizing that in the US context there is a great deal of ambiguity and debate about whether they constitute a racial or ethnic group (or both). On the one hand, Latinx as a pan-ethnic identity is closely tied to the political methodology of the US Census, which has long defined and measured "Hispanic origin" independently of how it defines and measures race. Nonetheless, we also acknowledge that Latinx and Hispanic are long-standing racialized categories distinct from how we often think about ethnic groups, especially White or European ethnic groups. As a racialized category, Latinx has to a large extent been imposed, assigned, and enforced externally by those more powerful in order to draw rigid, hierarchical boundaries and distinctions between themselves and others (Cornell and Hartmann 2004; Omi and Winant 1994; Rodriguez 2000). As Masuoka (2008) points out, Latinxs can and do identify as an ethnic group (pan-ethnic or national-origin specific) and a racial group; yet it is a politicized racial identity or group consciousness that has the most powerful influence on Latinx political behavior. With all this mind, we alternate between using the terminology of "race" and "race/ethnicity" to include and refer to Latinxs, as well as African Americans and Whites.[15]

From one chapter to the next, we trace multiple processes of representation— from the electoral outcomes that determine levels of descriptive representation, to the legislative activities that shape opportunities for substantive representation, to the policy outcomes that solidify the links between descriptive and substantive representation. We focus most intently and extensively on bill sponsorship as a form of policy leadership especially important for the substantive representation of marginalized groups and their interests. By introducing and sponsoring legislative proposals, lawmakers set the political agenda, identifying and defining important policy problems and how to address them. Bill sponsorship is arguably the most pro-active form of

---

[15] These are also the reasons we often classify legislators' racial/ethnic identities as mutually exclusive. Unless otherwise noted, the legislators we identify as African American/Black or White are not also publicly identified as Latinx/Hispanic.

representational advocacy available to legislators. It is also an activity that is available to *all* legislators, irrespective of their place within the demographics and power structure of the institution. Thus, investigating who sponsors what can tell us a lot about who represents whom, especially in terms of race and gender. Indeed, this is where existing research has found the strongest and most consistent links between descriptive and substantive representation. Most important, though, the sheer number and variety of policy proposals available to legislators and researchers alike—across many diverse legislative institutions—provide some of the best opportunities for contemplating and appreciating the multiplicity and complexity of race-gender representation. Bill sponsorship allows legislators to address a myriad of group interests and issues in a variety of ways, allowing us to see similarities among differences and diversity within commonality.

Toward a More Intersectional Approach

Our interest in examining the multiplicity and complexity of race-gender representation is grounded in and sustained by our interest in *intersectionality*. As defined by Hancock and applied here, intersectionality "refers to *both* a normative theoretical argument *and* an approach to conducting empirical research that emphasizes the interaction of categories of difference (including but not limited to race, gender, class, and sexual orientation)" (2007, 63–64). It is not simply a call out to multiple identities or a call for diversity and inclusion (Bowleg 2008; Hancock 2007; Jordan-Zachery 2007; May 2015; Nash 2019). It rejects any assumption that we can fully understand race, gender, and representation by simply adding what (we think) we know about one category (e.g., women) to what (we think) we know about another (e.g., Latinxs or African Americans). Rooted in over a century of Black feminist thought and other efforts by women of color to theorize and resist the many ways in which their lives are rendered both intolerable and unintelligible, intersectionality is about power: how multiple and interlocking "structures of domination" work to simultaneously privilege and oppress (Nash 2019, 6; Baca Zinn and Zambrana 2019; Collins 2000; Guy-Sheftall 1995; Hancock 2016; Moraga and Anzaldúa 1983; Simien 2006).[16] In studying race-gender

---

[16] Additional, foundational works we have found particularly illuminating include Anzaldúa 1987; Baca Zinn and Dill 1996; Cohen 1999; Crenshaw 1989, 1991; Glenn 1992; Higginbotham 1992; hooks 1981, 2000; King 1988; Mohanty 1991.

representation in American politics, intersectionality compels us to recognize and investigate how race and gender co-exist as intersecting and interdependent forces that shape people's lives, communities, and political interests as well as our representational institutions, processes, and outcomes—not simply in terms of difference but often in terms of inequality and injustice (Crenshaw 1989; Hancock 2007; McCall 2005; Simien 2007; Smooth 2011).

In all these ways, intersectionality raises questions about how we use "categories of difference" (e.g., race and gender, women and minorities) to think about, organize, and make sense of the world (Hancock 2007). Thus, rather than thinking about intersectionality as a phenomenon (e.g., race-gender identities) or even a particular explanatory theory (of, say, race-gender representation), we engage intersectionality as a critical research paradigm (Else-Quest and Hyde 2016a; Hancock 2007, 2013): an "analytic sensibility . . . a way of thinking about the problem of sameness and difference and its relation to power" (Cho, Crenshaw, and McCall 2013, 795); an "approach to understanding the world" (Hancock 2016, 32); an "invitation to think beyond (or against the grain of) familiar boundaries or categories, to perceive sites of omission, and to consider their meanings and implications" (May 2015, 4).

At its core, intersectionality is a critique of dominant single-axis frameworks and additive models that treat such things as gender and race as mutually exclusive, independent social forces and categories of analysis. Such frameworks are faulted for being both limiting and misleading. In failing to recognize, for example, how race is gendered and gender is racialized (Simien 2007, 266), they ignore important differences and hierarchies within categories like "women" or "Blacks." This in turn obscures the positions and perspectives of those, like women of color, who are situated in the intersections, "multiply burdened" by the simultaneity of racism and sexism (Crenshaw 1989, 140). At the same time, these dominant frameworks render the positions and perspectives of those who are relatively privileged (e.g., White women, men of color) as generic, normative, and definitive, as if "All the Women Are White and All the Blacks Are Men" (Hull, Scott, and Smith 1982).[17] Intersectionality is thus a "commitment to methodologies that

[17] Crenshaw (1989, 151) effectively uses single-axis anti-discrimination "doctrine" to elaborate on this point: "Because the scope of antidiscrimination law is so limited, sex and race discrimination have come to be defined in terms of the experiences of those who are privileged *but for* their racial or sexual characteristics. Put differently, the paradigm of sex discrimination tends to be based on the experiences of white women; the model of race discrimination tends to be based on the experiences of the most privileged Blacks. Notions of what constitutes race or sex discrimination are, as a result, narrowly tailored to embrace only a small set of circumstances, none of which include discrimination against Black women."

undo the empirical and evidentiary erasure of multiple marginalized groups" (Bowleg and Bauer 2016, 340). It calls our attention to who and what are left out, rendered invisible, deviant, or distorted in our research. It seeks out and attempts to remedy the gaps and flaws in our knowledge and the biases in our methodologies not only as an issue of empirical accuracy and theoretical validity but also as a matter of social justice (Jordan-Zachery 2007; May 2015). For more likely than not, the people and phenomena ignored and misrepresented by dominant approaches are the very ones multiply marginalized in the "real world."[18]

In applying this critical lens, our work demonstrates how intersectionality compels us to reevaluate the entire study of gender, race, and political representation—from the questions we ask, to the literature we engage, the concepts we define, the measures and categories we adopt, the hypotheses we test, the models we employ, the methods we use, the conclusions we draw, and the generalizations we make (Cole 2009). We ask not only empirical questions about race, gender, and representation but also epistemological questions about how we can know or learn about such things. Are existing, single-axis tools of analysis adequate to the task? How might alternative, intersectionally informed theories, hypotheses, concepts, measures, and models improve our understanding and appreciation of the complexities of raced-gendered representation, especially from the perspective of women of color and others positioned in the intersections of political, social, economic, and epistemic marginalization? *What can a more intersectional approach reveal?*

Our book addresses these epistemological questions head-on by systematically comparing the tools and products of single-axis approaches to those of a more intersectional approach. Chapters 2 and 3 re-evaluate existing single-axis theories of descriptive representation and concepts of group interests (women's issues, Black interests, Latinx interests) central to the study of substantive representation to "render visible their limits" (May 2015, 248). To what degree and how do these tools of analysis obscure the electoral fortunes and representational activities of women of color—revealing the fortunes and activities not of all women and minorities but of White women and minority men in particular? Chapters 4 and 5 dive further into the complexities of race, gender, and substantive representation by employing and exploring

[18] Closer to home, Sanbonmatsu (2015a, 1) warns that "scholarly neglect of this topic [the intersection of race and gender in statewide executive officeholding] risks naturalizing the dearth of women of color in statewide executive positions, sending the message that it is understandable that women [of color] lack access to those offices and/or that such offices aren't realistically obtainable."

alternative theories, concepts, and measures of race-gender policy leadership and intersectional policy design. How well can *these* tools of analysis capture the diversity and intensity of race-gender representation undertaken by women of color—as well as men of color, White women, and White men? Chapter 6 then directly compares an additive and an intersectional approach to incorporating gender into the study of race, representation, and state welfare reform. As May (2015, 223) argues, "It is this double pursuit (of disturbing and resisting hegemonic [single-axis] rationalities while also noting and fostering resisting [intersectional] rationalities) that is at the heart of intersectional orientations." We also believe it is the most effective way to demonstrate what intersectionality has to offer as a critical research paradigm.

It is important to note that this "double pursuit"—this particular move toward more intersectional approaches to the study of race, gender, and representation—requires us to critically engage rather than reject outright the theories, concepts, and methodologies often associated with dominant single-axis approaches. For example, we want to both challenge categories of difference, whether they be "women and minorities" or "women and men of color," and recognize their significance in people's lives (Jordan-Zachery 2007, 256; McCall 2005). Thus, we categorize legislators and legislative activities in such terms; but we do so in multiple and provisional ways, weighing the epistemological gains and losses—what we can and cannot "see" and learn—with each configuration (McCall 2005). In this way, we hope to navigate the "dilemma" often faced by scholars "studying marginalized populations . . . in intersecting political contexts of oppression": "documenting and giving voice to the experiences of people occupying these categories, [while respecting] . . . the competing imperative to go beyond the constraint of the categories themselves" (Junn and Brown 2008, 76). The power of identity politics (the notion that identity is often political) and the expectations surrounding the links between descriptive and substantive representation rest on the assignment of people to categories. If we want to study those concepts, assumptions, and claims, then we necessarily have to do category-based research—research structured (provisionally) by the very categories that we want to (con)test (McCall 2005; Spierings 2012, 334). At the same time, we must acknowledge that the underlying phenomena of group identities and interests that our analytic categories attempt to gauge are just as fluid, unstable, conditional, and complex as the power relations that construct them.

Nor do we reject quantitative methods as inherently inappropriate or antithetical to intersectionality (Alexander-Floyd 2012). Methods in and of themselves can be used for and adapted to many epistemologies or methodologies—positivist or critical, dominant or insubordinate, feminist or anti-feminist (Harding 1987). It is not the methods that are single-axis or intersectional; it is how we use and interpret them (Bowleg and Bauer 2016, 340; Cole 2009). We employ methods of data collection and analysis that are both quantitative and qualitative when and where they seem most useful for addressing the empirical and epistemological questions at hand. But we remain open to and aware of their shortcomings as well.

We are wary of the simplifying and generalizing assumptions about intra-categorical homogeneity and inter-categorical independence built into quantitative methods in particular, as well as the ways in which tests of statistical significance privilege inter-categorical differences (Bowleg 2008; Hancock 2007, 2013; Shields 2008). We are also well aware of how quantitative, statistical analyses are ill-suited for studies of "low frequency" groups such as Asian American and Native American state legislators (Else-Quest and Hyde 2016b, 325). That is one of the ways in which our own study of representation remains limited. Nonetheless, by critically employing such methodological tools, we are able to "disturb and resist" quantitative measures and models that embody single-axis concepts and additive, either/or models of race, gender, and representation "while also noting and fostering" quantitative techniques that can accommodate and gauge a variety of possibilities for more complex relationships between race, gender, and representation (May 2015, 223; see also Else-Quest and Hyde 2016a).[19] And when we confront the limitations of quantitative, hypothesis-testing methods (for our purposes), we turn to more qualitative and inductive approaches. We detail this "double pursuit" of interrogating and exploring the problems and promises of our methodological choices within each empirical chapter and assess their intersectional potential in the concluding chapter.

[19] Intersectional scholars have been particularly critical of multiple regression models that add "dummy variables" for, say, race (e.g., Black or not) or gender (e.g., female or not) as controls, as well as models that add interactions between such dummy variables (Bowleg and Bauer 2016; Cole 2009; Hancock 2007, 2013; Junn and Brown 2008; Simien 2007). Such models assume that categories of difference are mutually exclusive (or independent) and additive (or linear)—as if gender has the same effect across categories of race, or as if gender has more or less of an effect depending on some either/or (e.g., White vs. non-White) conception of race. We agree that such models are too rigid for intersectional analysis, for they cannot accommodate or capture a range of possible (non-additive or unranked) relationships and effects of categories of difference. For example, they cannot tell us whether or how the representational activity of Latina legislators is similar to or different from that of Black female, White female, or Latino legislators. Our regression models, which often incorporate "crossed dummies" (a series of dummy variables for each race-gender group of legislators), are designed precisely for this purpose: to allow for similar effects, different effects, distinct/unique effects, or any combination thereof (Spierings 2012).

Like Hancock (2013), we want to distinguish our use of intersectionality as a critical research paradigm from an "intersectionality-as-testable-explanation" approach. What makes this project an intersectional one is neither the theories and hypotheses we test nor the results we present. It is not contingent upon legislative women of color behaving any differently from their colleagues, for example. We test some theories that are informed by intersectionality and intersectional research and we do find evidence of distinctive representational leadership on the part of women of color; but that alone is not what makes our project intersectional. While we seek to demonstrate the critical, knowledge-building capacity of intersectional inquiry, we are not "testing" it as an empirical theory. If we are testing anything it is the meaning and significance of "identity politics" and the "categories of difference" (Hancock 2007) that drive it—in late 20th- and early 21st-century American politics. As in our previous work, our questions about and investigations of the election, behavior, and impact of women, people of color, and women of color are critical of over-simplified and over-generalized assumptions about similarities within and differences between identity groups often associated with identity politics and the study thereof (Haynie 2001; Reingold 2000). Our critical stance recognizes the complexity and contingency of the socially constructed and contested identities that give meaning and value to the concept of descriptive representation and the politically constructed and contested group interests that give meaning and value to the concept of substantive representation (Reingold and Swers 2011). Ultimately, we pursue such critical questions to see what these gendered, raced, and raced-gendered categories of analysis reveal and obscure about the politics and practice of representation in the American states. Intersectionality compels us to pursue such questions; it does not designate any particular answers or dictate particular conclusions.

A Look Ahead

Chapter 2: The Political Geography of Descriptive Representation

In the next chapter we examine which environments and institutional structures promote the descriptive representation of women of color and whether existing single-axis theories regarding the electoral fortunes of women or racial/ethnic minorities are useful. Such theories address two primary questions: Why are some state legislatures more racially, ethnically, or gender diverse than others? Why are some state legislative districts more likely than others to elect women or minorities? Significant bodies of research tell us that women, almost always undifferentiated by race or ethnicity, are more likely to hold state legislative office in more liberal states with larger "pools" of highly educated, professional women, lower levels of legislative professionalism, weak party organizations, and multi-member districts. Concomitantly, extensive research on the political geography of African American and Latinx officeholding shows that single-member majority-minority districts, or the number and geographic concentration of racial/ethnic minorities in the vote-eligible population, are key. When it comes to which conditions, institutions, and structures promote the descriptive representation of women of color, however, a great deal of uncertainty remains. There is little guidance for understanding or predicting how gender, race, and ethnicity interact to shape the electoral fortunes of minority women.

Studies by Bejarano (2013) and Scola (2014) are notable exceptions in their efforts to gain a more thorough, intersectional understanding of geographic variations in the descriptive representation of minority women. (See also, Silva and Skulley 2019.) These studies reveal how standard women-and-politics models and, to a lesser extent, standard race-and-ethnic-politics models do a better job identifying the correlates of state legislative officeholding for White women and men of color than they do for women of color. Yet it is still unclear *why* these single-axis models fall short at the intersections of gender and race/ethnicity, and how the electoral environment affects women of color in particular. We build upon this research by examining the structural implications of a theory of intersectional resistance and resilience particular to minority women in politics.

Drawing on research suggesting women of color possess certain strengths and advantages over White women and men of color (e.g., Bejarano 2013; Fraga et al. 2008), we hypothesize that the electoral fortunes of Black women and Latinas are systematically less constrained by political opportunity structures than standard, single-axis models of descriptive representation suggest. Our state- and district-level analyses of descriptive representation in all 49 state houses in 2005, however, suggest that the representation of minority women is no less constrained than that of their White female or minority male counterparts, but differently constrained. Like men of color but unlike White women, Black women and Latinas find few opportunities for officeholding outside of majority-minority districts. Yet similar to the experiences of many White women, women of color seem less likely than their male counterparts to garner the support they need (and most likely deserve) to successfully contest the opportunities that are available. Our results thus raise new questions about the electoral barriers Black women and Latinas confront and their ability to resist and overcome intersecting legacies of racial and gender subordination.

Chapter 3: Conceptions of Group Interests and the Links between Descriptive and Substantive Representation

In this chapter, we focus the critical lens of intersectionality on foundational concepts of marginalized group interests and issues. Definitions of women's interests, Black interests, and Latinx interests lie at the heart of any analysis of substantive representation or legislative activity on behalf of women and/or minorities. To gauge the links between descriptive and substantive representation, political scientists have employed a variety of definitions of group interests, often distinguishing between more narrowly defined "women-specific" or "racial" issues and broader issues, such as health and education, that are also salient but less explicitly or directly tied to gender, race, or ethnicity alone. To what extent, then, do our definitions of group interests affect who is or appears to be more or less willing to act for women, African Americans, or Latinxs? Does the relationship between descriptive and substantive representation depend on how we define and measure group interests? We are particularly interested in whether and how definitions of marginalized group interests affect the conclusions we draw about women of color in US state legislatures. Are legislative women, regardless of race and ethnicity, equally likely to take the lead on women's issues, regardless of how they are defined? Are Black and Latinx lawmakers, regardless of gender, equally likely to take the lead on racial issues, regardless of how they are defined?

Intersectionality cautions against generalizing about representation across differences in race and gender and suggests that any single-axis conception of marginalized group interests risks concealing or distorting the representational advocacy provided by women of color, while privileging that provided by White women and men of color. The more narrow and single-group specific definitions may be particularly problematic, especially compared to broader conceptions covering issues deemed highly salient to women, African Americans, and Latinxs alike (Smooth 2011). To test this proposition, we examine the agenda-setting behavior (i.e., bill sponsorship) of Democratic (and, to a lesser extent, Republican) state legislators in 15 state houses, in 1997 and 2005, across a variety of definitions of group issues/interests. We find that no matter what definition of group interests is at hand, legislative women of color never appear as secondary actors in efforts to place such issues on the policymaking agenda. Their bill sponsorship activity either matches or exceeds that of their White female or minority male colleagues. Yet we also find that relying only on narrowly defined, group-specific conceptions of policy interests will overlook and underestimate the truly distinct representational leadership of women of color in shaping healthcare and education policy to address the interests of women and people of color.

Chapter 4:   Race-Gender Policy Leadership

Chapter 4[20] looks beyond single-axis conceptions of group interests and substantive representation to explore what we call, "race-gender policy leadership." To what extent and how do representatives address both race and gender in their policymaking initiatives? Who is more or less likely to do so? Recognizing that various group interests (Black, Latinx, women's) can be (or at least appear to be) distinct, overlapping, or intersecting (Brown and Banks 2014; Minta and Brown 2014), we distinguish and measure multiple approaches to race-gender policy leadership among the same set of Democratic (and Republican) lawmakers serving in 15 US state houses in 1997 and 2005. Specifically, we test hypotheses that legislative women of color are more likely than others (including White women and men of color) to sponsor (a) bills that address narrowly targeted, group-specific women's interests and minority interests, *one-at-a-time*; (b) at least one bill that addresses multiple group-specific interests *simultaneously* (e.g., standard

---

[20] This chapter is adapted from Beth Reingold, Kirsten Widner, and Rachel Harmon, "Legislating at the Intersections: Race, Gender, and Representation," *Political Research Quarterly* (2019), OnlineFirst. doi:10.1177/1065912919858405.

anti-discrimination and affirmative action measures); and (c) one or more bills that address the particular interests of *disadvantaged subgroups* of women and/or minorities, such as poor women of color (Strolovitch 2007).

Although our conceptions of race-gender policymaking are fairly inclusive, our data show that relatively few legislators engage in this sort of leadership, even among Democrats. Nonetheless, women of color (in both parties) do play important, leading roles in addressing the policy needs of multiple and multiply disadvantaged groups. Depending on the measure of race-gender policy leadership, either Black women or Latinas stand out from their peers, sponsoring more race-gender legislation than their minority male or White female counterparts. In short, we provide additional evidence that policy leadership and substantive representation are raced-gendered (Hawkesworth 2003).

Chapter 5: Explorations in Intersectional Policymaking

In this chapter, we push even further beyond single-axis conceptions of substantive representation and dig deeper into the contours of race-gender policy leadership. The quantitative approach of Chapter 4 provides a broad overview of various ways in which legislative advocacy on behalf of women and minorities can occur—sequentially or simultaneously, with or without regard to those who are multiply or intersectionally disadvantaged. Yet, these approaches are by no means the only ways lawmakers might engage in race-gender policymaking. As others have indicated, there are numerous possibilities for re-framing what most consider a women's issue (e.g., domestic violence) or a racial issue (e.g., immigration) or a women-and-minorities issue (e.g., diversifying government contracting) as a race-gender issue (Brown 2014b; Frederick 2010.)

Drawing from a historically situated body of intersectional theorizing in law and public policy (e.g., Crenshaw 1989, 1991; Dill and Zambrana 2009; Hancock 2007; Hankivsky and Cormier 2011; INCITE! 2006; Roberts 1997, 2002; Spade 2013; Whittier 2016), Chapter 5 investigates these possibilities and many others. How might various women's interest bills, Black interest bills, and Latinx interest bills be formulated to address the concerns of women of color and others who are "intersectionally marginalized" (Brown and Banks 2014) or "multiply burdened" (Crenshaw 1989)? What do the varieties of intersectional policy proposals look like and who is more or less likely to undertake such initiatives? Addressing these questions, we argue, requires a more qualitative and inductive approach to the study of gender, race, and policy agendas. We therefore embark on an in-depth, qualitative content analysis of the bills sponsored by six subsamples of Democratic state legislators serving majority-minority constituencies in the same state-years. Thus, we compare the bills sponsored by similarly situated Latina, Latino, Black female, Black male, White female, and White male legislators who are "most likely" to craft intersectional proposals. Our analysis suggests that while single-axis approaches to policy problems are abundant, legislators are creating a wide variety of initiatives that appear cognizant of the many different ways in which multiple, intersecting categories of difference shape the lives and life-chances of their constituents. Such intersectional policy-making is by no means the province of women of color only; but once again, we find evidence to suggest that women of color are among its most reliable practitioners.

Chapter 6: Welfare Policy Outcomes: Comparing
Single-Axis and Intersectional Approaches

Under the guidelines of the federal Personal Responsibility and Work Opportunity Reconciliation Act of 1996, every state in the country undertook unprecedented efforts to "end welfare as we know it." Previous research shows that African American and Latinx state legislators were able to mitigate or ease some of the more stringent restrictions, demanding requirements, and harsher penalties associated with this wave of get-tough welfare reform (Fording 2003; Owens 2005; Preuhs 2006, 2007). In this chapter,[21] we ask whether the presence and power of women in state legislatures had similar effects. To address this question, we compare and contrast two alternative approaches to incorporating gender into the study of representation and welfare policymaking. A single-axis or additive approach suggests that female state legislators—regardless of race/ethnicity—will mitigate the more restrictive and punitive aspects of welfare reform, much like their African American and Latinx counterparts do. In contrast, an intersectional approach suggests

[21] This chapter is adapted from Beth Reingold and Adrienne R. Smith, "Welfare Policymaking and Intersections of Race, Ethnicity, and Gender in U.S. State Legislatures," *American Journal of Political Science* 56(1) (2012): 131–47.

that legislative women of color will have the strongest countervailing effect on state welfare reform—stronger than that of other women or men of color.

Our empirical analyses suggest that an intersectional approach yields a more accurate understanding of gender, race, and welfare politics in the states. Depending on which women and which policies one examines, the presence and power of legislative women had a liberal effect, a conservative effect, or no effect. Across the policy dimensions, however, legislative women of color had a distinctive effect. Though few in number, Latinas and Black women did more to alleviate the get-tough provisions of welfare reform than did their White female, Latino, or Black male colleagues. Once again, our research calls into question many overly broad assumptions and generalizations about women and racial minorities in politics. Plus, it demonstrates that a few, very committed and well-placed "critical actors" really can make a difference on major policy issues of the day (Childs and Krook 2006).

Chapter 7: Conclusion

The concluding chapter summarizes our main findings and highlights our contributions to the study of gender, race, and representation and the development of intersectionality as an analytic framework. We also discuss the questions and issues, both old and new, that warrant further intersectional research.

Even if the numbers of women, women of color, and men of color who run for and win public office continue to grow, the questions this book raises and addresses will remain central to debates about how open, receptive, and responsive American political institutions and American democracy itself are to groups long disenfranchised, disempowered, and under-represented, by law and by custom. Despite frequent protests against "identity politics,"[22] people care about who representatives are.[23] Political scientists pay attention to the presence of women and racial/ethnic minorities in government as a sign of democratic strength and stability (Bühlmann et al. 2012; Sigman and

[22] See, for example, https://www.thenation.com/article/archive/what-is-the-left-without-identity-politics/ (accessed 30 January 2020) from the left; and https://www.nationalaffairs.com/publications/detail/why-conservatives-struggle-with-identity-politics (accessed 30 January 2020) from the right.

[23] See, for example, contending remarks from Pete Buttigieg and Stacey Abrams during the 2020 presidential nomination race: https://thehill.com/homenews/campaign/444985-abrams-swipes-at-buttigieg-identity-politics-is-exactly-who-we-are (accessed 30 January 2020).

Lindberg 2018; Wolff 2018); democratic theorists consider it a marker of fairness and equity (Mansbridge 1999; Phillips 1995; Williams 1998). In varying ways and to varying degrees, ordinary people—women and racial/ethnic minorities especially—are more politically engaged or at least feel better represented when they see or anticipate having more people like them in public office (Atkeson 2003; Atkeson and Carillo 2007; Barreto 2010; Barreto, Segura, and Woods 2004; Bobo and Gilliam 1990; Burns, Scholozman, and Verba 2001; Campbell and Wolbrecht 2006; Hayes and Hibbing 2017; Pantoja and Segura 2003; Rocha et al. 2010; Sanchez and Morin 2011). People of color and women in office firmly believe their leadership makes a difference (Dittmar et al. 2017; Hardy-Fanta et al. 2016, 284); they and other activists organize and raise money for precisely that reason.[24] Often these desires for greater descriptive representation are colored and qualified by partisanship or ideology—as in EMILY's List, which supports only pro-choice Democratic women as candidates (Merolla, Sellers, and Fowler 2013; Reingold and Harrell 2010). Organizing to recruit and support women of color as candidates, however, is a relatively new phenomenon (Sanbonmatsu 2015b). Likewise, relatively few scholars pay attention to how race might inform the value placed on women's representation or how gender might inform the value placed on racial/ethnic representation (Dovi 2002; Gershon et al 2019; Simien 2015; Stokes-Brown and Dolan 2010; Uhlaner and Scola 2015;). What does the presence and activity of women of color in public office say about the quality of democratic representation in the United States?

Our study can help us begin to answer this question. By comparing how the political geography of electoral opportunities and constraints shapes the fortunes of women of color, men of color, and White women, Chapter 2 suggests that formidable race-gender barriers to equitable descriptive representation remain. By examining race-gender patterns of agenda-setting policy leadership (i.e., bill sponsorship) across a wide variety of issue-areas of interest to women, African Americans, Latinxs, women of color, the poor, and other intersectionality marginalized groups and communities, Chapters 3, 4, and 5 suggest that the continued shortage of legislative women of color undermines effective substantive representation of these marginalized and multiply disadvantaged groups. By distinguishing the impact of

---

[24] Benjy Sarlin, "'Giving Circles': Female Fundraisers Are Powering Women Candidates," *NBC News* (29 July 2018): https://www.nbcnews.com/politics/elections/giving-circles-female-fundraisers-are-powering-women-candidates-n895276 (accessed 9 February 2020).

legislative women of color on various dimensions of state welfare reform, Chapter 6 assures us that even small increases in the presence and power of women of color can make a difference in policy outcomes that are more responsive, fair, and just to those in need. In sum, our move toward a more intersectional approach to the study of political representation in the United States demonstrates how the presence and activity of women of color in public office functions as a bellwether of race-gender power and privilege— as embedded in our democratic institutions (Cooper 1892; Giddings 1984; May 2007).

We emphasize nonetheless that ours is only one of many "first steps" toward a more intersectional approach to the study of race, gender, and political representation. To claim otherwise, that our work should stand alone or be considered the final word, would undermine the integrity and power of intersectionality as a critical and productive research paradigm (Davis 2008).[25] As scholars and citizens we must continue to ask and pursue difficult, "messy," and "unsettling" questions about complex intersections of multiple axes of identity and power as they relate to political representation *and* our ability to understand it (May 2015; Smooth 2006b). Intersectional research must always be (considered) provisional, tentative, and partial; for we can always move toward a more—or different—intersectional approach (Carbado et al. 2013; May 2015, 251; McCall 2005). Race and gender, the central foci of this inquiry, are important, especially given the history of American politics and the study thereof. They are a good starting point. Yet there are undoubtedly multiple layers of intersectional complexity that warrant further investigation. Even within the confines of race and gender, we can do better and learn more by venturing beyond the limited and limiting categories of Black, Latinx, and White; male and female examined here. Paying more attention to additional racialized groups (e.g., Asian, Native, and Muslim Americans), non-binary conceptions of gender and gender identity, and other salient configurations of racialized gender and gendered race (e.g., queer of color) is much needed. Pushing against the boundaries of our theories, concepts, and methods—questioning and evaluating their biases and oversights—must also continue. As our research has taught us, what we know depends mightily on how we go about obtaining that knowledge.

---

[25] We take to heart Davis's (2008) argument that part of what makes intersectionality so "successful" is its open-ended, self-reflexive nature: "Intersectionality offers endless opportunities for interrogating one's own blind spots and transforming them into analytic resources for further critical analysis" (p. 77).

Postscript (June 2020)

This manuscript was submitted immediately before a period of great upheaval that included a global pandemic and associated lockdown, the murders of Ahmaud Arbery, Breonna Taylor, Tony McDade, and George Floyd, nationwide protests, and calls for sweeping changes to a wide range of institutions that embody, reproduce, and perpetuate systemic racism and inequality. The stage of the process we are in does not allow us the time or space to thoroughly explore the implications of this moment and its connection to the work we present here. We add this brief postscript to share a few initial reflections.

First, we stand in solidarity with the protestors and their calls for justice and change. Second, the findings of this book suggest that election of more Black and Latina women would be a significant step toward meaningful reform. Our data demonstrate that for decades, women of color have been proposing the types of measures sought by protestors; measures that are less punitive and more focused on building healthier and more equitable communities. We hope that our contribution helps to bring attention to their important work. However, we note that while women of color have long been the most likely and forceful advocates for intersectionally marginalized individuals and communities, they have not been—nor should they be—the only ones. We need to not only lift up their voices, but also to learn from their leadership and take up this work with them.

2

The Political Geography
of Descriptive Representation

Why are some state legislatures more racially, ethnically, and gender diverse than others? Why are some state legislative districts more likely to elect
women and minorities than others? A large, robust body of women-and-
politics (W&P) research tells us that women, almost always undifferentiated
by race or ethnicity, are more likely to hold state legislative office in more liberal states with larger "pools" of highly educated, professional women, lower
levels of legislative professionalism, weak party organizations, and multi-
member districts. Extensive race-and-ethnic-politics (REP) research on the
political geography of African American and Latino officeholding shows
definitively that single-member majority-minority districts, or the number
and geographic concentration of racial/ethnic minorities in the vote-eligible
population, are key.

When it comes to which conditions, institutions, and structures promote
the descriptive representation of women of color, however, a great deal of
uncertainty remains. There is little guidance, much less consensus, for understanding or predicting how gender, race, and ethnicity interact to shape
the electoral fortunes of minority women—or, for that matter, minority
men, White women, and White men. As scholars have lamented for decades,
women of color remain invisible in the predominant "single-axis" studies of
representation that group all women together, or all African Americans, or
all Latinos (Crenshaw 1989). Studies that do call attention to women of color
provide detailed accounts of the backgrounds, experiences, and electoral
accomplishments of officeholders (or, less frequently, potential candidates)
but rarely examine the contextual or institutional determinants of legislative
diversity directly or systematically (Carroll and Sanbonmatsu 2013; Darcy
and Hadley 1988; Fraga et al. 2006; Hardy-Fanta et al. 2006, 2007, 2016;
Montoya et al. 2000; Shah, Scott, and Juenke 2019; Smooth 2006a; Takash
1997; Williams 2001). Most are concerned with only Black women or only
Latinas and are therefore unable to draw comparisons or test generalizations

Race, Gender, and Political Representation. Beth Reingold, Kerry L. Haynie, and Kirsten Widner, Oxford University Press
(2021). © Oxford University Press. DOI: 10.1093/oso/9780197502174.001.0001.

across such differences. Thus, while suggestive, the indirect, fragmented, and often inconsistent evidence these studies offer makes drawing firm conclusions difficult at best.

Bejarano (2013), Scola (2014), and Silva and Skulley (2019) are notable exceptions in their efforts to gain a more thorough, intersectional understanding of geographic variations in the descriptive representation of minority women. These studies reveal how standard W&P models and, to a lesser extent, standard REP models do a better job identifying the correlates of legislative officeholding for White women and men of color than they do for women of color. Nonetheless, they offer limited theoretical insight into *why* these single-axis models fall short at the intersections of gender, race, and ethnicity, leaving us with little understanding of how the electoral environment affects women of color in particular.

We build upon this research by examining the structural implications of a theory of intersectional resistance and resilience particular to minority women in politics. Drawing on research suggesting women of color possess certain strengths and advantages over White women and men of color (e.g., Bejarano 2013; Fraga et al. 2008), we hypothesize that the electoral fortunes of Black women and Latinas are systematically less constrained by political opportunity structures than standard, single-axis models of descriptive representation suggest. We test our hypotheses using standard W&P and REP models to explain cross-sectional variation in the election of White women and men, Black women and men, Latinas, and Latinos to state legislatures, at the state *and* district levels. We are thus able to gauge the representational effects of both state- and district-level institutions, cultures, and communities, and to compare our results across multiple "categories of difference" (Hancock 2007, 63–64). This not only sheds new light on the political experiences and electoral fortunes of women of color, but also addresses important questions about generalizing across race/ethnicity in the study of gender and across gender in the study of race/ethnicity.

Congruent with our intersectional approach, we critically re-examine these single-axis frameworks and the extent to which they ignore important differences within categories, obscure the positions and perspectives of those who are "multiply burdened" (Crenshaw 1989, 140), and present the experiences and perspectives of those who are relatively privileged as characteristic of all (Cohen 2003; Haynie 2011; Junn and Brown 2008; Smooth 2006b). Our analysis demonstrates that single-axis approaches are, for these very reasons, fundamentally flawed; nonetheless, generalizing across intersectional differences is not always or universally unwarranted. We too find that standard models of women's representation are more applicable to the electoral fortunes of White women than to Latinas or Black women. But we also demonstrate that standard models of minority representation go a long way toward explaining the electoral fortunes of Latinx and African American women and men alike. So strong are the similarities between outcomes for women and men of color that our hypotheses find only limited empirical support. We conclude that the descriptive representation of women of color may be no less constrained than that of their White female and minority male counterparts, but differently constrained.

Our research, therefore, raises new questions about the alleged advantages of Black women and Latinas in politics and their ability to resist and overcome intersecting legacies of racial and gender subordination. Further evidence of "race-gender" constraints in electoral politics also has important and troubling implications for future growth in representational diversity and equality (Hawkesworth 2003). Much of the growth in both minority and female officeholding in recent decades can be attributed to the election of more women of color (Hardy-Fanta et al. 2016; Reingold 2014; Smooth 2006a). Thus, structural barriers that limit the opportunities for politically ambitious women of color, no matter how different in kind, place significant limitations on the descriptive representation of all women and people of color.

Single-Axis Approaches to Descriptive Representation

Research on descriptive representation in the United States has been primarily concerned with explaining why there are so few women or racial/ethnic minorities in elective office, relative to the general population. At the same time, W&P and REP scholars have long noted and attempted to explain why the relatively few women, African Americans, or Latinxs in office are not evenly distributed across states, districts, or municipalities. Indeed, the two phenomena—limited numbers and uneven distributions of elected women and minorities—are intricately connected. The same gender or racial/ethnic biases that prevent larger numbers of women and people of color from successfully running for public office also constrain the choices or options available to them—most notably the option of where to run (Haider-Markel 2010; Pearson and McGhee 2013). Geographic variation in descriptive

representation, therefore, highlights the numerous gendered or raced opportunity structures that channel the political ambitions and constrain the electoral fortunes of eligible women and minorities.

Women are more likely to run—and run successfully—in places where
they, as women, can anticipate and/or receive more support from voters,
donors, and political gatekeepers.[1] Thus, the presence of women in state
legislatures is strongly associated with not only large "eligibility pools" of
highly qualified, professional women, but also more "women friendly"
environments (Palmer and Simon 2008; Pyeatt and Yanus 2016): states
with more liberal electorates or a "moralistic" political culture that values
government activity promoting social welfare and full democratic participation and inclusion (Elazar 1984); and state legislative districts that are
more educated, professional/White collar, non-agricultural, and racially
or ethnically diverse (Hogan 2001). Women's officeholding also thrives in
multi-member districts, where balancing the ticket and achieving more
gender diversity may be easier for everyone to support (Darcy et al. 1997;
Darcy et al. 1994; King 2002).

Other institutions, such as state party organizations and legislative professionalism, are thought to deter women's representation. Fewer women
run for and win state legislative seats where party leaders—Democrats and
Republicans, who are often immersed in good old boy networks and prone
to underestimate the viability of female candidates—have more control over
the candidate selection process (Niven 1998; Sanbonmatsu 2006; see also
Crowder-Meyer 2013); and where higher salaries and superior policymaking
resources render such seats more powerful, desirable, and competitive. Term
limits, however, seem to have little effect on women's officeholding (Carey
et al. 2006; Carroll and Jenkins 2001a; Moncrief et al. 2007).

Explanations for the variation in African American and Latinx descriptive representation seem at first glance more parsimonious and powerful.
Here, the legacy of centuries of racial conflict and minority disenfranchisement looms large, as does the efficacy of the 1965 Voting Rights Act (VRA)
and subsequent amendments. There is, in this literature, relatively little concern about the "pool" of willing and able minority candidates, and much
more concern about racially polarized voting and institutionalized electoral
mechanisms (e.g., multi-member, or at-large, districts in which substantial

---

[1] In addition to the works cited below, we drew heavily from Arceneaux (2001), Camobreco and
Barnello (2003), Hill (1981), Norrander and Wilcox (2005), and Sanbonmatsu (2002).

minority communities are overwhelmed by White majorities) that have intentionally denied minority voters the opportunity to vote for candidates of their choice.

Thus, the bulk of the early research focused on the power of newly created single-member, majority-minority districts to overcome widespread minority vote dilution and under-representation, especially in the South (Davidson and Grofman 1994; Grofman and Handley 1989, 1991; Grofman, Migalski, and Noviello 1986; Jewell 1982; Moncrief and Thompson 1992; Rule 1992). To this day, gains in minority representation have occurred primarily in southern and southwestern states and in urban districts with large concentrations of VRA-empowered African American and/or Latinx voters (Davidson and Grofman 1994; Fraga et al. 2006; Hardy-Fanta et al. 2016; Lien 2006). Indeed, the size of the respective minority population is by far the most powerful determinant of Black and Latinx descriptive representation at all levels (Casellas 2011; Juenke and Shah 2015; King-Meadows and Schaller 2006; Lublin et al. 2009; Marschall and Ruhil 2006; Marschall et al. 2010; Meier et al. 2005; Preuhs and Juenke 2011; Shah 2014; Trounstine and Valdini 2008). Little else seems to matter in any consistent fashion, including the number of other racial/ethnic minority voters (Lublin et al. 2009; Marschall and Ruhil 2006; Preuhs and Juenke 2011). In short, politically ambitious African Americans and Latinxs have found many opportunities and much support within majority-minority districts—and very few opportunities elsewhere.[2]

There is even some doubt as to whether the remaining multi-member or at-large districts continue to dilute the influence of minority voters and weaken the relationship between minority populations and seats gained by minority candidates, especially in state legislatures (Engstrom and McDonald 1981; King-Meadows and Schaller 2006; Marschall et al. 2010; Meier et al. 2005; Trounstine and Valdini 2008). Similarly, most research discounts the ability of term limits to increase minority access to state legislatures (Carey et al. 2006; Moncrief et al. 2007). Casellas's (2011) report that term limits, much

---

[2] Research on the descriptive representation of African Americans and Latinxs rarely distinguishes minority candidacy from minority electoral success, most likely because large-scale data on the race and ethnicity of state and local candidates are unavailable. Thus, we know very little about where African Americans and Latinxs run—apart from where they win. A few recent studies, however, have shed new light on candidate emergence among racial/ethnic minorities, suggesting that "much of what we have considered to be benchmarks in theories of minority representation, including size of the minority population and electoral structures, are more crucial at the candidate entry stage" than at the winning (conditional on running) stage (Shah 2014, 267; Juenke and Shah 2015; Doherty, Dowling, and Miller 2019).

like single-member districts, increase Latinx representation by enhancing the voting power of large populations of Latinx citizens, is a notable exception.

Urban politics scholars have theorized about the potentially beneficial role of White "crossover" voters and indigenous group resources as well (Karnig 1979; Marschall and Ruhil 2006; Marschall et al. 2010; Shah 2014). Like liberal voters who support female candidates, well-educated Whites are expected to be more racially tolerant and, thus, more supportive of minority candidates. And much like the eligibility pools of professional women, higher-status minority communities are thought to have the civic, fiscal, and human resources necessary to field well-qualified candidates and mobilize support for them. While empirical support at the local level is mixed, such propositions have yet to be tested at the state legislative level.

Women of Color and Intersections of Race, Ethnicity, and Gender

The few attempts to understand how political opportunity structures shape the election of women of color reinforce warnings that the political behavior and experiences of women of color "cannot always be anticipated from what we know about Blacks [or other marginalized racial/ethnic groups] and women individually" (Darcy and Hadley 1988, 630). Intrigued by conflicting theories regarding the countervailing effects of multi-member districts on the election of women and minorities, early studies (Darcy et al. 1997; Rule 1992; Welch and Herrick 1992) revealed that multi-member districts enhanced the election of Black and White women alike and inhibited the election of men, regardless of race or ethnicity. Rule's analysis also indicated that the "ideal environments" for Black and White women legislators were quite similar in other respects (e.g., well-to-do northern states), while those for Black men (poor southern states) and women tended to differ (1992, 61, 65–66).

More recent attempts to understand these intersections of gender and race/ethnicity at the state and local level, however, reveal that the "ideal environments" for White women and women of color are not at all alike (Bejarano 2013; Scola 2014; Trounstine and Valdini 2008). A quick glance at the distribution of African American, Latina, Asian American, and Native American women across state legislatures in recent years further suggests that the electoral fortunes of women of color are quite similar to those of men of color: tethered to large concentrations of co-ethnic voters (Hardy-Fanta et al. 2006, 2016; see also Palmer and Simon 2008). Trends over time, meanwhile, have consistently shown that while women of color remain numerically underrepresented at all levels of public office (Hardy-Fanta et al. 2006, 17), their electoral gains have outpaced those of both White women and men of color.[3]

Together, these developments suggest the electoral environment for minority women is a complicated mix of relative disadvantages and advantages, where opportunities and obstacles are shaped by intersections of race/ethnicity and gender—not simply one or the other, or one plus the other (Brown 2014a). Nonetheless, it remains unclear just how gender and race interact to affect the electoral fortunes of women of color—theoretically or empirically. Part of the problem is that disparate research designs prohibit full and consistent comparisons across intersecting categories of difference. Rule (1992) compares Anglo women, Black women, and Black men; Bejarano (2013) compares all women, all Latinxs, and Latinas; Scola (2014) compares all women, White women, and women of color (African American, Latina, Asian and Pacific Islander, and American Indian combined). Generalizability is also compromised by inconsistencies in explanatory variables and samples.

Most puzzling, however, are the findings themselves. According to Bejarano and Scola, the presence of women of color in state legislatures has little or nothing to do with political culture, ideological climate, state political parties, legislative professionalism, multi-member districts, or term limits and everything to do with the size and socioeconomic status of the state's minority population. Questions about why women of color seem to be immune from the social structures and political institutions that constrain the electoral prospects of White women, whether minority women and men are equally dependent on the support of minority voters, and whether all "minority" voters are equally supportive of all minority candidacies, have yet to be explored.

Nonetheless, numerous attempts to account for Black women's and Latinas' electoral success (relative to White women, Black men, or Latinos) provide useful theoretical clues. Explanations vary a bit, but they all tell a story of disadvantages overcome and opportunities seized. From the crucible of gendered racism and the collective struggles against it, women of color

[3] Bryce and Warrick (1977) noted such trends as early as 1969–73, and almost every study of minority women as candidates or public officials since then highlights similar patterns.

emerged more politically ambitious and qualified than their White female counterparts—more motivated, confident, connected, and skilled; deeply rooted in community activism; and less constrained by traditional gender norms (Bejarano 2013; Darcy and Hadley 1988; Darling 1998; Frederick 2013; Montoya et al. 2000; Smooth 2006a; Takash 1997; Tate 2003; Williams 2001). In one recent and eloquent example, Atima Omara—a Black candidate and candidate recruiter/consultant herself—conveys how Black women's interest in running for public office is rooted in their struggles to overcome legacies of gendered racism.[4]

> Black women have engaged in politics in the United States for over 150 years, trying to protect their families and their communities by securing a seat at the table. Political savvy has often been a matter of life or death for a community that has overcome slavery, voter disenfranchisement, predatory lending, education inequity, and police brutality, to name just a few ongoing issues important to many Black people. As a result, Black women are known in their communities for their commitment to service, whether at church, in the schools, at a community organization, or in their local political parties—sometimes all four. They don't just go to vote for themselves, but they also ensure their family and friends go to vote.

As Omara concludes, "These are all ideal starting points for an aspiring candidate." Thus, when new VRA-enabled majority-minority districts are created, women of color are well positioned to take advantage of the many open-seat opportunities (Darcy and Hadley 1988; Tate 2003). Judging from their successes over the years, these candidates appear to draw cross-gender support within minority communities and cross-racial support from women outside those communities (Bejarano 2013; Philpot and Walton 2007; Smooth 2006a; Tate 2003). Of course, not without a fight. Indeed, as some of the most successful women of color candidates attest—to this day—they continue confronting and overcoming the barriers before them, with and without the help of others.

Celebrating her role in establishing the first female majority in a state legislature (both chambers), Nevada Senator Patricia Ann Spearman recalls: "It's been a long, hard fight. I'm starting to see some of the fruits of not just my

---

[4] Atima Omara, "Black Women's Political Leadership: Behind the Numbers," *Gender on the Ballot* (11 December 2019): https://www.genderontheballot.org/black-womens-political-leadership-part-1/.

labor, but the labor of so many other people whose names I don't know." As a Black woman, a lesbian, a lieutenant colonel in the army, and an ordained minister, she adds, "I've had to fight for everything that I have. All the titles, none of that was given to me." When Serena Gonzales-Gutierrez told people she was considering a run for the Colorado House in 2018, they would say things like, " 'Well, don't you have small children?'—as if to discourage me." Nay-sayers like that "made me want to fight more," Gonzales-Gutierrez told National Public Radio. "That's all the reason that I am doing this." With encouragement from friends and candidate training from Emerge Colorado, she won her race and helped women claim a historic majority of the seats in the Colorado House. That same year, the 2018 Year of the Woman, an unprecedented number of women of color won congressional races in majority-White districts. Among them was Lauren Underwood, undaunted by the odds and confident in her ability to win and represent. "I learned to be a black woman in this community," she said while campaigning. "This is my home, and the idea that I might not be a good fit is an idea I never gave a lot of consideration to."[5]

As these women attest, aspiring women of color candidates are often shunned by traditional gatekeepers such as party leaders and wealthy donors (Carroll and Sanbonmatsu 2013; Brown 2014a). Rather than go it alone, though, many turn to and build alternative sources of support. After narrowly losing her 2014 bid for a seat in the Michigan House of Representatives, Rebecca Thompson became a candidate "coach" and trainer herself, focusing on "motivating and preparing" women of color in particular.[6] Brown's (2014a, 89–90) feminist life histories of Black women serving in the Maryland state legislature illustrate the importance of " 'sista' networks"—"either as informal gatherings of women or organized as part of a sorority, church, or other Black women's association"—in building support for Black women candidates "in the absence of strong institutional backing."

This sort of intersectional resistance, resilience, and resourcefulness may be why the single-axis model of women's restricted pathways to public office does little to explain or predict the presence of women of color in state legislatures. If women of color like Senator Spearman, Representative

---

[5] Astead W. Herndon, "The Districts Are Mostly White. The Candidates Are Not," *New York Times* (19 July 2018): https://www.nytimes.com/2018/07/19/us/politics/minority-candidates.html.

[6] Linda Kramer Jenning, "Women of Color Face Significant Barriers When Running for Office. But They're Finding Support," *Yes Magazine* (31 July 2018): https://www.yesmagazine.org/democracy/2018/07/31/women-of-color-face-significant-barriers-when-running-for-office-but-theyre-finding-support/.

Gonzales-Gutierrez, and Representative Underwood are even more determined and politically ambitious than White women; and if they have alternative networks within minority communities and grassroots movements
in which to "facilitate their candidacies," then they may be less likely than
White women to be "victims of circumstance" (Bledsoe and Herring 1990,
220–21).[7] Women of color may be just as, if not more likely to encounter
skepticism, opposition, and discrimination from established gatekeepers
and donors, as so-called double disadvantage theories suggest (Beale 1970;
Githens and Prestage 1997; Moncrief, Thompson, and Schuhmann 1991);
but they may also be more willing and able to resist or overcome such
obstacles (Brown 2014a). Their electoral fortunes, therefore, may be less
dependent on the sorts of opportunity structures thought to constrain (all)
women's electoral participation (Carroll and Sanbonmatsu 2013, 105; Lien
and Swain 2013, 149).

And what of the standard models used to predict racial/ethnic diversity
in state legislatures? No doubt political women of color have benefited from
institutions like majority-minority districting and have gained a great deal of
experience and support from within their respective minority communities.
Yet there is reason to believe they may not rely on or enjoy the same level of
support from those communities as their male counterparts do.

If women of color have deeper roots in community-based organizations and activism than even men of color (Frederick 2013; Lien and Swain
2013; Williams 2001), and if they are more capable of building cross-racial
coalitions and gaining support from women outside their own racial/
ethnic communities (Bejarano 2013; Fraga et al. 2006, 2008; Smooth 2006a;
Tate 2003), then their electoral fortunes may be less dependent on group-
specific socioeconomic resources or large concentrations of co-ethnic voters.
Minority women also may have an especially hard time gaining co-ethnic
support when they are competing against minority men in high-stakes races
(McClain et al. 2005; Philpot and Walton 2007; Smooth 2006a). This too
suggests that women of color benefit less than their male counterparts do
from large, well-off co-ethnic populations—and that standard REP models
are less useful for women of color. On the other hand, if women of color are
more ambitious and resourceful, they might be more likely than men of color

---

[7] These two conditions—higher levels of ambition and deeper roots in community activism among
women of color—may not be found amongst post-civil rights generations of eligible candidates and
elected officials (Hardy-Fanta et al. 2007, 2016; Lawless 2012).

to tap into White "crossover" support, gain additional support from other racial/ethnic minority groups, and take advantage of new electoral opportunities, such as those provided by term limits (Hardy-Fanta et al. 2016).[8]

Thus, to provide a more comprehensive understanding of how political demographics, cultures, and institutions shape the descriptive representation of women of color, as well as those of men of color, White women, and White men, we test the following hypotheses.

H1: Compared to White women, the presence of African American women and Latinas in state legislatures is less dependent upon the size of their respective eligibility pool, the predominant political culture or ideology, legislative professionalism, the strength of party organizations, or the presence of multi-member districts.

H2: Compared to Black and Latino men, the presence of Black women and Latinas in state legislatures is less dependent upon the size or socioeconomic status of their co-ethnic population, or the prevalence of multi-member districts, and more likely to benefit from large concentrations of White crossover supporters, other minority voters, and term limits.

Research Design

Existing studies of descriptive representation in state legislatures have adopted numerous research designs. Most attempt to explain variation in the gender, racial, or ethnic composition of legislatures, paying close attention to the effects of state-level cultural, institutional, and demographic factors. A more unusual but equally useful approach takes the state legislative district—or, in the case of multi-member districts, the seat—as the unit of analysis to examine what sorts of constituencies are more or less likely to elect women and men of various racial and ethnic backgrounds (Casellas 2011; Hogan 2001; Lublin et al. 2009; Palmer and Simon 2008; Silva and Skulley 2019). We undertake both approaches. Theoretically, descriptive representation is a product of both state-level structural opportunities and constraints and the proclivities and resources of the district-level constituencies in which candidates emerge and run. Our multilevel analyses also provide a more robust test of our hypotheses.

---

[8] Existing attempts to gauge the effects of term limits on the election of women of color to state legislatures are inconclusive (Bejarano 2013; Carroll and Jenkins 2001b).

Employing standard W&P and REP models, we test our hypotheses regarding the unique positioning of women of color by comparing results across multiple single-axis and intersectional outcomes. At the state-level, we use the standard W&P model to predict four separate outcomes: the percentage of state legislative seats occupied by all women, White women, Black women, and Latinas. We test H1 by comparing the results/coefficients across outcomes/equations. Similarly, we employ two standard REP models to predict six separate outcomes: the percentage of seats occupied by all African Americans, African American men, African American women, all Latinxs, Latino men, and Latina women; and we test H2 by comparing results across outcomes. At the district/seat-level, we combine elements of both W&P and REP models to predict simultaneously the likelihood of the seat being occupied by a White man, White woman, Black man, Black woman, Latino, or Latina. We test both H1 and H2 by comparing results across relevant outcomes. This analytic strategy provides multiple tests of our hypotheses and enables us to assess directly the efficacy of single-axis and additive approaches to understanding the political geography of descriptive representation.[9]

We focus our analysis of descriptive representation on members of the lower chambers of 49 state legislatures in 2005 (excluding Nebraska's unicameral and nonpartisan legislature). Like most of the research we draw upon, ours is a cross-sectional design. We chose 2005 primarily because it is one of the first years for which much of our data is available from the US Census. Second, 2005 is a good midpoint in the redistricting cycle—one that accommodates changes made in district maps before and after the 2002 elections but does not come so late in the cycle that the 2000 census data are no longer optimal.

Operationalizing Descriptive Representation (Dependent Variables)

To gauge the presence of women (of various race/ethnicities) and people of color (women and men) in state legislatures, we rely primarily on our

---

[9] To account for the possibility that candidate emergence and success are fundamentally different across parties (Sanbonmatsu 2002) and acknowledge the fact that almost all Black and Latinx state legislators are Democrats, we also ran Democrat-only models. As noted below, these results do not differ significantly from those reported here.

own biographical database that identifies the gender and race/ethnicity of individual members of 28 state houses (lower chambers).[10] Our determination of gender was based primarily on pictures in the Blue Books (printed directories) or on state legislative websites, along with names and/ or pronouns used. To identify the race/ethnicity (White, African American, Latinx, Asian American, Native American) of legislators, we relied on information from multiple sources, including pictures and organizational affiliations, such as ethnic/racial caucuses or Historically Black Colleges and Universities (HBCUs), available in Blue Books and/or webpages of individual legislators; lists of African American or Latinx representatives published on state webpages or in other state documents; and explicit references to the racial/ethnic identity of legislators found in newspaper (Lexis-Nexis) and/or internet searches (e.g., "Representative XX is the first Latino to be elected the YY state legislature"). We also consulted directories of Asian American state legislators from the 2005–6 edition of the *National Asian Pacific American Political Almanac* (Nakanishi, Lai, and Kwok 2005– 6) and lists of Native American state legislators provided by the National Council of State Legislature's (NCSL's) State-Tribal Institute (personal communication, April 27, 2009).

To obtain data on the racial and gender composition of the remaining 21 state houses, we supplemented our own database with information made available to us by the Center for Women in American Politics (CAWP), the Joint Center for Political and Economic Studies (*Black Elected Officials Roster*, 2005), the National Latino Legislative Database Project (Ramirez 2006), the *National Asian Pacific American Political Almanac* (Nakanishi, Lai, and Kwok 2005–6), and the NCSL's State-Tribal Institute. All of these secondary sources employ methods similar to ours to determine the racial, ethnic, and/or gender identity of state legislators. We took advantage of the availability of multiple, overlapping data sources and cross-referenced our Latinx identified legislators with those of the National Latino Legislative Database Project (Ramirez 2006) and the National Association of Latino Elected and Appointed Officials' (NALEO's) annual directory. Any discrepancies were resolved by conducting further online searches and, ultimately, the weight of the resulting information.

---

[10] Only those legislators who were elected to fill the seat in the most recent regular election are included our district/seat and state level analyses; those who entered office "late" as midterm replacements are excluded.

For our purposes (here and throughout), "White" refers to any legislator who is not identified as African American, Latinx, Asian American, or Native American. Our coding scheme allows for legislators to be identified as members of multiple racial/ethnic groups. In our database of 2005 legislators, there are four who are coded as both Black and Latinx; one who is coded as Latinx and Asian American; and three who are coded as Latinx and Native American. In our state-level analyses (Tables 2.1 and 2.2a–b), these multi-ethnic legislators are counted as Black or Latinx whenever appropriate, for each corresponding dependent variable. For our district/seat-level model (Table 2.3), however, we chose to exclude all multi-ethnic legislators (N = 8) from the analysis rather than include them in a separate category (one too small for any quantitative analysis) or choose one racial/ethnic category over another. For similar reasons—very small numbers and arbitrary choices—we also exclude all Asian American (N = 59) and Native American (N = 40) legislators from the district/seat-level analysis.[11]

By classifying legislators into these mutually exclusive race-gender categories, we do not mean to suggest or assume that these identities are static, essential ones (Hancock 2007). Rather, we aim to capture legislators' contemporaneous, publicly acknowledged identities. This is why we rely so heavily on indicators of *publicly identified and/or identifiable* race, ethnicity, and gender. These are the sorts of socially constructed and recognized identities that give meaning to the concept of descriptive representation. Our subsequent analyses of the representational activity and impact of legislators are premised on—and, indeed, reinforce—the assumption that descriptive representation as conceived and measured here is no guarantee of uniformity in behavior, attitudes, or interactions with others.

Operationalizing Political Opportunity Structures (Independent Variables)

Data for many of our independent variables are drawn from the extant research literature, as our primary analytic goal is to re-evaluate existing

---

[11] Asian American and Native American legislators are also concentrated in very few states. Over half (N = 33) of all Asian American state legislators serve in the Hawaiian state house; almost three-quarters (N = 42) are found in either Hawaii or California. Two-thirds (N = 27) of all Native American state legislators serve in four states (Alaska, Montana, New Mexico, and Oklahoma).

knowledge produced by single-axis approaches to descriptive representation in the states. To measure the liberal/conservative ideological climate in the states, we rely upon Erikson, Wright, and McIver's (2006) updated (1996–2003) "meanideo" scores, which are derived from aggregated national public opinion polls.[12] Scores are the average difference between the percentage of respondents who identify as "liberal" and the percentage who identify as "conservative" (%liberal–%conservative).[13] Newly available measures of "constituent policy preferences" (Tausanovitch and Warshaw 2013) allow us to include constituent ideology in our district/seat-level analysis (Table 2.3) as well.[14] We also use Elazar's (1984) typology (moralistic, traditionalistic, individualistic) to measure political culture, the NCSL's typology (professional, hybrid, citizens) to measure legislative professionalism (Hamm and Moncrief 2008),[15] and Mayhew's (1986, 197) state "traditional party organization" (TPO) scores to measure the strength of state party organizations (Sanbonmatsu 2006).[16] To gauge the effect of term limits, we rely on NCSL data indicating which states had legislative term limits (of any length) in effect in 2004.[17]

District type (single-member vs. multi-member) was determined using a combination of the CQ *Almanac of State Legislative Elections* (Lilley et al. 2008), the State Legislative Election Return Project,[18] and our own searches on state legislative webpages. At the state level, we employ a dummy variable that simply distinguishes all states that have any (≥1) multimember districts

[12] Data available at http://mypage.iu.edu/~wright1/correctappendix.xls (last accessed July 30, 2009).
[13] We obtained very similar results (in Table 2.1) using Enns and Koch's (2013) measure of state-level citizen political ideology in 2005. The Berry et al. (1998) 2005 Citizen Ideology Scores, the primary alternative measure used in existing research, are not related to any of our measures of descriptive representation in numerous bivariate and multivariate analyses.
[14] Tausanovitch and Warshaw's (2013) estimates of state legislative district ideology are based on responses to surveys conducted by the Annenberg National Election Study and the Cooperative Congressional Election Study, 2000–11.
[15] For the most recent NCSL rankings, see http://www.ncsl.org/legislatures-elections/legislatures/full-and-part-time-legislatures.aspx.
[16] Alternative measures for political culture and party strength (Cotter et al. 1984, 28–29) are either ignored in the extant literature or unavailable for all 49 states. The main alternative for state legislative professionalism, Squire's (2007) updated continuous measure, was in almost every instance unrelated to descriptive representation in our analyses—bivariate or multivariate.
[17] NCSL data are available at www.ncsl.org/programs/legismgt/about/termedout.htm (accessed on April 20, 2009). More nuanced, continuous measures of "term limitedness" (Sarbaugh-Thompson 2010) provided no additional insight or advantage over the NCSL's dummy variable, especially since our primary interests are in the conditioning effects of term limits.
[18] State Legislative Election Returns, 1967–2003, Thomas M. Carsey, William D. Berry, Richard G. Niemi, Lynda W. Powell, and James M Snyder, Release Version 5. Codebook and data available at http://www.unc.edu/~carsey/research/datasets/data.htm (last accessed May 3, 2009).

of any sort (N = 10). Our results do not differ if we use alternative measures, including continuous measures of the percentage of state legislative districts that are multi-member and/or measures that count only "free-for-all" multi-member districts and not post-designated ones (see Hogan 2001; Richardson and Cooper 2003).

Demographic data used to gauge the racial/ethnic composition of state populations, the race-gender composition of state civilian labor forces, the size of states' college-educated White populations (measuring potential White "cross-over" support for minority candidates), and group-specific measures of socioeconomic status (including occupational status, unemployment rates, college education, and median income) were all obtained from the 2000 US Census.[19] Parallel demographic measures for state legislative districts also were obtained from the 2000 US Census.[20]

To gauge the size of the state and district Latinx population, we rely on Census estimates of Hispanic *citizens* only, excluding those who are classified by the Census as "not a citizen." Though the representational effects of the full (citizen and non-citizen) Latinx population tend to be a bit weaker than those for the citizen-only population, the general patterns remain the same and our conclusions do not differ. We opt for the Latinx citizen measure because it has greater face validity. In our models, the variables measuring the racial/ethnic composition of the state or district are meant to gauge racially polarized voter support for Latinx and African American candidates as well as the size of candidate eligibility pools. Thus, in this context, it makes sense to exclude non-citizens who can neither vote nor hold office. Descriptive statistics and more detailed information on data sources are available in Appendix Tables A.2a–d.

[19] US 2000 Summary File 3 (Sample) downloaded from http://factfinder.census.gov/servlet/DatasetMainPageServlet?_lang=en (July 2009; September 2011). State-level occupational measures were obtained from the US Census 2000 Special EEO Tabulation Files, downloaded from http://www.census.gov/hhes/www/eeoindex/eeoindex.html (August 4, 2009). Documentation for the Special EEO Tabulations can be found at http://www.eeoc.gov/stats/census/index.html.

[20] US Census 2000 State Legislative District Summary File 4 (Sample), downloaded from http://factfinder.census.gov/servlet/DatasetMainPageServlet?_lang=en (August 25, 2009) and from http://factfinder2.census.gov/faces/nav/jsf/pages/searchresults.xhtml?refresh=t   (October–November 2013). Districts containing no African American men, no African American women, no Latino men, or no Latinas (N = 626 or approximately 11.5% of our observations) are excluded from the district/seat-level analysis (Table 2.3), for they have no group resources to gauge.

Results

State Level: Women's Representation Across Racial/Ethnic Categories

According to standard W&P models, gender diversity in state legislatures is primarily a function of citizen ideology, state political culture, women's employment in the professions, legislative professionalization, the strength of state party organizations, and the presence or absence of multi-member districts. Our results strongly suggest, however, that this model is not generalizable across race/ethnicity. As intersectional critiques maintain, this single-axis model of a highly constrained, gendered electoral environment is in many respects more applicable to the fortunes of White women than it is to those of women of color.

As seen in Table 2.1, White women's representation is significantly lower in states with more conservative electorates, a traditionalistic political culture, a professionalized legislature, and stronger party organizations—as the existing, single-axis research suggests.[21] Overall, the results for White women are quite similar to those for all women combined.[22] The results for women of color, however, differ markedly in almost every respect.[23]

As expected, the presence of Black women and Latinas in state houses is unaffected by ideology, political culture, or party organizational strength.[24] Rather, the representation of minority women appears to be almost entirely a function of the size of their respective eligibility pool. Given the almost perfect correlation between the size of Black/Latina women's professional labor force and their racial/ethnic group's share of the state population (r = .94 and .98, respectively), this is precisely what the REP literature would suggest.

---

[21] The effect of party organizational strength is statistically significant with a 90% confidence interval (p = 0.107). Given the heavily censored nature of the distribution of minority state legislators (i.e., many state houses with no African Americans or no Latinxs), we chose tobit over ordinary least square regression models for our state-level analyses. To account for heteroskedasticity in our models, we use robust standard errors. Our results do not differ significantly when we employ seemingly unrelated regression or tobit (pairwise) models. However, we do use the "seemingly unrelated" post-estimation routine in Stata to gauge the statistical significance of differences in our results across equations in Tables 2.1, 2.2a, and 2.2b.

[22] Results for predicting the percentage of White *Democratic* women in state houses are also very similar. See Appendix, Table A.3.

[23] Unless noted otherwise, all differences between coefficients for White women and those for Black women or Latinas are statistically significant (p ≤ .05 in post-estimation chi-square tests).

[24] The differences in the effect of ideology on White women and Latinas and in the effect of party organization on White and Black women are statistically significant at p = .0605 and p = .0688, respectively.

Table 2.1 Descriptive Representation in State Houses, 2005
Women-and-Politics Model
Tobit (robust standard errors)

	% All Women	% White Women	% Black Women	% Latina Women
Ideology	.381*	.277*	−.009	.044
	(.151)	(.113)	(.046)	(.045)
Moralistic Political Culture	1.417	1.913	.026	1.215
	(3.563)	(3.392)	(1.202)	(.952)
Traditionalistic Political Culture	−3.711	−6.116^	1.481	.783
	(3.521)	(3.412)	(1.170)	(.997)
% Labor Force that Is Professional Women	.180	NA	NA	NA
	(.963)			
% Labor Force that Is Professional White Women	NA	.477	NA	NA
		(.628)		
% Labor Force that Is Professional Black Women	NA	NA	2.023***	NA
			(.315)	
% Labor Force that is Professional Latinas	NA	NA	NA	4.046***
				(.421)
Professional Legislature	−3.686^	−5.016*	1.731*	−.430
	(2.159)	(2.179)	(.818)	(.754)
Citizens' Legislature	−.520	.361	.017	−1.157
	(2.349)	(1.952)	(.692)	(.805)
Party Organizational Strength	−1.185	−1.275	.327	.430
	(.851)	(.774)	(.304)	(.270)
Multi-member Districts	2.312	3.009	−1.286^	.631
	(2.715)	(2.199)	(.661)	(.772)
Constant (Intercept)	29.717^	21.564*	−1.305	−3.060*
	(16.654)	(10.182)	(1.367)	(1.260)
No. of States	49	49	49	49
	F(8, 41) = 9.59***	F(8, 41) = 20.44***	F(8, 41) = 14.40***	F(8, 41) = 20.49***
	Pseudo R^2=0.0757	Pseudo R^2=0.1165	Pseudo R^2=0.2470	Pseudo R^2=0.3604
# left-censored observations	0 @0	0 @0	15 @ 0	32 @ 0

^p ≤ .10; *p ≤ .05; **p ≤ .01; ***p ≤ . 001

Joint effects of moralistic/traditional political culture are significant for White Women (p = .0037).

Joint effects of professional/citizen legislature are significant for White Women (p = .0748) and Black women (p = .0913).

Moreover, we cannot differentiate the impact of minority women's eligibility pools from that of intra-racial/ethnic communities as a whole. Either way, our hypothesis that professionalized eligibility pools are more important for White women than for women of color does not find support here.

The two remaining predictors have varying effects on women's representation across race/ethnicity. While state legislative professionalism works against the election of White women, it has no effect on the election of Latinas and a small but significant positive effect on the election of Black women.[25] And while multi-member districting has no apparent effect on either White women or Latinas, it has a small but marginally significant negative effect on African American women (as the standard REP model would suggest). Thus, while Black women's representation is not immune from legislative professionalism or multi-member electoral structures, as hypothesized, it is impacted in ways not anticipated by standard single-axis models of (White) women's representation.

State Level: African American and Latinx Representation Across Gender

According to standard REP models, racial/ethnic diversity in state legislatures is primarily a function of the racial/ethnic composition of the citizenry: the larger the minority population, the larger the minority delegation in the legislature. The strength of that population-seat relationship, however, can be weakened by the presence of large, multi-member districts (which make it harder to construct majority- or near majority-minority districts) or by a lack of legislative turnover. Accordingly, Table 2.2a tests the population-seat model conditioned on the presence of multi-member districts and Table 2.2b tests the population-seat model conditioned on having term limits in effect. Further analysis (not shown) also explores the effects of White crossover support and group resources.[26]

---

[25] The difference between the coefficients for White women and Latinas is not significant (p = .1232).

[26] Given our limited number of observations and degrees of freedom, our state-level models of African American and Latinx representation (Tables 2.2a and 2.2b) are necessarily restricted. First, we cannot test simultaneously the conditioning or interactive effects of both multi-member districting and term limits. Second, beyond the racial/ethnic population and conditioning variables presented in Tables 2.2a and 2.2b, we can include only one additional independent variable. Even with only one additional independent variable, we are unable to estimate confidence intervals for point estimates. Thus, measures of White crossover support and group-specific resources were introduced one at a time to the base models presented in Tables 2.2a and 2.2b. Following Casellas

Table 2.2a Descriptive Representation in State Houses, 2005 Race-and-Ethnic Politics Multi-Member District Conditional Model Tobit (robust standard errors)

	% Black (All)	% Black Men	% Black Women	% Latinx (All)	% Latino Men	% Latina Women
% Black	.773***	.577***	.245***	.071^	.027	.040
	(.048)	(.041)	(.039)	(.041)	(.037)	(.035)
% Latinx Citizens	.077*	.017	.063^	1.154***	.851***	.382***
	(.036)	(.049)	(.033)	(.084)	(.060)	(.032)
Multi-member Districts	-.874	-.126	-1.731	.533	.048	-.414
	(1.026)	(1.017)	(1.216)	(1.403)	(1.372)	(1.301)
MMD * % Black	.102	.023	.120*	.005	.037	.054
	(.067)	(.086)	(.051)	(.055)	(.053)	(.052)
MMD * % Latinx Citizens	-.022	-.041	.030	.035	-.055	.157**
	(.067)	(.164)	(.088)	(.115)	(.092)	(.058)
Constant (Intercept)	-.632	-1.245*	-.459	-4.610***	-3.406***	-2.939***
	(.720)	(.611)	(.712)	(.906)	(.735)	(.768)
No. of States	49	49	49	49	49	49
	$F_{(5, 44)} = 139.61$***	$F_{(5, 44)} = 56.10$***	$F_{(5, 44)} = 30.79$***	$F_{(5, 44)} = 153.78$***	$F_{(5, 44)} = 139.17$***	$F_{(5, 44)} = 269.84$***
	Pseudo $R^2 = 0.3436$	Pseudo $R^2 = 0.3560$	Pseudo $R^2 = 0.2014$	Pseudo $R^2 = 0.4083$	Pseudo $R^2 = 0.4058$	Pseudo $R^2 = 0.3730$
# left-censored observations	8 @ 0	13 @ 0	15 @ 0	18 @ 0	21 @ 0	32 @ 0

^$p \leq .10$; *$p \leq .05$; **$p \leq .01$; ***$p \leq .001$

Table 2.2b Descriptive Representation in State Houses, 2005 Race- and Ethnic-Politics Term Limits Conditional Model Tobit (robust standard errors)

	% Black (All)	% Black Men	% Black Women	% Latinx (All)	% Latino Men	% Latina Women
% Black	.765***	.567***	.248***	.048	.013	.046
	(.041)	(.037)	(.034)	(.032)	(.030)	(.030)
% Latinx Citizens	.091*	.005	.088***	1.108***	.824***	.352***
	(.038)	(.058)	(.025)	(.109)	(.076)	(.028)
Term Limits	-4.018**	-2.872**	-3.195^	-9.323***	-9.412***	-2.023*
	(1.340)	(.968)	(1.839)	(2.348)	(1.573)	(.847)
Term Limits * % Black	.454***	.221*	.405***	.557***	.654***	-.102*
	(.102)	(.087)	(.111)	(.142)	(.092)	(.044)
Term Limits * % Latinx Citizens	.023	.082	-.004	.422**	.324**	.243***
	(.074)	(.066)	(.083)	(.133)	(.101)	(.052)
Constant (Intercept)	-.704	-1.014^	-.822	-3.897***	-2.968***	-2.553***
	(.545)	(.557)	(.562)	(.833)	(.674)	(.696)
No. of States	49	49	49	49	49	49
	$F_{(5,44)} = 106.91$***	$F_{(5,44)} = 68.35$***	$F_{(5,44)} = 17.60$***	$F_{(5,44)} = 185.55$***	$F_{(5,44)} = 111.19$***	$F_{(5,44)} = 60.40$***
	Pseudo R^2=0.3657	Pseudo R^2=0.3645	Pseudo R^2=0.2335	Pseudo R^2=0.4353	Pseudo R^2=0.4525	Pseudo R^2=0.3858
# left-censored observations	8 @ 0	13 @ 0	15 @ 0	18 @ 0	21 @ 0	32 @ 0

^$p \leq .10$; *$p \leq .05$; **$p \leq .01$; ***$p \leq .001$

Results in Tables 2.2a–b and Figures 2.1a–b confirm much of the previous research on African American and Latinx representation: the racial/ethnic composition of the state population is key. The electoral fortunes of African American men and women alike depend heavily on the size of the Black population, and the electoral fortunes of Latinos and Latinas alike depend heavily on the size of the Latinx citizenry. However, women of color reap significantly fewer electoral benefits from their co-ethnic communities than their male counterparts do, especially in the majority of states without multi-member districts (Figure 2.1a) and in the majority of states without term limits (Figure 2.1b). Only in states where term limits are in effect does Black women's representation get as much of a boost from the state's Black population as Black men's representation does (see Figure 2.1b, left panel).

As in previous research, we find only limited evidence of significant interracial effects. Regardless of electoral structures, the size of the Latinx population has no effect on the election of Black men, and only a small, positive

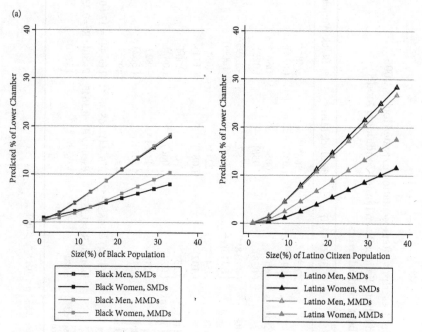

Figure 2.1a Effects of State Racial/Ethnic Composition on Descriptive Representation—With and Without Multimember Districts
(SMD = Single-member District; MMD = Multimember District)

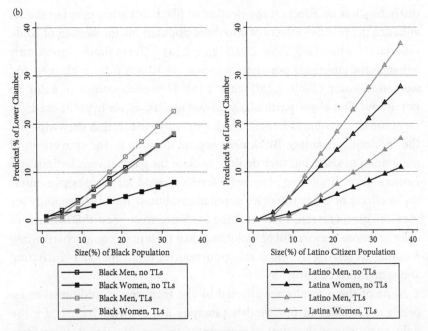

Figure 2.1b Effects of Racial/Ethnic Composition on Descriptive Representation—With and Without Term Limits

(TL = Term Limits)

effect on the election of Black women. While the difference in the estimated effects is not statistically significant, it is congruent with our hypothesis that women of color will benefit more from cross-racial support than men of color. On the other hand, the most significant inter-racial effects run counter to our hypothesis. In states with term limits, Latino male representation benefits tremendously from larger African American populations while Latina representation actually suffers a bit. In states without term limits, the size of the Black population has no discernible effect on Latino or Latina officeholding.

Electoral structures themselves have curious effects on minority representation, according to our results. Contrary to H2, multi-member

(2009, 2011), we also substituted legislative professionalization for term limits as the turnover-related conditioning variable. However, we found no evidence to suggest that professionalization inhibits the conversion of population to seats. Contrary to results in Table 2.1, we also found that professionalization has no significant first-order or direct effects on Black or Latinx descriptive representation, regardless of gender.

districting has no effect on the election of Black or Latino men but it does enhance the positive effects of co-ethnic populations for women of color, especially Latinas (see Table 2.2a/Figure 2.1a).[27] Term limits significantly enhance the co-ethnic population-to-seat relationship for both men and women of color (Table 2.2b/Figure 2.1b). However, women of color do not always find them particularly advantageous, as we hypothesized. As mentioned, term limits benefit Black women so much that they wipe out the "normal" advantage Black men appear to enjoy in the conversion of population to seats; but they do little to close the gap between Latinos and Latinas. Term limits can also create fertile ground for the positive, inter-racial effects of other minority populations, but as noted above, only for men of color. Overall, there is some evidence to suggest that women of color are more resourceful or ambitious than their male counterparts when it comes to seizing the electoral opportunities multi-member districting and term limits can provide.

None of these results are affected by the inclusion of additional inde-pendent variables in our models (analysis not shown). Latinas are the only ones whose descriptive representation benefits significantly from larger populations of well-educated White populations, providing only limited support for H2. Group-specific resources also have very lim-ited effects, and in the opposite direction expected. Black resources, especially those of Black men, have significant negative effects on Black representation, but only in the multimember-districting. And there is no evidence to suggest that Black women are any less dependent on such resources.

Modeling Gender, Race, and Ethnicity at the District/Seat Level

Our hypotheses find even less support in our district/seat level anal-ysis (Table 2.3). Here, we incorporate insights from both the predominant W&P and REP models to see how the likelihood of all six representational outcomes (a state house seat being occupied by a White man, White woman, Black man, Black woman, Latino, or Latina) is shaped by the following district-level characteristics: racial and ethnic composition (percentage

---

[27] Gender differences in the conditioning effects of multi-member districting are statistically sig-nificant for Latinx representation (p = .0562), but not for Black representation (p = .3880).

Table 2.3 Descriptive Representation of State House Seats, 2005
Multinomial Logit (standard errors)

	White Woman/ White Man	Black Man/White Man	Black Woman/ White Man	Latino/ White Man	Latina/ White Man
Policy Conservatism	−.690*** (.176)	−.756 (.513)	−.904 (.606)	−1.136^ (.591)	−.665 (.804)
% White College Educated	.008 (.008)	−.031 (.027)	−.008 (.032)	−.039 (.026)	−.016 (.037)
% Urban	.003* (.002)	.021*** (.005)	.033*** (.007)	.023* (.010)	.018 (.012)
% Black	.001 (.004)	.112*** (.008)	.119*** (.011)	−.003 (.016)	.024 (.019)
% Latinx Citizens	.008 (.007)	.040* (.016)	.045* (.020)	.138*** (.011)	.140*** (.014)
Multi-Member District	.448*** (.095)	.179 (.350)	.128 (.405)	.486 (.363)	1.157** (.444)
Resources/SES of White Women	.219* (.109)	.033 (.237)	.080 (.257)	.475^ (.255)	.446 (.321)
Resources/SES of Black Men	−.021 (.074)	.686^ (.388)	.300 (.655)	−.080 (.377)	−.063 (.483)
Resources/SES of Black Women	.012 (.073)	−.906* (.404)	−.525 (.654)	.056 (.334)	.110 (.433)
Resources/SES of Latinos	−.134^ (.079)	−.383 (.286)	−.433 (.334)	.404 (.452)	−1.414 (.870)
Resources/SES of Latinas	.035 (.079)	−.032 (.232)	.043 (.276)	−.537 (.507)	.159 (.735)
Constant (Intercept)	−1.877*** (.227)	−7.178*** (.810)	−9.620*** (1.084)	−7.020*** (1.210)	−8.428*** (1.587)

No. of seats = 4685
LR chi²(55) = 3074.16***
Pseudo R² = 0.3292

SES = socioeconomic status
^p ≤ .10; *p ≤ .05; **p ≤ .01; ***p ≤ .001

Black, percentage Latinx citizen); ideology; size of the White college-educated population; level of urbanization; resources or socioeconomic status
of each race-gender group (excluding White men); and electoral structure
(multi- or single-member).[28] The results of this more integrated approach

---

[28] Multicollinearity prevents us from distinguishing the effects of district racial/ethnic composition from those of non-White eligibility pools or the effects of White crossover support from

further clarify how political opportunity structures channel the electoral fortunes of women of color in ways that are both familiar and distinctive.

Again, we see little evidence suggesting the determinants of women's descriptive representation are the same regardless of race/ethnicity and a good deal of evidence suggesting the determinants of African American and Latinx descriptive representation do not differ dramatically by gender.[29] Post-estimation Wald tests for combining alternatives (Long and Freese 2006, 239–40) indicate that the independent variables as a group significantly differentiate between all possible pairs of alternative outcomes *except* the Black-man/Black-woman and Latino/Latina pairs. In other words, state house seats occupied by Black men and women, or by Latinos and Latinas, are statistically indistinguishable with respect to the variables in our model. Yet those occupied by White women, Black women, and Latinas are quite different. These patterns are largely attributable to the effects of districts' racial/ethnic makeup.

As Figures 2.2a–b illustrate, much depends on the size of the Black and Latinx citizen populations in the districts. Across gender, African American representation benefits tremendously from the presence of large Black populations; Latinx representation is equally dependent on large populations of Latinx citizens; and White representation suffers in both scenarios. Moreover, the marginal effects of district racial/ethnic composition follow similar patterns for women and men in the same racial/ethnic group. For Black men and women alike, the size of the district's Black population has practically no effect until it reaches a threshold of about 30%; and it has its strongest impact in the critical, majority-minority range of 45–55%. For Latinos and Latinas alike, the size of the district's Latinx citizen population has no effect until it reaches a threshold of about 25% and its strongest effect is in the range of 35–55%.[30] And for White men and women alike, the probability of descriptive representation starts to decline at the same thresholds and takes a proportionately similar dive in the same majority-minority ranges.

---

those of White women's eligibility pools. Controlling for state fixed effects results in hugely inflated coefficients and standard errors for the estimated effects of Multi-Member District on African American Woman, Latino, and Latina outcomes, and for the constants for all outcomes except those for White Woman. With few exceptions, however, the patterns seen in Table 2.3 remain quite similar.

[29] Results for *Democratic*-held seats only do not differ significantly from those reported here. See Appendix, Table A.4.

[30] The effects of co-ethnic populations on African American and Latinx representation are so profound that no other variable has a significant, non-zero effect unless and until the respective district populations are well within the "critical thresholds" identified.

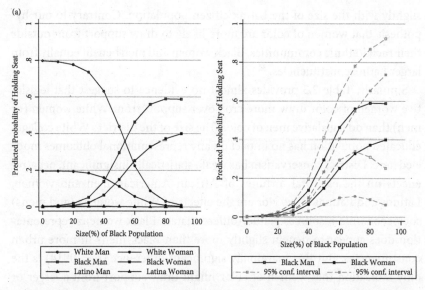

Figure 2.2a Effects of District Black Population on Descriptive Representation

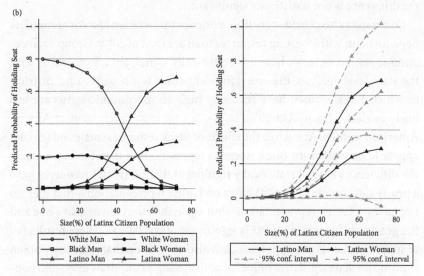

Figure 2.2b Effects of District Latinx Citizen Population on Descriptive Representation

As in the state-level analysis, evidence of cross-racial/ethnic support among minorities is quite mixed. The probability of Latino or Latina representation is unaffected by the size of the African American population, and the probability of Black female or Black male representation increases slightly with the size of the Latinx citizen population. Contrary to our hypothesis that women of color are more likely to draw support from outside their racial/ethnic communities, Black women and men benefit equally from larger Latinx constituencies. [31]

Similarly, Table 2.3 provides almost no evidence to suggest that legislative women of color draw more crossover support from White women (or men) than do legislative men of color. The size of the district's White college-educated population has no impact on any representational outcomes modeled here. District conservatism has weak, statistically insignificant, negative effects on the electoral fortunes of African American men and women, Latinos and Latinas alike. Nor are the effects of White women's (and men's) socioeconomic resources gender-differentiated. Black women's representation does appear to benefit slightly more than Black men's in more urban constituencies. But this marginally significant difference ($p = .0914$) is the only indication that women of color might draw support from a larger or more diverse pool of voters. If anything, more urban districts give a slightly stronger boost to Latino representation than to Latina representation, but the difference is not statistically significant.

Our results also provide very little evidence that women of color are any less dependent on within-group resources than are men of color. Group socioeconomic resources rarely have any statistically significant effect, and as with the state-level analysis, the one significant effect is a negative one: districts in which Black women have relatively high socioeconomic status are less likely to elect African American men—but no more likely to elect African American women. And while the effects of Black resources (male and female) appear to be weaker for Black women's representation than for Black men's, the differences are not statistically significant. Latino (male) resources have a nearly significant ($p = 0.104$) effect on Latina representation—that they do not have on Latino representation—but again the effect is a negative one and the gender difference in effects is significant at $p = 0.0557$. These results fail to support not only our hypothesis, but also any notion that minority women running for state legislative office (or considering a run) draw upon and benefit disproportionately from the support of well-to-do minority women in their districts.

---

[31] No within-group gender differences in the representational effects of %Black and %Latinx citizen are statistically significant ($p \leq .05$ in post-estimation chi-square tests).

Clearly, whether Latina, Black, or White, women's descriptive representation is highly constrained by district-level politics of race—albeit in very different ways. But beyond the effects of district racial/ethnic composition, are the electoral fortunes of White women any more constrained by the political geography of state legislative districts than are those of Latina and African American women—as we hypothesized? Results in Table 2.3 suggest not.

As noted above, no one's electoral fortunes depend on the size of the district's White college-educated population. White women's chances of gaining a state legislative seat are significantly dependent upon district ideology and their own socioeconomic status, while those of Latinas and African American women are not; but none of the differences in effects are statistically significant. Both White women's and Latinas' chances of getting elected are significantly enhanced in multimember districts. But contrary to H1, Latina representation is, if anything, *more* dependent on such electoral institutions than is White women's (p = 0.1134); and while Black women's representation does appear to be "free" of such constraints, the difference in the estimated effects of multi-member districts on Black and White women is not statistically significant.[32] Similar patterns of contradictory and insignificant racial/ethnic differences can be seen in the effects of district urbanization on women's chances of gaining a state legislative seat.

Conclusions

Black women can experience discrimination in any number of ways . . . that are both similar to and different from those experienced by white women and Black men. (Crenshaw 1989, 149)

Together, our state- and seat-level models of descriptive representation in state legislatures demonstrate the utility of a critical intersectional approach to re-evaluating single-axis theories. First, they highlight the perils of generalizing about gender across categories of race/ethnicity. In numerous

---

[32] The difference in the effects of multi-member districts on Black women's and Latinas' chances of electoral success is significant at p = 0.0775.

instances, we see that the conditions that foster or impede White women's representation do not necessarily affect that of African American women or Latinas in the same ways—and vice versa. The state-level conservatism, traditionalism, legislative professionalism, and party organizational strength that impede White women's representation have little or no effect on Black women's or Latinas' representation. The district-level racial and ethnic diversity that propels women of color into state legislative office inhibits the election of White women.

Nor is it always safe to generalize about "women of color." Some evidence suggests that while multi-member districting is particularly advantageous for Latinas, term limits are particularly advantageous for Black women. Though the differences are not always statistically significant, African American women may benefit more from the crossover support of Latinxs than Latinas do from that of African American women and men; and Latina representation may benefit more from White crossover support than does Black women's representation. Of course, the same can be said for generalizing about "minority" men. The politics of race and gender are too complex for such generalizations or assumptions to go unchallenged.

Having tested such assumptions, however, we can say with more confidence that conclusions regarding African American or Latinx representation are often equally applicable to the experiences of women of color and men of color. This is especially so when it comes to the effects of the racial/ethnic composition of state and district populations and, by implication, racial redistricting. Thus, even when the null hypothesis rules the day, an intersectional approach can contribute to our knowledge. Evidence that the electoral fortunes of minority men and women are so closely tied to the support of their own racial/ethnic communities can speak volumes about the politics and history of race, and even gender, in the United States.

Nonetheless, our findings are not all that cut and dried. In our seat-level analysis, for example, we uncover a number of similarities in the kinds of districts in which White women, Black women, and Latinas find electoral opportunities and challenges. Also noteworthy are the very significant differences in the ability of women and men of color to reap the benefits of the population-to-seats relationship at the state level. Larger African American and Latinx populations somehow translate into more seats for Black and Latino men than for Black and Latina women, respectively—especially in the majority of states without multi-member districts or term limits. While women of color may not need much larger concentrations of minority voters

to get elected in any given district, our results suggest they are not successfully contesting those districts at equivalent rates.

Our research thus sheds much needed light on—and raises additional
questions about—the experiences of women of color in electoral politics.
Building on existing theories and evidence suggesting the comparative
strength, ambition, and resilience of minority women in politics, we hypothesized that Latina and African American women would be less constrained
by most of the opportunity structures thought to channel the electoral
fortunes of women and racial/ethnic minorities in general—and more likely
to take advantage of new opportunities, such as term limits, and untapped resources, such as crossover support from White women (and men) and other
women (and men) of color. Our state level analyses provide some support for
these hypotheses: the presence of women of color in state legislatures is less
dependent on state ideology, political culture, party organizations, and legislative professionalism than is the presence of White women. We also find
that Black women are particularly effective at taking advantage of term limits
while Latinas are pursuing opportunities in (states with) multi-member
districts. Each of these opportunity structures may help explain how the
numbers of state legislative women of color have increased so rapidly in recent years (compared to the numbers of White women and men of color),
but still remain low.

We hesitate, moreover, to conclude that large co-ethnic populations are
any less important for the electoral success of minority women than for minority men. First, we uncover no evidence that women of color get more seats
out of smaller co-ethnic populations than do men of color, thus making them
less dependent on larger co-ethnic populations. Second, there is very little
and no consistent evidence in either our state- or district-level analyses that
women of color have the intersectional advantage of gaining support from
elsewhere—that is, from either White women (and men) or other women
(and men) of color.

All of this further suggests that, compared to White women especially,
the electoral fortunes of women of color are no less constrained by political opportunity structures, just differently constrained. For whereas
women of color may be relatively immune from the constraints of state
political cultures, party organizations, and legislative institutions, they are
profoundly more constrained by the racial/ethnic politics of state and district demographics. Plus, there are some indications that women of color
find less support from within their co-ethnic communities than their male

counterparts do. In short, this is not what the political geography of intersectional advantage or resilience would look like. The 2018 election of Lauren Underwood and other women of color to majority-White congressional districts gives hope that circumstances have changed since the first Year of the Woman. Whether this is a reflection of long-lasting systemic changes in race-gender opportunity structures remains to be seen. Our results suggest that, without such structural or institutional change (say, in party recruitment of candidates), unusually high levels of community activism (Hardy-Fanta et al. 2007, 2016) and political ambition (Lawless 2012) are not enough to propel 21st-century women of color into public office. Further investigation and theorizing is clearly needed.

Indeed, future research on gender, race, and descriptive representation could and should be even more intersectional in its approach, especially with respect to theory-building. Our research draws upon and tests single-axis theories, models, hypotheses, and variables developed with either women (undifferentiated by race or ethnicity) or African Americans and Latinxs (undifferentiated by gender) in mind. Theorizing about the descriptive representation of Black women and/or Latinas remains relatively under-developed, leaving us with too few models, hypotheses, or variables that might be uniquely or particularly applicable to them. Development of such intersectional research tools could help address many of the questions our research uncovers or resurrects. Why, for example, is the state-level population-seat relationship so often weaker for women of color than for men of color? Why is there so little evidence of cross-racial coalition building to further diversify public officeholding, by which political women could draw upon the support of other women (and men) across racial/ethnic boundaries? Are intersecting and compounding systems of marginalization undermining rather than facilitating such efforts? In short, what are we leaving out of our models?

3

Conceptions of Group Interests and the Links between Descriptive and Substantive Representation

Once women and minorities are elected to public office, what difference does it make—especially for the women and minorities they descriptively represent? Decades of research make it quite clear that descriptive representation matters (Griffin 2014; Reingold 2008, 2014; Swers and Rouse 2011). Public officials who "stand for" women, African Americans, and Latinxs in terms of shared identity are more likely to "act for" them as well, thus reinforcing many of the hopes and expectations that have long fueled efforts to elect more women and minorities (Pitkin 1967; Williams 1998). Nowhere is this link between identity and representational activity more clearly and consistently demonstrated than in the research on legislators' policy leadership.

Across time, level of office, and political parties, female representatives are the ones more likely to care about, talk about, and legislate women's issues and interests (Berkman and O'Connor 1993; Bratton 2002, 2005; Bratton and Haynie 1999; Carroll 2008; Dodson 2006; Dodson and Carroll 1991; Dolan and Kropf 2004; Fridkin and Woodall 2005; Gerrity, Osborn, and Mendez 2007; Holman 2015; MacDonald and O'Brien 2011; Orey et al. 2006; Osborn 2012; Osborn and Mendez 2010; Pearson and Dancey 2011; Reingold 2000; Saint-Germain 1989; Swers 2002, 2013; Thomas 1994; Wolbrecht 2002). These gender gaps in women's substantive representation are revealed in interviews, surveys, press releases, and newsletters, in committees and on the floor, and—most forcefully—in the bills lawmakers sponsor. Likewise, Black and Latinx legislators are the ones most attentive to Black and Latinx constituents and interests, respectively—across time, level of office, and practically every dimension of policymaking activity, from legislative oversight, to directing "pork barrel" government resources, to committee deliberations and floor speeches, to bill sponsorship (Baker and Cook 2005; Bratton 2006; Bratton and Haynie 1999; Broockman 2013; Canon 1999; Casellas 2011;

Race, Gender, and Political Representation. Beth Reingold, Kerry L. Haynie, and Kirsten Widner, Oxford University Press (2021). © Oxford University Press. DOI: 10.1093/oso/9780197502174.001.0001.

Gamble 2007; Grose 2011; Haynie 2001; Minta 2011; Rouse 2013; Wallace 2014; Wilson 2010, 2017).[1]

Despite this wealth of data, relatively little is known about the representational activity or policy leadership of women of color. How do African American women and Latinas "fit in," if at all? Do they act for women *and* minorities—more so than their White female or minority male counterparts? If so, how? How might they address multiple group interests in their policy initiatives? How, even, would we know? Intersectional theorists argue that the single-axis tools of analysis used in all the research cited above to address single-axis questions about race, gender, and representation are inadequate to the task.

Collins (2000, 5–6), for example warns: "Theories advanced as being universally applicable to women as a group upon closer examination appear greatly limited by the White, middle-class, and Western origins of their proponents." Crenshaw (1989, 139) vividly illustrates some of those limitations in her groundbreaking "Black Feminist Critique of Antidiscrimination Doctrine, Feminist Theory and Antiracist Politics": the "problematic consequence of the tendency to treat race and gender as mutually exclusive categories of experience and analysis"—embodied in the very terminology of "women and minorities"—is the erasure of those who are "multiply-burdened" by intersecting forces of sexism and racism. In case after case reviewed by Crenshaw, Black women's claims of discrimination were denied; they had no legal standing as women harmed by sex discrimination, as Blacks harmed by racial discrimination, or as Black women harmed by sex and race discrimination. Just as dominant legal conceptions of discrimination obscure "claims that cannot be understood as resulting from discrete sources of [sex or race] discrimination" (Crenshaw 1989, 139), so too can single-axis theories and concepts of political representation distort, discount, and even deny the experiences, perspectives, and interests of women of color.

---

[1] There is also a wealth of research that gauges legislators' preferences on women's issues or racial/ethnic issues via surveys or, more often, roll-call votes on proposed legislation (e.g., Baker and Cook 2005; Canon 1999; Casellas 2009; Frederick 2009; Griffin and Newman 2008; Hero and Tolbert 1995; Juenke and Preuhs 2012; Lublin 1997; Osborn 2012; Reingold 2000; Swain 1993; Swers 2002; Wallace 2014; Whitby and Krause 2001; Wilson 2017). From this perspective, evidence of the link between descriptive and substantive representation is mixed and relatively weak. Partisanship and constituency often account for all or almost all explained variation. Due to the relatively passive and highly selective nature of such behavior, we do not consider these expressions of policy preferences or support as forms of policy leadership.

Smooth's (2011) conundrum illustrates this very problem, as applied to the study of women's political representation and notions of women's interests upon which it rests.

In conducting interviews with female African American state legislators, I found that the great debates among women and politics scholars over the meaning of women's issues have not captured a major issue that surfaced time and again in the interviews. The African American women I interviewed affirmed that "women's issues" constituted a top priority on their legislative agendas and understood themselves as representatives of women's interests. But when they began to discuss the issues they championed on behalf of women, these issues were not the "usual suspects." They often mentioned proposed legislation that I would have coded as a "children's issue" or, at times, a "race issue." These legislators articulated a political agenda reflecting crosscutting issues that were not easily codified along a single issue axis. Instead, the legislators articulated their legislative priorities as complex and multifaceted. They saw their legislative priorities affecting constituents across their districts, but they also keenly expressed the impact of these issues on the lives and well-being of women in particular. (Smooth 2011, 436)

Our ability to gauge the links between the descriptive and substantive representation of Latinxs, African Americans, and women necessarily rests on how we define and measure group interests—what it means to "act for" a marginalized group. And that is our most daunting challenge. Our goal in this chapter and the next two is to confront that challenge head on. What exactly are the problems that make the task so challenging and how can we address them? We begin our analysis of the relationship between race, gender, and representational behavior by taking an intersectionally critical examination of various single-axis conceptions of group interests—women's, Blacks', and Latinxs'. To what extent and how do these definitions and resulting measures of representational activity distort, discount, and even deny the initiatives of women of color? In particular, we explore Smooth's (2011, 437) assertion that the more narrowly defined group-specific conceptions (e.g., violence against women, racial discrimination, immigration) are more problematic than broader, overlapping conceptions of group interests and issues (e.g., health and education).

With a firmer grasp of the limitations of single-axis approaches, we move toward a more intersectional approach to confront the challenge of group interests and substantive representation. How do we recognize the complexity and multiplicity of group interests that are forged by the dynamic and intersecting powers and privileges of race and gender? Chapter 4 takes an important step in the right direction to examine what we call *race-gender policy leadership*: legislative activity that addresses matters specific to both women/gender and minorities/race. Rather than impose one singular model of race-gender policy leadership, we examine multiple approaches that could be characterized as more or less additive or intersectional. Again, the key question remains, what can this race-gender framework reveal about the representational priorities of women of color (and others) that existing single-axis frameworks obscure? Chapter 5 then takes a more in-depth, qualitative, and inductive approach to examining the race-gender nature of state legislators' policy proposals. Here our main task is to explore the intersectional contours of race- and/or gender-inflected policy itself. What might intersectional initiatives look like? Who crafts such legislation and whom does it serve?

All three chapters, therefore, offer an intersectional response to the challenges of studying who represents whom and conceptualizing race-gender political interests and advocacy. They do so by deconstructing and reconstructing the categories of analysis we use to classify and analyze the social identities of policymakers and the group interests they champion. Such intersectional approaches, we argue, are key to revealing the distinctive representational impact of women of color as well as the complexity and multiplicity of race, gender, and representation.

Concepts of Representation: Single-Axis Approaches to Group Interests and Policy Leadership

To observe the substantive representation of women, African Americans, or Latinxs in the policy leadership of elected officials, political scientists have carefully considered and employed a variety of conceptual and operational definitions of group issues and interests. Most begin with the notion of salience and look to group-specific research and reports on public opinion, public policy, social movements, advocacy organizations, and even candidates and officeholders themselves for insights into what issues are of most concern to group members (objectively and/or subjectively). Nonetheless, scholars often differ on how directly and uniquely salient those issues are. Some women's issues, for example, are salient because they primarily or most directly concern or affect women as women, while others are salient because they reflect the more "traditional" concerns (or interests) that women as primary caretakers presumably have about others, especially children and those in need. Accordingly, some studies distinguish "women's" or "women-specific" issues like abortion, domestic violence, sexual harassment, and child care from more general social welfare issues, such as education, healthcare, and poverty assistance (MacDonald and O'Brien 2011; Osborn 2012; Reingold 2000; Saint-Germain 1989; Swers 2002, 2013; Thomas 1994).

Conceptions of Black and Latinx political interests/issues make very similar distinctions regarding group salience, *or how directly, specifically, or explicitly an issue or bill concerns the group in question* (Minta and Brown 2014). Rouse (2013), for example, identifies four issue areas "of concern to Latinos" (p. 49): "specific Latino interests, education, health, and welfare policy" (p. 53). In this conception, "specific" Latino interest bills include "such measures as prohibiting ethnic discrimination, protecting migrant workers, issues relating to new legal and illegal immigrants, and addressing the specific health and welfare needs of Latinos" as well as "education programs to help limited English proficiency (LEP) students" (p. 54). Education, health, and welfare policy, on the other hand, are much broader categories that address general issues of access and opportunity in the quality, quantity, and/or equity of government provided or regulated social benefits and needs. (See also Bratton 2006; Casellas 2011; Griffin and Newman 2008; Wallace 2014; Wilson 2010.)

Similarly, almost every study of African American representation builds on Kinder and Sanders' (1996, 29) distinction between "matters of policy that bear unambiguously and uniquely on race" and "'implicit' or 'covert' racial issues . . . [that] do not explicitly mention race but may be widely understood to have a racial implication." Canon (1999, 166), for example, distinguishes "racial" issues or bills "dealing with civil rights, discrimination, minority businesses and historically black colleges" from "part-racial" ones "concerning public housing, food stamps, welfare, inner-city revitalization, and gun control." Again, the main distinction is often between racially targeted measures and more general social welfare policies that likely have indirect and disproportionate impacts on African Americans and/or other racial/

ethnic minorities. (See also Bratton and Haynie 1999; Griffin and Newman 2008; Haynie 2001; Minta 2011.)

Studies also differ in whether they draw ideological lines, especially when dealing with issues more directly salient to women or racial/ethnic minorities. Studies of women's representation often distinguish and compare leadership on feminist initiatives that promote women's rights or equality and more general, liberal *or* conservative, social welfare issues (MacDonald and O'Brien 2011; Saint-Germain 1989; Swers 2002, 2013). Others restrict designated women's issues to only those that are feminist (and women-specific), or at the very least not anti-feminist (Bratton 2002; Bratton and Haynie 1999; Dodson and Carroll 1991; Wolbrecht 2002). Still others impose no ideological restrictions (Gerrity, Osborn, and Mendez 2007; Osborn 2012; Reingold 2000; Thomas 1994). Studies of racial/ethnic representation follow similar patterns, though most adopt Bratton and Haynie's (1999, 665) lead and define specific group interests "in an explicitly liberal fashion" and with an eye toward combating racial discrimination and inequalities (e.g., Bratton 2006; Bratton, Haynie, and Reingold 2006; Haynie 2001; Orey et al. 2006; Rouse 2013; Wallace 2014; Wilson 2017).[2] Only a few examine conservative or "anti"-group activity targeted toward women or racial/ethnic minorities as a separate or distinct category of analysis (Reingold et al. forthcoming; Osborn 2012; Swers 2002; Swers and Larson 2005; Wilson 2010).

Remarkably, all these studies show that descriptive representation makes a difference regardless of which definition of group interests is employed. Some studies note, however, that the size of the gender or racial/ethnic differences, or the strength of the relationship between identity and representational leadership may vary depending on how group interests are defined (Bratton 2006; Bratton and Haynie 1999; Brown and Banks 2014; Canon 1999; Haynie 2001; Minta and Brown 2014; Osborn 2012; Reingold 2000; Rouse 2013; Swers 2002; Thomas 1994; Wilson 2010). Overall, these studies suggest that descriptive representation is more powerful the more narrowly or explicitly group interests are defined. Swers's (2002) study of the 103rd and 104th Congresses (1993–96), for example, finds that gender differences in policy leadership are more pronounced on feminist issues than on social welfare

---

[2] Canon (1999) is not explicit with regard to ideological screening; however, the examples he provides suggest that he too is restricting his analysis of "racial" and "part-racial" bills to those that would combat racial discrimination and promote the welfare and status of African Americans. Minta (2011; Minta and Brown 2014) may be the exception to the rule, though he too does not offer an explicit statement regarding ideology.

issues. At the same time, a few studies have paid close attention to variation among descriptive representatives, most notably differences related to partisanship (Baker and Cook 2005; Osborn 2012; Swers 2002, 2013; Wilson 2017), generation (Brown 2014b; Canon 1999), national origin (Bratton 2006; Wallace 2014), and race or gender (Bratton, Haynie, and Reingold 2006; Brown and Banks 2014; Minta and Brown 2014; Orey et al. 2006).

These studies raise very important questions about the generalizability and reliability of the findings and conclusions of this extensive body of research across differences in measurement and differences in representatives. Others have rightly cautioned, moreover, that these differences may be interdependent; different women/African Americans/Latinxs may have different conceptions of women's/Black/Latinx interests. Dodson (1998, 148), for example, argues that women in Congress "differ in the solutions they see to the problems women face, they differ in the kinds of women they represent, and they differ in the extent to which these concerns are salient." As a result, Carroll (2002, 66–67) adds, "even when women members of Congress act in ways that they perceive as representing women, their actions may not always look the same." (See also Reingold 2000.) This is precisely what Osborn (2012) finds to be the case among Democratic and Republican women in state legislatures. Yet precious few scholars have only recently begun contemplating the empirical or methodological implications of such possibilities.

If different descriptive representatives have different conceptions of group interests, then it is likely that researchers' decisions about how to define those interests will have significant effects on who appears more or less willing to act for those they descriptively represent. To what extent, then, do our conclusions about the relationship between descriptive and substantive representation depend on how we define group interests? In this chapter, we are particularly interested in whether and how single-axis definitions of women's, Blacks', and Latinxs' interests affect the conclusions we draw about women of color in US state legislatures. Are legislative women, regardless of race and ethnicity, equally likely to take the lead on women's issues, no matter how they are defined? Are Latinx and Black legislators, regardless of gender, equally likely to take the lead on Latinx and Black issues, regardless of how they are defined? To what degree have various single-axis definitions of group interests discounted or obscured the representational advocacy provided by women of color, while privileging that provided by White women and men of color?

Theory and Hypotheses: Intersectional Biases
of Single-Axis Concepts

Theories of intersectionality and secondary marginalization (Cohen 1999) suggest that any attempt to identify or construct common group interests, especially among marginalized groups, will reflect intra-group power differentials. The interests of those who are subject to multiple, overlapping, intersecting, interlocking, and compounding axes of inequality and subordination will differ from—and perhaps even be at cross-purposes with—the interests of those who are relatively privileged (Crenshaw 1989, 1991; Dovi 2002; Haynie 2011; hooks 2000; King 1988). Indeed, the privileges of one subgroup may even depend on the marginalization and deprivations of another (Glenn 1992; Cohen 1999). At the very least, group members who are relatively privileged may have the luxury of being unaware of such conflicting or diverging interests, while those who are "multiply burdened" (Crenshaw 1989) may be all too aware (Collins 2000; hooks 1981). Thus, the perspectives of more privileged group members will likely outweigh those of others in any public formulations and political assertions of group interests (Cohen 1999; Strolovitch 2007). To the degree we as researchers rely on these dominant, single-axis conceptions of group interests, our definitions will be more likely to capture the representational commitments of White women and men of color than those of women of color.

The few studies that do provide valuable insight into the legislative priorities of African American women and Latinas, however, suggest that it would be a mistake to assume that women of color do not share a commitment to women's issues, Black interests, or Latinx interests. Much like Smooth (2011), Carroll (2002, 57) notes that, in interviews with female members of the 103rd and 104th Congresses, the commitment to representing women was widely shared, though the congresswomen of color "talked in somewhat different ways" about that responsibility. Some "expressed the inseparability of their identities as, and their responsibilities to, people of color and women"; others expressed a particularly strong sense of responsibility to poor and working-class women, or to women outside the United States. (See also, Dittmar et al. 2017; Garcia Bedolla, Tate, and Wong 2005.)[3] Reviewing

---

[3] Ten Congresses and 20 years later, congresswomen of color are telling us much the same. "We have our agenda, which is very similar to all women, but then on top of that we have the unique perspective that we bring coming from the African American experience," says Representative Barbara Lee (D-CA) (Dittmar et al. 2017, 25).

the research literature on "Latinas as advocates and Representatives," García et al. (2008, 30) theorize that "Latinas, like most women, will demonstrate a propensity to advocate for women and families. But, different from most women, Latinas will also advocate for issues affecting the Latino community." In their study of the Mississippi state legislature, Orey et al. (2006, 112) argue that the "unique perspectives" of African American women as "doubly disadvantaged" by racism and sexism "result in a legislative commitment to representing the interests of both African Americans and women." (See also Brown and Gershon 2016, 103.)

Closer examination of the behavior of legislative women of color often confirms the expectation that they will take a "both/and" rather than an "either/or" approach to addressing multiple issues of gender and race/ethnicity. Orey et al. (2006), for example, found that in the Mississippi legislature, African American women were *more* likely than any of their other colleagues to introduce "progressive" women's interest bills, as well as progressive measures addressing Black interests, welfare, and children. Nonetheless, trying to do it all may require a balancing act: strategies and choices—perhaps even difficult choices or trade-offs—that make leadership on some types of group interests more compelling than others (Gay and Tate 1998). Takash's (1997) survey of Latina public officials in California led her to conclude that "the majority of Latina officeholders support feminist agendas and may be expected to promote legislation on women's rights," but they "express more concern with issues facing the Latino community as a whole, such as employment, access to education and retention, and safe neighborhoods" (p. 429). Bratton and Haynie (1999) discovered that, compared to their Black male and White female colleagues, Black female state legislators sponsored fewer (narrowly defined) Black interest bills or women's interest bills, but just as many (broadly defined) health, education, welfare, and children's bills.

Other studies also report that legislative women of color are just as, if not more, committed to issues that address both gender and racial/ethnic interests more broadly conceived. Comparing the three "public policy issues that are of greatest concern" to the Black and White, male and female Democratic state legislators in her survey, Barrett (1995, 226) found that "the greatest difference is not in the issues per se, but rather in the level of agreement among black female legislators" (pp. 233–34). Thus, while education and health care issues were the most frequently cited priorities among all four groups of legislators, Black women were more likely than any others to mention them. Fraga et al. (2008) asked a very similar question in their 2004 survey of Latinx state legislators. Once again, education and healthcare were at the top of the list for both Latino men and Latinas, with nearly identical percentages ranking each as either their most important issue or among their top three. (See also García et al. 2008.)

Together, the empirical research and theories of intersectionality reinforce Smooth's (2011) argument that the more narrowly defined, single-axis conceptions of group interests may be the most problematic—precisely because they neglect "crosscutting," "multifaceted" issues that address "the material consequences of race, class, and sexual identities" as well as gender (p. 437). To avoid what Crenshaw (1991, 1252) calls "political intersectionality," or having "to split one's political energies between two sometimes opposing groups," legislative women of color might eschew issues framed primarily or exclusively in terms of one single-axis group or another in favor of broader issues or issue-areas than can accommodate more complex, overlapping, or intersecting issues of gender, race, and ethnicity. Thus, the more narrow and group-specific our analytic categories, the more likely we are to overlook and underestimate the representational efforts of women of color. As García et al. (2008, 17) caution, it is important to note that "because the activities of Latinas tend not to be gender-specific, their activism is not included in the broader analysis of women's activism." Latina political leadership, in other words, may be rendered invisible by dominant, single-axis categories of analysis.

In the schematic outlined above, conceptions of group interests that identify issues or bills directly salient to or explicitly targeted for women, Black, or Latinx individuals, organizations, or communities come closest to this more "narrow," single-axis category of policy leadership. Thus, we hypothesize that these narrower, group-specific definitions of legislative activity will be most likely to underestimate the representational leadership of women of color and overestimate that of White women or men of color. More capacious, social welfare-oriented definitions of group interests, however, are expected to have the opposite effects. Precisely because they contain the overlap in the purported interests of African Americans, Latinxs, and women alike, conceptions of group interests that include general public health, education, and welfare/poverty policy will be more likely to capture the representational efforts of women of color.

In this chapter, we focus on the sponsorship of women-specific, Black-specific, and Latinx-specific bills on the one (narrow) hand and health and education bills on the other (broad) hand. We reserve the sponsorship of welfare/poverty bills, which invariably address the needs of those who are "intersectionally marginalized" in terms of race, gender, and class (at least), for the analysis of race-gender policy leadership in Chapter 4 so that we can concentrate on the more single-axis, overlapping, and non-over-lapping conceptions here (Brown and Banks 2014; King 1998; Strolovitch 2007). Assuming that women of color do not avoid narrowly-defined, group-specific bills altogether and that the biases of our analytic catego-ries are differences in degree only, our specific expectations are outlined in Table 3.1.

Minta and Brown (2014) provide an alternative theory worth noting, however. They argue that minority *men* are just as attentive to women's is-sues as are White women and minority women for two reasons. First is the similarity and overlap between women's interests and "racial and ethnic minority interests" (Minta and Brown 2014, 254). Second, interactions between men and women of color in various minority caucuses raise awareness of such overlapping (or even intersecting) interests and "facilitate agenda coordination" and coalition building not only among members of the minority caucus but also with members of the women's caucus (p. 257). Minta and Brown's analysis reveals that "the presence of minority men is just as important as the presence of women, specifically minority women, in increasing attention to women's issues in the House" (2014, 261). Their results are supported by the findings of Lavariega Monforti et al. (2009) that Black male Democrats in Texas sponsor more

Table 3.1 Expectations for Observed Race-Gender Differences in Policy Leadership

	# of Women-Specific Bills	# of Health and/or Education Bills	# of Black-Specific Bills	# of Latinx-Specific Bills
Most Active Sponsors	White women	Women of color	Black men	Latinos
	Women of color	White women, Men of color	Black women	Latinas
	Men of color		Latinos	Black men
			Latinas	Black women
Least Active Sponsors	Men (all)	White men	Whites (all)	Whites (all)

progressive bills, including women's issue bills, than all other legislators, and Latino legislators sponsor more women's and children's interests bills than do Latinas. Thus, we might find the differences between men and women of color to be more muted than we would otherwise expect.

At the same time, it is important to acknowledge that there is some potential overlap between all four categories of bill sponsorship in Table 3.1. As we explain below, we did not code or create these categories to necessarily be mutually exclusive. For example, a civil rights bill that provides protections against discrimination on the basis of sex/gender, race/color, and national origin was coded as a women-specific, Black-specific, *and* Latinx-specific bill. Likewise, health and education bills addressing the targeted needs and interests of women/girls and/or racial/ethnic minorities were coded as both health/education and group-specific measures. This presents an opportunity to further explore the observational effects of ever-narrowing categories of analysis. More precisely, we expect that differences between legislative women of color and others (White women and men of color) will increase as we move toward defining these categories of bills sponsorship as mutually exclusive. For example, women of color (and men of color, for that matter) may be even less likely than White women to sponsor women-specific bills when we exclude bills that address Black- and/or Latinx-specific concerns as well. They may be still less active on women-specific issues when we also exclude bills related to health or education. Conversely, women of color may be particularly attracted to health or education bills that specifically target the needs or concerns of women or racial/ethnic minorities as a way of addressing or balancing the complex and perhaps intersecting interests of both.[4]

Data, Measures, and Models

To test these hypotheses, we draw from two inter-related databases created for this project on identity and representation in US state legislatures: one

---

[4] There are very few health or education bills in our database that address the needs of *both* women and racial/ethnic minorities (or women of color) specifically. Nonetheless, we explore the possibility that women of color will prioritize group-targeted health or education bills even though the vast majority of such bills address (on their face, at least) only women (regardless of race/ethnicity) *or* racial/ethnic minority groups (regardless of gender).

on individual state legislators and their constituencies, and the other on bills sponsored by those legislators.[5] We concentrate our analysis on 15 state houses (or lower chambers) in 1997 and 2005: Arizona, California, Florida, Maryland, Minnesota, Mississippi, Nevada, New Jersey, New Mexico, North Dakota, Ohio, South Carolina, Tennessee, Texas, and Utah.[6] As explained in Chapter 1, these states and years were selected to increase the generalizability of our study and provide maximum variation in legislator identity, constituency characteristics, party control, ideology, and region.[7] Despite our efforts, however, there were too few Asian American or Native American legislators serving in our state house-years to accommodate quantitative analysis as distinct groups.[8] We therefore exclude them from our analysis.

Operationalizing Legislator Race-Gender Identity

For this sample of state houses, we rely exclusively on our own biographical database, as described in Chapter 2. The flexibility of this database allows us to measure the intersecting gender and racial/ethnic identities of the state legislators in two ways. Our fully specified, disaggregated models classify legislators into six mutually exclusive categories: White man, White woman, Black man, Black woman, Latino, and Latina. Because our theory and hypotheses do not always distinguish among minority women (or men), we also employ a set of models in which legislators are grouped into four mutually exclusive categories: White men, White women, men of color (Black and/or Latino), and women of color (Black and/or Latina).[9] In all our regression analyses, the reference category is White men.

[5] National Science Foundation SES #0618368; Kathleen A. Bratton, Kerry L. Haynie, and Beth Reingold, Principal Investigators.

[6] For the New Jersey Assembly, which has odd-year elections, we examine bills introduced in 1998 and 2006 to maintain comparability across states. Thus, in all 13 states with two-year election cycles, we examine bills introduced during the first and often more productive year following each election. In the two states with four-year election cycles (MD and MS), 1997 and 2005 fall midway within a span of four discrete annual sessions.

[7] See Appendix Table A.1 for detailed state-year information on legislative race and gender diversity, party control, and ideology.

[8] Of the 2,987 legislators in our sample, there are 23 Asian Americans (0.77%) and 15 Native Americans (0.50%). One Asian American and four Native American legislators were identified as also having Latinx backgrounds; they are included in our sample as Latinx.

[9] In analyses employing these aggregated models, we are able to include three legislators identified as both Black and Latinx who are excluded from the disaggregated analyses.

Operationalizing Policy Leadership

Policy leadership can occur throughout the legislative process and, as highlighted earlier, studies of representation have observed activity at many of stages of the process. In this project, we examine policy leadership at the agenda-setting stage of bill introduction and sponsorship for several reasons. In the existing literature, the links between descriptive and substantive representation are strongest and most consistent in patterns of bill sponsorship. It is at this agenda-setting stage, where policymaking activity is much less constrained by party leaders, committee chairs, and other institutional pressures, when legislators seem most willing and able to express their commitments to certain groups and group interests—and to do so in a variety of ways (Bratton and Haynie 1999; Canon 1999; Lavariega Monforti et al. 2009; Reingold 2000; Wallace 2014; Wilson 2017). Like roll-call votes, bill sponsorship is a consequential form of position taking (Mayhew 1974). But unlike roll-call votes, bill sponsorship signals both the direction and the intensity of a legislator's preferences; as such, it is often a more costly investment of time, effort, and political capital (Rocca and Gordon 2010; Schiller 1995; Sulkin 2011; Tamerius 1995). On a more practical level, bill sponsorship provides the most accessible and comparable measure of substantive representation available, especially when observing legislative behavior across multiple state-level institutions.

For "institutionally disadvantaged" legislators in minority caucuses who have relatively few opportunities to claim credit for favorable roll-call votes, bill sponsorship is particularly important (Rocca and Sanchez 2008, 133). Bill sponsors, moreover, are the policy leaders who not only shape the agenda but also assume primary responsibility for whatever policy outcomes ensue (Kingdon 1984; Schiller 1995). But even if most bills introduced "die" in committee deliberations and never come up for a floor vote, putting an issue of concern to women and/or minorities on the legislative agenda is an important representational activity in and of itself. If keeping issues off the table is one of the most effective (and often hidden) ways of establishing and maintaining political power, then getting issues on the table is one of the most effective mechanisms for marginalized groups to gain and assert their own power (Bachrach and Baratz 1963; Cobb and Elder 1983; Gaventa 1980; Kingdon 1984; Schattschneider 1960).

To measure each legislator's propensity to sponsor women-specific, Black-specific, Latinx-specific, health, and education bills, we identified the primary sponsor(s) of every bill introduced in our sample of state-years.[10] Most of these state legislatures allowed only one primary sponsor or lead author for any given bill. However, in the few state-years (FL97, FL05, NV05) that allowed for multiple primary sponsors and offered no systematic way of distinguishing their roles, we coded multiple legislators as primary sponsors of the bill in question. To focus on legislators' more substantive policy-oriented proposals, we analyze only regular/general bills introduced during regular sessions; more symbolic or commemorative resolutions, memorials, and such were not included.[11] Our dependent variables, therefore, are counts of the number of regular bills in each group-interest category that legislators introduced as primary sponsors during the designated year.

Coding Bill Issue Content

To identify the types of group interest bills outlined in Table 3.1 (as well as welfare/poverty measures for Chapter 4), we began by hand-coding the issue content of all bills introduced in any given state house-year. Trained coders read summaries or synopses of bill proposals and assigned however many content codes necessary to capture the topics or issues presented.[12] They chose from 122 content codes organized under 12 general headings: health; education; groups; civil rights and liberties; social welfare; family; crime; business, commerce and labor; agriculture, environment, and transportation; campaigns, voting, and elections; immigration, military, and foreign affairs; and general government.[13] We then selected non-exclusive subsets of bill content codes (across the 12 headings) to constitute each type of group

[10] Each state legislature's online bill tracking database proved to be the most valid and reliable source of information regarding sponsors and committee referrals. They were especially useful for differentiating primary/lead sponsors from other types of sponsors.

[11] A number of other bills are excluded from our analysis because they lack either individual sponsors or meaningful content. In the Florida 1997 session, for example, "local" bills do not have any designated sponsors. Committee- or local delegation-sponsored bills are also excluded when they do not have a named legislator as a (co-)primary sponsor. Several state houses (CA, NM, TN, and UT) permitted "spot," "placeholder," or "caption" bills—empty vessels waiting to be amended with "real" proposals when needed, usually after the deadline for bill introductions. Such bills, when left un-amended, are omitted.

[12] Summaries or synopses were available in the bill's caption (or long title), the state's bill-tracking database, or at the beginning of the bill text. Full text was consulted in very few cases in which such summaries/synopses were either unavailable or prohibitively vague. Whenever possible, coders analyzed bills as they appeared when first introduced.

[13] Periodic intercoder reliability exercises on random samples of 25 bills revealed agreement rates ranging from 51% to 84%, with an average of 65%.

interest: women-specific, Black-specific, Latinx-specific, health, education, and welfare/poverty. (Appendix Table A.5 provides a full list of all six subsets of bill content codes used to identify each type of group interest legislation.) In many cases, bills that received these content codes were further screened and filtered to make sure they fit our definitions of group-specific, health, education, and welfare/poverty policy. This method of hand-coding bills was used in 22 of the 30 state-years examined here.

To expand our database and increase the validity and reliability of our initial coding protocol, we used these bill content codes and the group interest bills they identified to develop a series of keyword search terms with which to identify legislation archived in the Lexis-Nexis State Capital online database.[14] In an iterative process, we created keyword dictionaries that would most efficiently capture the same sets of group interest bills the hand-coding procedures did. (See Appendix Table A.6 for a full listing of these keyword dictionaries.) We then used the Lexis-Nexis keyword searches, with further screening, to compile a comparable database of women-specific, Black-specific, Latinx-specific, health, education, and/or welfare-poverty bills introduced in another eight state-years (AZ05, CA05, FL05, MD97, MD05, NJ06, SC05, TX05).[15] We also used the keyword dictionaries and Lexis-Nexis searches to identify a small number of group interest bills that our hand-coding method missed.

Each bill in our database was identified and coded as a women-specific, Black-specific, Latinx-specific, health, education, and/or welfare-poverty bill independently. Thus, any single bill can address one or more categories of group interest at a time. For example, a measure requiring healthcare insurers to cover breast reconstructive surgery (TN97 HB517) is classified as both a women-specific bill and a health bill. An environmental justice bill ensuring that hazardous waste facilities are not disproportionately concentrated in minority or low-income communities (MS97 HB447) is classified as a Black-specific, Latinx-specific, welfare/poverty, and health bill. This allows

---

[14] Lexis-Nexis discontinued all access to its State Capital database in September 2019 and replaced it with its new StateNet database. Fortunately, all of our work for this project was completed beforehand. We nevertheless expect that our keyword dictionaries will prove useful for future research, regardless of the platform used.

[15] Our keywords captured an average of 93% of the hand-coded bills. To screen the Lexis-Nexis bills captured, two coders independently classified every bill as "extraneous" or not. Coders could also classify a bill as unclear. Disagreements between coders (extraneous vs. not extraneous), which occurred in less than 6% of the bills coded, were resolved by the lead author. Bills coded as unclear by either coder were also investigated and resolved by the lead author. For more detailed information on keyword capture rates and intercoder reliability rates, see Appendix Tables A.7 and A.8.

us to examine, in this chapter and the next, whether and how overlap (or the lack thereof) in issue-content affects the relationships between descriptive and substantive representation we observe.

The combination of bill content codes and keyword search terms used to identify women-specific, Black-specific, and Latinx-specific bills was selected to reflect as closely as possible extant *narrow* conceptions of group interests that include only those issues that explicitly, directly, or most disproportionately concern or affect women, African Americans, or Latinxs. As a result, women-specific bills engage issues of family law (divorce, child support/custody), child care, family/maternity leave, domestic violence, sexual violence, abortion and reproductive health (including sex education), sex discrimination (including sexual harassment and ameliorative affirmative action measures), and anything explicitly or clearly targeted (exclusively or primarily) toward women and/or girls. Black-specific bills address multiple issues of racial discrimination and civil rights/racial equality including voting rights and redistricting, racial profiling, hate crimes, and other forms of racial violence, as well as efforts to teach or promote Black history and culture, or racial tolerance and inclusion. Of course, measures targeting African American/Black individuals, communities, organizations, or institutions (e.g., HBCUs) were also classified as Black-specific. Latinx-specific bills address the same issues of racial/ethnic discrimination and civil rights, as well as multicultural education and promotion (as long as they are inclusive of Latinxs, ethnic/language minorities, or immigrant groups). In addition to measures targeting Latinxs as a group, bills dealing with immigration, immigrants, migrant laborers, or refugees, border relations/regions, and language policy (including bilingual education) are classified as Latinx-specific (as long as they are not specific to other immigrant/language groups).

In contrast, our coding scheme was designed to produce very *broad* and inclusive sets of health and education proposals considered highly salient to women, African Americans, and Latinxs alike. Health bills address a wide array of healthcare matters: anything related to health insurance (including medical assistance for the poor and/or elderly), healthcare provision, healthcare professionals, or healthcare organizations like hospitals and nursing homes. Proposals related to mental health, occupational health (including workers' compensation), reproductive health, substance abuse/addiction treatment and prevention, and HIV/AIDS are all included. We also

included various issues of public health and safety such as emergency services (other than law enforcement), disaster relief and emergency prepared-
ness, food and drug safety, and the regulation of hazardous/toxic substances.
Education bills include all manner of curricular, administrative, and finance
issues concerning the provision of public (and occasionally private) primary,
secondary, and higher education. Programs, personnel, and funding for adult
literacy, sex education, bilingual and LEP education, multicultural awareness
and diversity training, and workforce/vocational/job training were also designated as education policy.

We do not attempt to distinguish more liberal "pro"-group measures from
more conservative "anti"-group measures, at least, not directly. Coding the
ideological direction of individual bills proved too unreliable and time-
consuming given the sheer quantity of bills and our reliance on bill synopses.
Instead, we devote the bulk of our analysis of bill sponsorship to the policy
agendas of Democratic legislators only. Because the vast majority of Black and
Latinx legislators in our sample are Democrats, excluding Republicans (and a
few Independents) not only alleviates concerns about whether conservative
measures qualify as substantive representation, but also allows for more valid
comparisons of White and minority legislators.[16] Nonetheless, we also present and compare additional analyses of group-related policy leadership on
the part of Republican legislators serving in our sample of state houses. This
allows us to assess the generalizability of our findings across party lines.

Control Variables

To estimate the relationship between legislator identity and bill sponsorship,
we use negative binomial regression, controlling for a number of possible
confounding factors that previous research and Chapter 2 suggest can influence both descriptive representation and policy leadership on women's issues and racial issues (see especially Bratton 2002; Bratton and Haynie 1999;
Bratton, Haynie, and Reingold 2006; Haynie 2001; Rouse 2013; Swers 2002;
Wilson 2017).[17] As mentioned, we control for partisanship by analyzing

[16] All but four (99%) of African American legislators and 87% of Latinx legislators in our sample of
state houses are Democrats. In contrast, Republicans outnumber Democrats in our sample of White
legislators: 50% of White women and 63% of White men are Republican.
[17] Given that our dependent variables are event counts restricted to positive integers, ordinary least
squares (OLS) regression is inappropriate for our multivariate analysis. Poisson regression is often

Democrats and Republicans separately. Data on legislators' party affiliations were obtained from the State Legislative Election Returns (SLER) database (Klarner et al. 2013). We also control for several constituency characteristics, including racial and ethnic composition (percentages of constituents who are African American and Latinx) and socioeconomic status (average household income). All district demographic data are taken from multiple editions of Congressional Quarterly's *State Legislative Elections* almanac (Barone et al. 1998; Lilley et al. 2008) and are derived from the decennial US Census.[18] We also control for "Democratic strength" in the district, or the percentage of the two-party vote cast for the Democratic state house candidate(s) in the preceding election, using district-level SLER data (Klarner 2018; Preuhs and Juenke 2011).[19]

In addition, we take into account various aspects of legislators' professional status that are likely to influence the opportunities for group-interest policy leadership. First, we control for whether the legislator chaired a relevant committee. A "relevant committee" is a house standing committee to which the group interest bills under consideration were referred on a regular basis. More precisely, a committee is defined as "relevant" when at least 10% of the bills in the designated policy area are referred to it. Committee referrals of bills were obtained from online state legislative bill tracking databases, and

recommended as an alternative for event count models (G. King 1988) but it rests on the assumption that distinct events are statistically independent, which is highly unlikely in the case of content-specific bill introductions. A legislator who introduces one group interest bill clearly has an increased probability of introducing more group interest bills. As a result, all of our dependent variables are over-dispersed: the variance in the distribution is greater than the mean. In such instances of over-dispersion, negative binomial regression is the most appropriate statistical model—and the one we employ here. On occasion when sponsorship rates are extremely low, we also rely on secondary logistic regression analysis of the probability of sponsoring at least one bill.

[18] Given the results of Chapter 2, suggesting that more urban districts are more likely to elect White women and legislators of color, we considered controlling for the percentage of constituents residing in urban areas. We do not include an urban control variable here, however, primarily due to data availability issues. The 1998 Congressional Quarterly (CQ) almanac provides this information for our 1997/98 districts but the 2008 edition does not. We can obtain a 2005 measure of state legislative district population density directly from the 2000 Census (https://factfinder.census.gov/faces/nav/jsf/pages/index.xhtml), but it is not comparable. Unlike CQ, it does not define "urban" or "urban area" as distinct from "suburban" and "rural." Supplementary analysis that combines these two measures indicates that %Urban does often have a significant positive effect on bill sponsorship; but including it in our models does not change our main results significantly. If anything, it enhances group differences slightly. Thus, if excluding %Urban from our analysis introduces any bias, it is a conservative one—one that favors falsification.

[19] This measure of Democratic strength serves as a proxy for both district liberalism and Democratic legislators' electoral security. No other measure of district ideology is available for our full sample.

information regarding who chaired which state house standing committees was obtained from annual editions of the *State Yellow Book*.

We also control for the legislator's seniority. To gauge seniority, or tenure in office, we used the SLER database to identify the most recent year each legislator was elected to the state house as a non-incumbent, and then subtracted that from the year their legislative activity was observed.[20] Thus, our seniority variable indicates the number of years each representative had served consecutively, prior to the observed session. Finally, we control for the legislator's overall level of policymaking activity by tallying the total number of regular house bills she/he introduced as primary sponsor during the entire legislative session.[21] Congressional studies of bill sponsorship reveal significant but mixed patterns across race and gender: in anticipation of their lack of institutional influence, Latinx and Black members sponsor fewer bills; women sponsor more (Rocca and Sanchez 2008; Volden, Wiseman, and Witmer 2013). To account for differences between states and changes over time, we include state and year fixed effects in all models. Descriptive statistics for our independent and control variables can be found in Appendix Table A.9a-b.

Results: How Conceptual Lenses Shape Patterns of Race-Gender Representation

To gauge the effects of changing definitions of group interests on the relationship between descriptive and substantive representation across the intersections of race and gender, we begin our analysis with the more narrowly defined group-specific issues and then proceed with an examination of more broadly defined issues of health and education. Our general expectation is that as we move toward broader, overlapping definitions of group interests, legislative women of color will appear increasingly more active as agenda-setters and policy leaders vis-à-vis their White female and minority male colleagues.[22]

---

[20] We thank Adrienne Smith for designing this measure and writing the Stata code used to implement it.

[21] To compensate for outliers and a very thin distribution at the high end, we convert the raw tally of total bills sponsored (plus one) to a natural log.

[22] Throughout our analysis, comparisons of race-gender group differences are made from postestimation predictions calculated using average marginal effects, following Long and Freese (2014). Predicted counts for each of our six race-gender groups of legislators, and their 95% confidence intervals, are displayed in the figures. Tests of statistical significance were executed with the "mchange" sPost command in Stata (Long and Freese 2014). Note that while the confidence intervals

While our precise expectations regarding the distribution of policy leadership across legislators' race-gender identities (outlined in Table 3.1) vary for each set of group-specific issues, they are the same for health and education issues. Thus, we examine race-gender differences in the number of bills legislators sponsor that address issues of health and/or education combined.[23] Again, we focus first and foremost on Democratic state legislators.

Throughout our analysis of Democratic policy leadership, control variables either behave as expected or are insignificant. The racial/ethnic composition of the legislator's district tends to have a significant positive effect on the sponsorship of group-specific bills in ways we would expect: legislators with more diverse districts sponsor more women-specific bills; those with larger proportions of African American constituents sponsor more Black-specific bills; and those serving more Latinx constituents sponsor more Latinx-specific bills. Sponsorship of health and education bills, however, is unaffected by district diversity. Other district characteristics—namely, income levels and Democratic vote share—rarely affect bill sponsorship activity of any type. Not surprisingly, legislators who tend to sponsor a lot of bills also tend to sponsor more group interest bills, of all types. Those who chair relevant committees are also more frequent sponsors of women-specific and health/education bills, but they sponsor approximately the same number of Black-specific and Latinx-specific bills as other legislators. Beyond chairing a relevant committee, seniority has no independent effect on bill sponsorship patterns observed here.

Group-Specific Issues

Sponsoring bills addressing issues specific to women is something relatively few Democratic state legislators in our sample undertake. More than half (59%) sponsor no such bills; only a fifth (19%) sponsor more

for some of the statistically significant differences appear to overlap in the figures presented, "visual examination of whether 95% confidence intervals overlap will result in Type II errors and is not a reliable way of testing differences in point estimates" (Karpowitz, Monson, and Preece 2017, 932; see also Bolsen and Thornton 2014).

[23] Supplementary analysis indicates that the observed relationships between descriptive and substantive representation are very similar when we examine the sponsorship of health and education bills separately.

than two. On average, they sponsor slightly less than one (.89) bill each in any given year. Nonetheless, as the figures in Table 3.2 and Figure 3.1 demonstrate, female legislators are much more active sponsors of women-specific bills than their male colleagues are, all else being equal.[24] In this case, women's descriptive representation matters, regardless of race/ethnicity. Contrary to our expectations, women of color sponsor, on average, just as many women-specific bills as do White women: 1.5 each. Latinas sponsor slightly more (1.7 each), Black women slightly less (1.4), but the differences among these women are not statistically significant. Black male and Latino legislators sponsor significantly fewer women-specific bills (.9); and White male legislators sponsor by far the fewest (.6). Thus, while men of color are significantly more active on women-specific issues than White men are, they are not as active as Minta and Brown's theory would suggest.[25]

Sponsorship of Black-specific and Latinx-specific bills is even less frequent. The vast majority of these Democratic lawmakers initiate no such legislation: 85% sponsor no Black-specific bills; 83% sponsor no Latinx-specific bills. On average, each legislator sponsors only .22 Black-specific and .24 Latinx-specific bills per year. Congruent with previous research, however, racial/ethnic identities matter a great deal. Regardless of gender, African Americans sponsor significantly more Black-specific bills and Latinxs sponsor significantly more Latinx-specific bills than do White representatives.[26] (See Table 3.3 and Figures 3.2–3.3.) Contrary to our hypothesis and intersectional critiques of narrowly defined single-axis conceptions of substantive representation, women of color are no less active than men of color on these racially specific issues. Black men sponsor slightly more

---

[24] The difference between Black women and Latino men is the only gender difference that is not statistically significant at $p \leq .10$. Because the number of legislators in each of the minority race-gender categories in the sample is relatively small and the rates of race-gender bill sponsorship are low, detecting significant differences can be challenging. For this reason, we set a significance level of $p \leq .10$ for this study, rather than the more common $p \leq .05$. Supplementary analyses using boot-strapped standard errors yield very similar results.

[25] Logistic regression analysis of the likelihood of sponsoring at least one group-specific bill (with the same set of control variables) provides very similar results. We note throughout this section the few exceptions. With regard to women-specific bills, the one exception is that, in the disaggregated models, the differences between White men and men of color are not statistically significant.

[26] All such racial/ethnic differences are statistically significant.

Table 3.2 Sponsorship of Any Women-Specific Bill(s)

	Dependent Variable # of Bills Sponsored	
	(1)	(2)
White Woman	.962***	.958***
	(.103)	(.103)
Man of Color	.423***	
	(.138)	
Black Man		.415**
		(.178)
Latino		.401**
		(.183)
Woman of Color	.946***	
	(.156)	
Black Woman		.837***
		(.208)
Latina		1.073***
		(.207)
People of Color in District	.005*	
	(.003)	
Blacks in District		.006*
		(.004)
Latinxs in District		.003
		(.003)
Average Income in District	.005*	.005
	(.003)	(.003)
Democratic Vote-share in District	−.000	−.000
	(.002)	(.003)
Legislator Seniority	−.006	−.007
	(.006)	(.006)
Chair of Relevant Committee	.401**	.389**
	(.164)	(.164)
Total Bills Introduced (logged)	1.264***	1.263***
	(.069)	(.069)
Constant	−4.509***	−4.465***
	(.417)	(.426)
Observations	1,453	1,450
Log Likelihood	−1556.4298	−1554.2959
Pseudo R^2	0.1669	0.1674

Negative Binomial Regression with state and year fixed effects *p < 0.1; **p < 0.05; ***p < 0.01

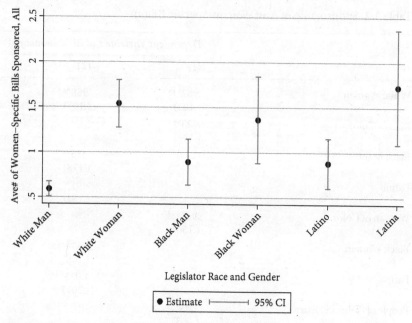

Figure 3.1 Sponsorship of Any Women-Specific Bills
(Ave = Average)

Black-specific bills (.6 each) than Black women do (.4 each), but the difference is not significant. Latinas actually sponsor *more* Latinx-specific bills (.7 each) than Latinos do (.4 each), and the difference is statistically significant. Latinas are also slightly more likely than Latinos to sponsor *any* Latinx-specific legislation (p = .104).[27]

Given the overlap in how we delineate Black-specific and Latinx-specific issues (e.g., issues of racial/ethnic discrimination included in both), it is not surprising that, compared to White legislators, Latinx legislators sponsor a bit more Black-specific legislation and Black legislators sponsor more Latinx bills. Yet again, women of color do not appear any less committed than men of color to sponsoring such cross-group specific bills. Black men and women sponsor comparable numbers of Latinx-specific bills (.3 each) and again, Latinas sponsor *more* Black-specific bills than Latinos do (.3 vs. .1), though the difference is not statistically significant

---

[27] Logit analysis not shown.

Table 3.3 Sponsorship of Any Black-Specific or Latinx-Specific Bill(s)

	Dependent Variable # of Bills Sponsored	
	Black-Specific	Latinx-Specific
White Woman	.225 (.242)	.433** (.210)
Black Man	1.801*** (.288)	1.018*** (.301)
Black Woman	1.510*** (.348)	.851** (.367)
Latino	.341 (.352)	1.095*** (.272)
Latina	1.086*** (.388)	1.719*** (.300)
Blacks in District	.012* (.006)	.011* (.006)
Latinxs in District	.004 (.006)	.009* (.005)
Average Income in District	.005 (.006)	.002 (.006)
Democratic Vote-share in District	.006 (.005)	.005 (.005)
Legislator Seniority	−.000 (.011)	−.002 (.010)
Chair of Relevant Committee	.276 (.285)	.239 (.248)
Total Bills Introduced (logged)	.980*** (.112)	.977*** (.111)
Constant	−6.299*** (.912)	−6.697*** (.885)
Observations	1,450	1,450
Log Likelihood	−652.05279	−725.37818
Pseudo R^2	0.1777	0.1630

Negative Binomial Regression with state and year fixed effects *p < 0.1; **p< 0.05; ***p < 0.01

(p = .119).[28] In fact, Latino sponsorship of Black-specific bills is so low, it is statistically indistinguishable from the sponsorship rates of White women and men.

---

[28] Also unexpected is that White women sponsor significantly more Black-specific bills than do White men. In logit analysis, however, this gender gap is reduced and no longer statistically significant (p = .104).

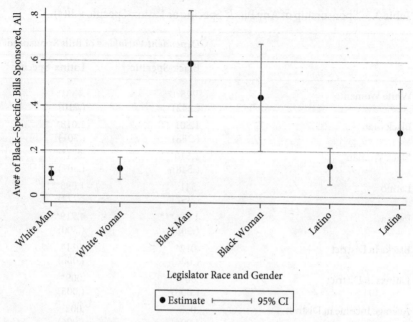

Figure 3.2 Sponsorship of Any Black-Specific Bills
(Ave = Average)

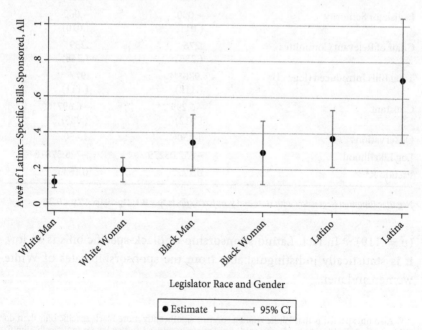

Figure 3.3 Sponsorship of Any Latinx-Specific Bills
(Ave = Average)

Health and/or Education Issues

Many Democratic state legislators—regardless of race-gender identity—engage in agenda-setting policy leadership on health and education issues. Two-thirds sponsor at least one health policy bill, almost as many (62%) sponsor one or more education bills, and a full 80% sponsor either health or education legislation (or bills that address both issues simultaneously). On average, Democratic state lawmakers sponsor almost five (4.71) health/education bills each in any given year. Some, however, are a lot more active than others. As we hypothesized, legislative women of color stand out as the most active health/education policy leaders of all. Indeed, all of our expectations delineated in Table 3.1 are borne out in the aggregate model shown in Table 3.4 (column 1): women of color are most active (with an estimated 6.6 bills each), followed by White women and men of color (at 5.2 and 4.8 bills, respectively); White men are the least active (4.3 bills each).[29] The disaggregated model of health/education policy leadership (shown in Table 3.4, column 2 and Figure 3.4), however, reveals significant variation among women and men of color. All else being equal, Black women sponsor the most health/education bills: approximately 7.4 bills each. Latina legislators sponsor an average of 5.9 bills each, which is comparable to the sponsorship rates of Black men (5.3 bills) and White women (5.2 bills).[30] Latinos meanwhile are just as inactive as White men (4.4 and 4.3 bills, respectively). In fact, Latinos—along with White men—sponsor significantly fewer health/education bills on average than any other group of lawmakers.

Overall, our results reveal that women of color—Latinas, Black women, or both—are among the leading advocates for the interests of women and minorities across all these single-axis conceptions of group interests, no matter how narrow or broad. Black women stand out as the most active policy leaders on broadly defined health and education issues (with Latinas not far behind); and Latinas stand out as the most active policy leaders on narrowly defined Latinx-specific issues. If women of color are opting for broader policy arenas (like health and education) that can better accommodate the complex, overlapping, or intersecting issues of gender, race, and ethnicity, they are not doing so at the expense of taking on leading roles in more

---

[29] All group differences, except that between White women and men of color, are statistically significant.

[30] The difference between sponsorship levels of Black women and Latinas is not quite statistically significant (p = .109).

Table 3.4 Sponsorship of Any Health and/or Education Bill(s)

	Dependent Variable # of Bills Sponsored	
	(1)	(2)
White Woman	.205***	.204***
	(.052)	(.052)
Man of Color	.122*	
	(.065)	
Black Man		.215**
		(.088)
Latino		.025
		(.085)
Woman of Color	.449***	
	(.078)	
Black Woman		.549***
		(.107)
Latina		.324***
		(.105)
People of Color in District	−.000	
	(.001)	
Blacks in District		−.001
		(.002)
Latinxs in District		.001
		(.002)
Average Income in District	.001	.001
	(.002)	(.002)
Democratic Vote-share in District	.001	.001
	(.001)	(.001)
Legislator Seniority	−.004	−.004
	(.003)	(.003)
Chair of Relevant Committee	.504***	.501***
	(.072)	(.072)
Total Bills Introduced (logged)	1.063***	1.065***
	(.032)	(.032)
Constant	−1.784***	−1.772***
	(.184)	(.188)
Observations	1,453	1,450
Log Likelihood	−3021.4541	−3011.6107
Pseudo R^2	0.2129	0.2136

Negative Binomial Regression with state and year fixed effects *$p < 0.1$; **$p < 0.05$; ***$p < 0.01$

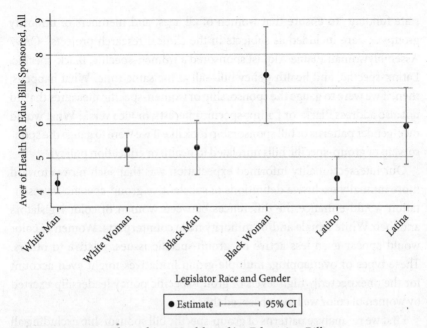

Figure 3.4 Sponsorship of Any Health and/or Education Bills
(Ave = Average)

group-specific policy arenas. Nonetheless, if we were to examine substantive representation only in terms of narrowly defined group-specific interests, we would underestimate the full extent of Black women's and Latinas' distinctive contributions. By our count, White women are among the leading advocates only on women-specific issues; Black men are leading advocates only on Black-specific issues; and Latinos are never ranked among the most active sponsors of group-interest legislation. In these terms, the contrast is quite striking.

Toward More Narrow, Mutually Exclusive Conceptions of Group-Specific Interests and Substantive Representation

Thus far, our concepts of group interests and measures of substantive representation have been defined in single-axis terms, but not as mutually exclusive. So, for example, by introducing AB 1341, which requires those receiving state funding "to ensure that women of all ages, and members of minority groups . . . are included as subjects in the clinical research projects," CA97 Assemblywoman Elaine Alquist sponsored a women-specific, Black-specific, Latinx-specific, and health policy bill—all at the same time. What happens, then, if we were to gauge the sponsorship of women-specific measures that do not also address Black- or Latinx-specific interests, or vice versa? What would race-gender patterns of bill sponsorship look like if we were to gauge the sponsorship of group-specific bills unrelated to health or education policy?

Our intersectionality informed expectation was that such moves toward more mutually exclusive definitions of substantive group-specific representation would enhance the differences between women of color legislators and their White female and/or minority male counterparts. Women of color would appear even less active on group-specific issues, relative to others. These types of overlapping, multiple-group initiatives might even account for the unexpectedly high levels of group-specific policy leadership exerted by women of color we have observed thus far.

First we re-analyze patterns of group-specific bill sponsorship excluding all legislation that addresses women's specific interests and Black/Latinx-specific interests simultaneously. Overall, this does nothing to dislodge women of color from the ranks of most active sponsors or to further differentiate them from White women (as sponsors of women-specific bills) or men of color (as sponsors for Black- or Latinx-specific bills). At most, it reduces the relative standing of Black male legislators (a bit) as sponsors of women- and Latinx-specific bills, putting them in the least active category along with White men.[31] It also makes the Latinx-specific sponsorship levels of Black women and White women statistically indistinguishable from those of White men.

Next, we exclude group-targeted health and education bills as well and re-analyze patterns of group-specific bill sponsorship once more. Here we find some evidence suggesting that extremely narrow, single-axis conceptions of group interests—ones that exclude such issues as women's health or racial disparities in educational opportunities—underestimate the representational leadership of women of color. Black women are no longer among the leading sponsors of women-specific bills and are no more active on such issues than any of the men. Latinas meanwhile sponsor only slightly more Latinx interest bills than do other legislators, and none of the differences are statistically significant.

---

[31] As Chapter 4 will demonstrate, this is because very few legislators sponsor bills that address women-specific and Black/Latinx-specific interests simultaneously; and Black male legislators are the most likely sponsors.

Latina sponsorship of Black-specific bills also becomes indistinguishable from that of everyone else (besides Black men and women) in the least active tier. Similarly, Latinas' role as leading sponsors of health and education bills is diminished somewhat (relative to others) when we exclude group-targeted measures from the analysis; they sponsor significantly fewer measures than do Black women and their activity level is equivalent to that of every other legislator.

Further analysis confirms that the main reason for these apparent drops in group-interest policy leadership on the part of women of color is that women of color sponsor the most group-targeted health and education bills of anyone.[32] As shown in Figure 3.5, Latina legislators sponsor an average of one such bill per year and Black women are not far behind with an average of .8 bills per year. At only .15 bills each, White men sponsor the least. In the middle tier are White women (.5 bills each), Black men (.4), and Latinos (.3). In the Texas 2005 regular session, for example, women of color sponsored a disproportionate share of Democrats' group-specific health and education bills: while only 21% of the Democratic caucus, they sponsored 42% of these bills.

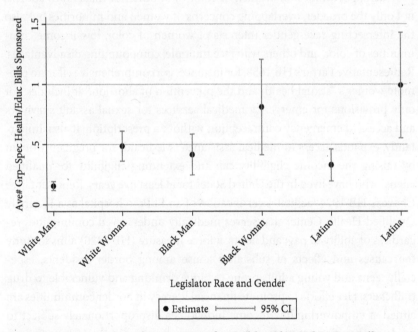

Figure 3.5 Sponsorship of Group-Specific Health and/or Education Bills
(Ave = Average)

---

[32] All differences between women of color and other legislators are statistically significant—except that between Black women and White women (p = .148).

These TX05 bills address a wide variety of health and education issues of particular concern to women and communities of color. Representatives Jessica Farrar (Latina) and Senfronia Thompson (African American) sponsored multiple bills (8 altogether) addressing women's reproductive healthcare, including measures to provide emergency healthcare to sexual assault survivors, mandate health insurance coverage of human papillomavirus (HPV) and cervical cancer screenings, expand access to emergency contraception, and promote breast-feeding. Representative Norma Chavez (Latina) alone sponsored seven bills addressing the health and education needs of her predominantly Mexican American constituents living in the border region (El Paso), including measures to improve public healthcare for "one of the most medically underserved regions in the United States" (HB 2420, HRO Bill Analysis), establish a Binational Alcohol and Substance Abuse Task Force, develop a financial literacy curriculum for public high schools in the region, and convene a Higher Education Border Work Group.

A closer look at these bills (and supporting documents) suggests they may provide opportunities for women of color (and other lawmakers) to address not only the broader, overlapping concerns of women and minorities but also the intersecting race-gender interests of women of color, low-income communities of color, and others who face multiple, compounding disadvantages. Representative Farrar's HB 1658, for instance, is a comprehensive effort to promote women's "sexual health and the prevention of abortion." It includes not only provisions for emergency medical services for sexual assault survivors and access to emergency contraception without a prescription; it also, importantly, expands access to medical assistance (Medicaid) for pregnant women by raising the income eligibility cap and extending eligibility to "qualified aliens" who have lived in the United States for at least five years. Representative Chavez's HB 1924 facilitates certification of an El Paso hospital as a Federally Qualified Health Center that serves medically underserved communities regardless of ability to pay; and her task force measure (HB 3426) aims to study the causes and effects of substance abuse among border residents, especially teens and young adults prone to binge drinking and vulnerable to drug traffickers. Her efforts to promote financial literacy in border communities are aimed at empowering low-income individuals disproportionately subject to predatory banking practices such as sub-prime mortgages.[33]

---

[33] Chapter 5 will further explore the intersectional potential of legislation sponsored by these two women of color and many other representatives who served majority-minority constituencies.

Generalizable to Republicans?

Very few of the race-gender patterns of group-interest bill sponsorship found among Democrats are reflected in our sample of Republican state lawmakers—and not simply because there are so few African Americans and Latinxs among them.[34] Perhaps reflecting a conservative aversion to identity politics, Republicans sponsor even fewer group-specific bills than do Democrats. Approximately two-thirds (68%) sponsor no women-specific bills in any given year; only 12% sponsor more than two. On average, they sponsor slightly more than half a bill (.59) each year. Hardly any GOP (Republican) legislators sponsor a Black- or Latinx-specific bill: 94% sponsor no Black-specific bills; 90% sponsor no Latinx-specific bills. On average, each legislator sponsors only .08 Black-specific and .14 Latinx-specific bills per year. Even with these low levels of group-specific activity, however, there is still meaningful variation among Republican lawmakers.[35]

On women-specific matters, the eight Latinas and one Black man are by far the most active GOP legislators. Latina lawmakers sponsor an average of 1.75 bills each in any given year, with only one refraining altogether. The Black man, who served in the 1998 New Jersey Assembly, sponsored one such bill. In contrast, White GOP women sponsor an average of only .8 bills each and most (59%) do not sponsor any women-specific legislation. White men and Latinos sponsor .5 bills each, with only a third (29% and 36%, respectively) participating in women-specific policy leadership at all. None of the three Black women sponsor a single women-specific measure. These patterns remain much the same when we control for the same set of district and legislator characteristics: all else being equal, Latinas sponsor significantly more women-specific bills (2.75) than anyone else;[36] White women sponsor significantly more than White men do (.9 vs. .5), with Latinos situated in

[34] In our sample of Republican legislators, there are 28 Latinos, eight Latinas, three Black women, and one Black man.

[35] Given the very low numbers of Republican legislators of color, we place less emphasis on tests of statistical significance, especially when comparing African Americans to others. For the same reason, we employ multivariate analysis—controlling for the same variables as we did for Democrats—secondarily, to confirm the race-gender patterns observed in the raw frequencies. In these multivariate models of Republican policy leadership, district characteristics matter little; their regression coefficients are almost always insignificant. The only control variables that have consistent effects are overall legislative activity and chairing a relevant committee.

[36] Given the very small number of Latinas, the difference between their women-specific sponsorship activity and that of White women is not statistically significant (p = .110).

between (.65 each). Black women, of course, remain completely inactive. Thus, there are no clear race-gender patterns. Women of color and men of color are among the most likely and the least likely sponsors. White women's activity level is comparable to that of men of color but significantly higher than that of White men—and Black women. Compared to their Democratic counterparts, GOP Latinas engage in women-specific policy leadership much more frequently; everyone else participates less frequently.

GOP legislators of color, like their Democratic counterparts, can often be counted on to sponsor at least one racially specific piece of legislation. Black legislators are, by our measure, fairly reliable sponsors of bills addressing Black- and Latinx-specific interests simultaneously. The lone Black man and one Black woman each sponsored two such measures. Similarly, a quarter of Latino Republicans (7 of 28) sponsored a single bill targeting either Latinx-specific interests or the interests of racial/ethnic minorities in general. This is considerably more effort than that exhibited by White women or men, less than 10% of whom sponsor any such legislation. Yet, none of the Latina lawmakers sponsored a single Latinx-specific or racially-targeted bill. This is in stark contrast to Democratic Latinas, who are the most active sponsors of Latinx-specific legislation. Unlike their Democratic counterparts, GOP Latinas seem to be devoting all of their group-specific sponsorship activity to women-specific issues.

GOP policy leadership on health and education issues is much more frequent, often matching Democratic levels of sponsorship activity. Overall, 60% sponsor at least one health policy bill, 61% sponsor at least one education bill, and a full 80% sponsor at least one or the other. On average, Republican state lawmakers sponsor 3.37 health and/or education bills each in any given year. Unlike their Democratic counterparts, however, GOP women of color are the least active sponsors, not the most active; but the differences between them and other Republicans are not significant. Latinas sponsor an average of 2.5 health/education bills each, and Black women sponsor 1.7; White men, Latinos, and White women all sponsor about 3.5 bills each (3.3, 3.6, and 3.7, respectively). The Black man is particularly prolific at 11 bills sponsored; but once we control for the total number of bills sponsored (among other things), his level of health/education policy leadership is similar to those of comparable White men, Latinos, and White women—and only slightly higher than those of Black women and Latinas. The only statistically significant difference is between White women (at 4.3 bills each) and White men (at 3.2 bills each).

Thus, among White Republicans, we see gender gaps in women's substantive representation that are consistent with existing theory and empirical research. Republican Latinos (and the one Black man) also appear to be more reliable sources of racially targeted policy initiatives than their White colleagues. Arguably, existing single-axis conceptions of group interests work well in highlighting the representational efforts of these legislators. The few Republican women of color, however, appear to be relatively unreliable sources of group interest legislation, both narrowly and broadly defined. Black women avoid women-specific issues and Latinas avoid Latinx-specific issues altogether; and neither group seems to opt for higher levels of activity on broader, overlapping issues of health or education.

There is one group-interest policy arena in which GOP women of color do stand out. Much like their Democratic counterparts, they appear particularly committed to sponsoring group-specific health and education bills. Together, Republican Latinas and Black women are at least twice as likely as their co-partisans to sponsor at least one health or education bill targeting either women/girls or racial/ethnic minorities: 36% of minority women sponsor such legislation (37.5% of Latinas, 33% of Black women) compared to only 18% of White women, 10% of minority men, and 8% of White men.[37] On average, GOP women of color each sponsor .36 of these bills; White women sponsor .24, and White men and men of color both sponsor .1.[38]

Again, though few in number, these group-targeted health/education bills sponsored by women of color offer a variety of race, gender, and race-gender initiatives, including efforts to enhance pre-college minority students' math and science skills, to incorporate a "Parenting and Paternity Awareness" component into the high school health curriculum, and to restrict access to contraceptives. A bill requiring provision of HIV/AIDS information, voluntary testing, and counseling for women seeking annual gynecological or family planning services, sponsored by CA05 Representative Bonnie Garcia, provides another example of how these targeted health and education measures can address the intersectional needs of women of color in particular. Written in collaboration with a local organization founded to address "the lack of resources available to women—especially Hispanic women—with

---

[37] None of the Republican Black man's 11 health/education bills is group-specific.

[38] Differences between women of color and others are statistically significant, with one exception: their average count (.36) is not significantly higher than that of White women (.24). Introducing our battery of control variables does not alter these patterns, though it does render all differences statistically insignificant.

HIV," the bill's statement of purpose notes that African American and Hispanic women account for a disproportionate share of new HIV diagnoses among heterosexual women but are often reluctant to seek care.[39]

Discussion and Conclusions

The relationship between descriptive and substantive representation is not a simple one. As this chapter begins to illustrate, it depends in no small part on which group members and which definition of group interests one considers.[40] But do some definitions of group interests spotlight the representational leadership of some members while obscuring that of others? More specifically, are definitions of group interests and measures of substantive representation race-gender biased? This chapter explores that possibility by examining systematically the inferential effects of varying definitions of group interests in analyses of US state legislative agenda-setting behavior.

Relying on the critical framework of intersectionality as well as extant research on Latina and African American women in public office, we speculated that such race-gender bias would be more likely to occur when group interests are defined narrowly in terms of issues that affect women or minorities most directly and primarily. Gauging legislative leadership on such group-specific issues (only), we hypothesized, may overestimate the representational commitments of White women and men of color, while underestimating those of women of color. In contrast, broader, overlapping conceptions of group interests, such as health and education, might capture the representational activities of legislative women of color more accurately, revealing a stronger commitment or higher level of policy leadership than we might otherwise observe.

Our analysis of bill sponsorship activity among Democratic state legislators, where the overwhelming majority of legislators of color are located, confirms these expectations to some extent. As expected, Democratic women of color

---

[39] For information about the founder of Working Wonders of Cathedral City, see http://www.hivpositivemagazine.com/wonders.html (accessed 15 January 2020). Information about the purpose of the bill is contained in the Assembly Committee report (4 April 2005), available on the state's bill tracking website.

[40] No doubt the relationship between women's descriptive and substantive representation also depends on where (i.e., which legislative body or bodies) and when (i.e., which year or years) one looks.

(especially Black women) sponsor significantly more health and education legislation than do their co-partisan colleagues. Somewhat unexpectedly, we also find that women of color—in both parties—are particularly invested in policy proposals that address the targeted health and educational interests of women and/or minorities. Thus, overlooking such sponsorship activity or failing to recognize it as part and parcel of what it means to act for women and people of color will result in underestimating the representational leadership of women of color.

Equally important, though, is our most consistent finding: no matter what definition of group interests we employ, Democratic women of color never appear disengaged from or any less committed to the groups' substantive representation than anyone else. They are among the leading sponsors of every type of group-interest legislation examined. As US Representative Maxine Waters, chair of the House Financial Services Committee (and one-time member of the California state house), recently asserted: "we take on everything" (Dittmar et al. 2017, 38).[41] When these legislative women of color are distinguished, it is because they provide *higher* levels of leadership on group-interest issues—and this is the case regardless of how narrowly or broadly those issues or interests are defined. Latinas sponsor more Latinx-specific bills than anyone else, even Latinos. Black women and Latinas sponsor more health and education bills than anyone else, especially when those bills are targeted to address the interests of women or racial/ethnic minorities in particular.

Only among Republican women of color do we see any sign of reluctance to take the lead as a sponsor of group-interest legislation: Latinas avoid Latinx-specific bills altogether; Black women sponsor no women-specific measures; both are among the least active sponsors of general health and education bills. Yet these same women provide higher levels of leadership in other areas of group interest: Latinas are far and away the most active sponsors of women-specific legislation; Latinas and Black women both sponsor more group-targeted health and education bills than any other group of Republican lawmakers. Again, these patterns are unrelated to how narrowly or broadly group interests are defined. Why GOP women of color assume policy leadership roles on some group-interest issues and not others is an interesting puzzle worthy of future research (see Ward 2016).

---

[41] Only when we exclude group-targeted health and education bills—one possible mechanism by which women of color manage to "take on everything"—do women of color appear less active as sponsors of group interest bills.

Our intersectional analysis of single-axis definitions of group-interest representational activity also reveals significantly more variation among race-
gender groups of legislators than we might otherwise observe. Most notably,
African American women and Latinas do not always pursue the same paths
to substantive representation, as the "women of color" moniker often implies.
Among Democrats, Black women focus a bit more of their agenda-setting
efforts to health and education issues than their Latina counterparts do, and
each group of women (along with Black men and Latinos) focuses more attention to the interests of their own racial/ethnic group. Among Republicans,
Latinas seem to devote almost all of their group-interest energy into women-
specific bills, while Black women concentrate on racially specific bills. Thus
are significant partisan differences among Latinas and African American
women revealed. Democratic Latinas are the most active sponsors of Latinx-
specific issues while GOP Latinas steer clear. Democratic Black women are
among the most active bill sponsors across nearly all definitions of group
interests while GOP Black women limit their efforts to racially targeted
measures. Among Democrats, women of color sponsor the most health and
education bills; among Republicans, they sponsor the fewest. We thus return
full circle to the conclusion that the relationship between descriptive and
substantive representation is a complex, contingent, and intersectional one.

To paraphrase Smooth (2006b), this is a mess worth capturing in our research designs. If our findings are any indication, no simple, single-axis,
single-shot, or one-size-fits-all approach to defining and measuring group
interests will do justice to the very real complexity of the phenomena we
hope to understand. Different definitions can and do yield different results.
Allowing for and even embracing such complexity is, of course, especially
valuable and appropriate for an intersectional approach to political representation (Hancock 2007; McCall 2005). It also recognizes the complexity and
contingency of the very political, socially constructed nature of group interests
themselves (Reingold and Swers 2011). Perhaps, then, the best strategy is to
maintain the one we developed for this study: identify multiple definitions
of group interests; theorize about the meaningful conceptual and empirical
differences (and similarities) between them; and empirically test propositions
derived from such theorizing. We do just that in Chapter 4 by introducing a
new, multidimensional concept of race-gender policy leadership.

4

Race-Gender Policy Leadership

Women of color in public office often speak of their commitment to representing the under-represented. Jill Carter, for example, ran for the Maryland House of Delegates in 2002 to champion "the causes of people that need champions," to speak out for those who are "intentionally ignored."[1] Senfronia Thompson, the longest-serving woman, African American, and Democrat in the Texas House, fights to, as she puts it, "let the little dogs eat." In a 2011 *Texas Tribune* profile, we are told that she counts among her most important accomplishments "measures to help low-income people pay their electric bills, stave off cuts to nursing homes, provide support for rape victims and prevent racial profiling."[2] Catherine Cortez Masto, the first Latina ever elected to the US Senate, recalls what propelled her into running in her first race for Nevada's attorney general back in 2006: "fighting for vulnerable people who were looking for somebody to stand up for them." Shortly after winning her Senate seat in 2016, she was reminded of who those vulnerable people are and why they still command her attention.[3]

> On Election Day, . . . I was walking through the hotel where we held our party, and these young Hispanic men and women were coming up to me and crying. They were concerned about their future, their parents, concerned that families would be torn apart. Even to this day, I will be in a convenience store or out in Southern Nevada or in Reno, and people will come up to me and cry. It reminds me that I am here to represent them, their stories, their struggles, their fight. I know that when my grandfather crossed the Rio Grande, somebody was there to support him and to fight

[1] Aliza Friedlander, "'I Was the Squad Before "The Squad"'—Meet Jill Carter, Running for Congress," *Jewish Insider* (3 February 2020): https://jewishinsider.com/2020/02/i-was-the-squad-before-the-squad-meet-jill-carter-running-for-congress/

[2] Emily Ramshaw, "Defending 'Little Dogs' but Playing Both Sides," *The Texas Tribune* (21 July 2011): https://www.nytimes.com/2011/07/22/us/22ttthompson.html.

[3] "Sen. Catherine Cortez Masto: It Was Time to Be My Own Boss: The First Ever Latina Elected to the U.S. Senate on How a Box of Chocolate Can Make All the Difference." As told to Mattie Kahn, *Elle* (23 February 2017): https://www.elle.com/culture/career-politics/a43287/catherine-cortez-masto-interview-senator/.

Race, Gender, and Political Representation. Beth Reingold, Kerry L. Haynie, and Kirsten Widner, Oxford University Press (2021). © Oxford University Press. DOI: 10.1093/oso/9780197502174.001.0001.

for him. I know when my dad was discriminated against because he was a Hispanic, somebody opened doors for him, and that's why he opened doors for others. That's what we do as Americans. If we've succeeded then we help others who are still struggling.

Right now, there are 21 female senators in the Senate, and that is more than we have ever had at any one point. It's not enough. We have different perspectives that we bring to the conversation, different issues that we push forward. But we're *still* fighting for equal pay for equal work. We're still fighting for our right to decide what happens to our bodies. We are hearing from members in Congress who still don't understand what Planned Parenthood *does* for members of our communities. Women need more seats at the table. Period.

Like Representative Thompson, Senator Cortez Masto includes both racial/ethnic minorities and women among those whose interests she intends to champion. Is this something a lot of women of color in office have in common? To what extent do other elected representatives stand up for *multiple* groups whose causes need championing? Who fights for those who are *multiply disadvantaged*? These are questions the single-axis analysis of policy leadership in Chapter 3—and elsewhere—cannot adequately address. We could see who fights for women's interests, who fights for Black interests, and who fights for Latinx interests. But we could not see clearly who fights for women *and* people of color, or for women of color and others who face multiple forms of marginalization.

This chapter marks a turn toward more intersectional approaches and tools of analysis so that we can investigate these "both/and" questions about race, gender, and representation. To better understand the role of women of color—and men of color, White men, and White women—we must engage more intersectional concepts of substantive representation and ask a different set of questions. Rather than simply pondering whether women and racial/ethnic minorities in office are more likely to advocate on behalf of other women and minorities, respectively, this chapter asks, to what extent and how do representatives address both race and gender in their policymaking initiatives? Are policy agendas and legislative advocacy raced-gendered in this respect (Hawkesworth 2003)?

A growing body of research focused on the representational behavior of women of color in office has begun shedding light on these questions. Our earlier research, for example, finds that across 10 state houses, Black women are more likely than their Black male or White colleagues to sponsor at least one Black interest bill and one women's interest bill (Bratton, Haynie, and Reingold 2006). In their analysis of congressional websites, Brown and Gershon (2016, 101) report that while "all the legislators examined implicitly connected their identity to an advocacy issue, . . . minority congresswomen are most likely to include more than one marginalized identity (such as their race, class, and/or gender) to illustrate their concern for a disadvantaged sub-population." Similarly, Brown, Minta, and Banks examine how lawmakers' race-gender identities affect their and their institutions' attention to "joint issues" that directly or indirectly affect both women and racial minorities in the Maryland state legislature and in Congress (Brown and Banks 2014; Minta and Brown 2014; see also Barrett 1995). Taking a more in-depth case study approach, Brown (2014b) and others have explored the intersectional complexities of how the identities and experiences of legislative women of color shape their representational activities on behalf of women, minorities, and minority women in particular (García et al. 2008; Takash 1997; Williams 2016).

In this chapter, we build on these and other studies of race, gender, and representation to further operationalize and test theories of intersectional identity and legislative behavior (Brown 2014b; Hawkesworth 2003; Smooth 2011; Strolovitch 2007). Taking advantage of our extensive database of sponsored bills, we aim primarily for a deeper and more generalizable understanding of raced *and* gendered, or "race-gender" policymaking through a unique combination of conceptual innovations and data-gathering advances.

The concept of *race-gender policy leadership*, defined here as sponsoring bills that address the specific interests of both women and racial/ethnic minorities—or disadvantaged subgroups thereof—offers a more inclusive and complex understanding of representational policymaking. Focusing on multiple patterns of bill sponsorship, our analysis recognizes that legislators can approach the interests of various groups (Blacks, Latinxs, women) as distinct, overlapping, or intersecting. Thus, we examine not only the likelihood that legislators advocate for women *and* minorities at all, but also *how* they choose to do so: sequentially (one group's interest at a time), simultaneously, or with greater attention to intersectional disadvantages.

These innovations allow for a more thorough examination of theories of intersectional representation across multiple conceptions of race-gender policy leadership. Specifically, we test hypotheses that Black female and Latina legislators are more likely than all other legislators to sponsor (a) both women-specific bills and minority-specific bills; (b) bills that address multiple groups' interests simultaneously, such as standard anti-discrimination measures; and (c) bills that address the particular interests of multiply disadvantaged subgroups of women or minorities, such as poor women of color (Strolovitch 2007). Indeed, it is in the realm of race-gender policy leadership where we expect to see women of color make many of their most distinctive representational contributions.

We find that intersectionality does matter—both as an analytic approach and as a political phenomenon. In the single-axis analysis of Chapter 3, women of color appear to behave very much like other women when we consider narrowly defined women-specific issues and very much like co-ethnic men when we consider Black-specific issues. And even though Latinas sponsor more Latinx-specific bills than do Latinos, they are equally likely to sponsor at least one such measure. Here, where we take a more intersectional approach to policy leadership, women of color really stand out. While few legislators engage in race-gender policy leadership, Black women or Latinas are more likely to do so than their minority male or White female counterparts, depending on the measure. Thus, women of color play distinctive, leading roles in addressing the policy needs of multiple and multiply disadvantaged constituencies. This suggests that the increasing numbers of women of color in legislative bodies has particular significance for the most marginalized constituencies.

Theories of Intersectional Representation

Theoretically, social identity links descriptive and substantive representation (Brown 2014b; Reingold 2000; Swers 2002). Above and beyond partisanship, ideology, and even constituency, it is the legislators' own identities and lived experiences as women or racial/ethnic minorities that is the primary driver of "acting for" others like them (Pitkin 1967). How, then, should we think about representation in the context of multiple, intersecting identities? While all legislators can identify themselves in terms of both gender and race/ethnicity and draw on that dual identity in their representational decision making, research suggests that women of color are most likely to do so (Brown and Gershon 2016). The particular intersections of race, gender, and class and experiences with racism, sexism, and economic deprivation that shape the identities and perspectives of legislative women of color enable and empower them to advocate on behalf of multiple constituencies, especially those that are "intersectionally marginalized" (Brown and Banks 2014; D. King 1998; Strolovitch 2007) or subject to "secondary marginalization" within marginalized communities (Cohen 1999).

As Brown and Banks (2014, 166) argue, Black women legislators have a "race/gender identity advantage"; their race/gender identities "better position . . . [them] to recognize the needs of multiple communities than White men and women and Black men. . . . ['Ihus,] Black women are uniquely positioned to use their intersecting raced and gendered identities to advocate for the needs of racial/ethnic minorities, women, and specifically minority women." (See also Orey et al. 2006.) "Because I am female and African American," explains US Representative (and one-time member of the Ohio General Assembly) Joyce Beatty, "I know that I have a laser eye on gravitating to women's issues, issues for minorities, [so] that I can make sure that they are included more" (Dittmar et al. 2017, 21). Similarly, Fraga and colleagues (2008, 163) coin the term "strategic intersectionality" to theorize "the unique position that Latina legislators may occupy, relative to Latino males." Their intersectional identity provides a distinct "set of interests, resources, and strategies" by which they "are positioned to be the most effective advocates on behalf of working-class communities of color" (p. 157; see also Bejarano 2013; García et al. 2008, 30; Rocha and Wrinkle 2011).[4]

Brown (2014b) goes one step further. Black women legislators, she argues, often "use an intersectional approach to formulating public policy" (p. 73). Drawing upon their firsthand knowledge of multiple intersecting systems of oppression, they reject policy proposals that treat race and gender "as mutually exclusive categories" and thus further obscure and marginalize women of color (p. 73). Rather than seeing issues as simply gendered *or* raced, Black women legislators are more likely to frame them as "race-gender" issues in order to "advocate for African-American women who are marginalized and disempowered" (p. 91). US Representative Donna Edwards, for example, illustrates how she thinks about pay equity differently:

[O]ne of the elements that I brought to the discussion around equal pay for equal work, for example, was to always put that in terms of what those

[4] Legislative women of color, unlike their White and/or male counterparts, may also face additional, external pressure from constituents, interest groups, colleagues, etc. to represent both women and minorities (Brown and Gershon 2014, 87).

overall numbers mean for Black women, for Latinas. Because I think just articulating the difference between saying a general number like 78 cents on the dollar [for women overall compared to white men] and saying 64 cents [for Black women] or 49 cents for Latinas helped my district relate to an issue that was thought of as a broader women's concerns, but not really a concern for women of color. And I think that helped our [Democratic] caucus to understand that as well. (Dittmar et al. 2017, 21)

Other studies provide evidence that Black women and Latina leaders are particularly attuned to the interests of those who are "multiply burdened" (Crenshaw 1989), especially poor women of color. Brown and Gershon (2014, 94–95), for example, find that minority congresswomen are unusual in drawing attention to their "humble backgrounds" and "communicating their empathy for minorities, women, and the economically disadvantaged." Similarly, Strolovitch (2007, 9) suggests that without the shared experiences of intersecting marginalization and discrimination that women of color bring to the table, advocacy organizations fighting on behalf of women or minorities are likely to discount "disadvantaged-subgroup" issues like welfare reform as too "narrow and particularistic" to warrant their full attention. Instead, they will focus much more attention and resources to "consensus," "majority," or even "advantaged-subgroup" issues framed only in terms of gender *or* race/ethnicity and thought to be of more central and widespread concern to their constituencies (Cohen 1999).

For these reasons, we hypothesize that legislative women of color will be more likely than all other lawmakers to engage in race-gender policy leadership—more likely to introduce both women-specific bills and minority-specific bills; more likely to introduce bills that address the specific interests of women and minorities simultaneously; and more likely to introduce bills that address the particular interests of disadvantaged subgroups of women or minorities. Congruent with theories that expect women of color to take more intersectional approaches to issue framing and advocacy, we also expect that their leadership will be most distinct when it comes to sponsoring bills that address the interests of disadvantaged subgroups. To the extent that bills addressing multiple groups' interests simultaneously are standard anti-discrimination measures, we expect the behavior of women of color to be least distinctive. White women and men of color might sponsor such bills as a matter of course, even when their focus is only on one particular group or protected category. Moreover, such measures are more likely to be framed as benefiting the entire group, even when the opportunities they address (e.g., government contracting or higher education) are most available to relatively advantaged subgroups (Strolovitch 2007).

Minta and Brown (2014) provide an alternative theory worth noting here as well. In addition to positing that minority men are equally effective at calling attention to women's issues, they find that the presence of minority men is even more important in drawing congressional attention to "joint issues" that directly or indirectly affect both women and minorities. Thus, we might find men of color to be equally, or even more likely than women of color to engage in race-gender policy leadership.

Conceptualizing and Operationalizing Race-Gender Policy Leadership

Adopting standard definitions of women's interest bills, Black interest bills, Latinx interest bills, and emerging conceptions of intersectional policy issues (Brown and Banks 2014; Cohen 1999; Hancock 2007; Minta and Brown 2014; Strolovitch 2007), we identify three mutually exclusive ways legislators could engage in race-gender policy leadership.[5] First, they could take an additive, *one-of-each* approach, sponsoring at least one women's interest only bill and one minority interest only bill.[6] Second, they could sponsor one or more bills that address the interests of women and at least one racial or ethnic minority *simultaneously*. Many civil rights or affirmative action measures embody this approach by addressing discrimination, hate crimes, or other inequalities related to sex/gender and race, color, ethnicity, national origin, etc. For example, Texas 1997 House Bill 1258 prohibits discrimination in "any education program or activity on account of ethnicity, color, gender, sexual orientation, religion, or national origin."[7] New Jersey 1998 Assembly Bill 2034 establishes the Task Force on Equitable Compensation to, among other things, review job titles "dominated by a single sex, race or national

---

[5] To be clear, the three types of race-gender policy leadership are operationalized to be mutually exclusive. However, an individual legislator could engage in more than one type of race-gender policy leadership activity.

[6] A women's interest *only* bill is one coded as a women-specific bill, but not as a Black- and/or Latinx-specific bill, or a welfare/poverty bill. A minority interest *only* bill is one coded as a Black-and/or Latinx-specific bill, but not as a women-specific bill or a welfare/poverty bill.

[7] Bill text: https://capitol.texas.gov/tlodocs/75R/billtext/html/HB01258I.htm (accessed 19 January 2020).

origin . . . [that is] when at least 70% of the incumbent employees are of one sex or when . . . one race or national origin is disproportionately represented."[8] *Simultaneous* bills may also address race and gender simultaneously—and intersectionally—by targeting the interests of women of color (or men of color). Yet, only 7% of the Democratic-sponsored *simultaneous* bills in our database do so (four targeting women of color, one men of color).[9] Like the New Jersey and Texas examples cited here, the vast majority of these bills seek to expand, clarify, expedite, or otherwise strengthen more traditional, single-axis approaches to combating or remedying sex/gender and racial/ethnic discrimination and violence.

The third approach to race-gender policymaking focuses more specifically on the interests of *disadvantaged subgroups* of women and of racial/ethnic minorities—including poor women of color. As we elaborate in Chapter 6, both the incidence of poverty and the history of welfare policy in the United States are deeply gendered and raced (Abramovitz 1996; Hancock 2004; Hawkesworth 2003; Mink 1995; Roberts 1997). Thus, sponsoring one or more bills that address the interests of poor, low-income, or economically disadvantaged individuals and communities constitutes an inherently intersectional approach to race-gender policy advocacy, even though such measures rarely reference women, racial/ethnic minority groups, or women of color explicitly. Importantly, it is the interests of such intersectionally marginalized subgroups that are so often framed as too risky, controversial, or narrow to be fully embraced by most single-axis-oriented advocates for women and minorities (Cohen 1999; Strolovitch 2007).

These three approaches are by no means the only ways lawmakers might engage in race-gender policymaking. As Brown's in-depth analysis illustrates, Black women can and do frame what is often considered a women's issue only (e.g., domestic violence) as a race-gender issue and work diligently to "advocate for African-American women who are marginalized and disempowered" (2014b, 91; see also Frederick 2010; Williams 2016). Similarly, bills that address the interests of women and racial/ethnic minorities simultaneously may do so in ways that are more or less intersectional.

---

[8] Bill text, summary statement: https://www.njleg.state.nj.us/9899/Bills/A2500/2034_I1.HTM (accessed 19 January 2020).

[9] New Jersey 1998 AB 2423, for example, establishes a Black Infant Mortality Reduction Education and Research Program. Ohio 1997 HB 335 establishes a program for family members or other volunteers to provide support services to adults and juveniles in state correctional institutions—as recommended by the state Commission on African-American Males.

For example, affirmative action measures could propose separate quotas or application procedures for women and minorities, or they could include remedies that recognize the intersecting and mutually constitutive nature of race-gender discrimination (Brown 2014b). We will explore these and other possibilities for intersectional policymaking in more depth in Chapter 5. Our approach here is a starting point, one that provides a relatively broad and inclusive overview of various ways in which legislative leadership on behalf of women and minorities can occur: from a predominantly additive, one-at-a-time approach, to a more traditional simultaneous approach, to a fully intersectional approach that places the interests of disadvantaged subgroups front and center.[10]

Operationalizing Bill Types

Operationalizing race-gender policymaking begins with defining and identi-fying different types of bills: women's interest, Black interest, Latinx interest, and welfare/poverty bills.[11] For the purposes of this chapter, we restrict "women's interest," "Black interest," and "Latinx interest" bills to those that are commonly thought to be more group-salient because they directly, spe-cifically, or explicitly target women and/or minorities—the group-specific bills we introduced in Chapter 3. These bills are the building blocks from which we operationalize our "one-at-a-time" and "simultaneous" approaches to race-gender policy leadership. To capture our third approach, which addresses the interests of intersectionally marginalized subgroups of women, African Americans, and/or Latinxs, we focus on bills addressing welfare policy, poverty, and the needs of low-income individuals and communities. This includes a wide variety of initiatives regarding the distribution of need-based (or means-tested), public assistance in the form of cash, healthcare, food, and housing as well as services, programs, and regulations for unem-ployed and minimum-wage workers. We follow Strolovitch (2007, 34–35) in choosing welfare/poverty issues in particular because they were high on the agendas of relevant policymaking institutions during the years covered by our study. Notably, these are also among the issues so often framed and

[10] Other measures of race-gender policy and policymaking, such as Minta and Brown's (2014) and Brown and Banks's (2014) direct and indirect "joint issues," cannot distinguish between these dif-ferent approaches.

[11] Again, we examine only bills introduced by individual legislators during the regular session.

discounted—by scholars and advocacy organizations alike—as less salient or central to group interests (Strolovitch 2007).

As in Chapter 3, we do not attempt to distinguish more liberal "pro"-group measures from more conservative "anti"-group measures. Instead, we analyze the policy agendas of Democratic and Republican legislators separately, focusing primarily on the former. Doing so allows for more valid comparisons of and generalizations about White and minority legislators within and across ideologically similar parties. We rely on the same combination of content coding by hand and keyword searches described in Chapter 3 to identify and collect all welfare/poverty bills as well as group-specific bills.[12]

Each bill in our database was coded as a women-specific, Black-specific, Latinx-specific, *and/or* welfare/poverty bill independently. Thus, any single bill could receive any combination of group-specific or welfare/poverty codes, from a single group-specific or welfare/poverty code to all four codes. In our analysis, we are particularly interested in both the single group-specific bills (i.e., bills coded as women-specific but not Black-specific, Latinx-specific, or welfare/poverty) and the bills that were coded as both women-specific and minority-specific (Black and/or Latinx). To examine policy leadership on behalf of disadvantaged subgroups of women and minorities, we consider all welfare/poverty bills regardless of whether they also received a group-specific (women's, Black, and/or Latinx) code.

Initial counts of bills introduced by individual legislators as primary sponsors reveal just how infrequent race-gender policymaking is in our sample of Democratic state representatives. Given the paucity of legislators who sponsored more than one bill or combination of bills that meets the definitions for each of our four dependent variables, we use dichotomous indicators that distinguish whether the legislator did or did not engage in the given type of race-gender bill sponsorship. *One-of-Each* is coded as 1 for those legislators who sponsored at least one women-specific only bill AND at least one Black-specific only, Latinx-specific only, OR Black- and Latinx-specific bill, and 0 otherwise. Fewer than one in 10 (8.6%) legislators in our Democratic sample sponsored at least *One-of-Each* women-specific and minority-specific bill. *Simultaneous* is coded as 1 for those legislators who sponsored bills that were coded as (women- AND Black- specific) OR (women- AND Latinx-specific) OR (women- AND Black- AND Latinx-specific), and 0 otherwise.[13] Only 4% of the sample sponsored at least one

---

[12] See Appendix Table A.6 for the list of welfare/poverty keyword search terms.
[13] None of these *Simultaneous* bills received a welfare/poverty code.

Simultaneous bill, and no one sponsored more than two. *Disadvantaged*, our broadly defined measure of policy leadership on behalf of disadvantaged subgroups of women and/or minorities, is coded as 1 if the legislator sponsored any welfare or poverty focused bills, and 0 otherwise. This was the most frequent area of activity; quite a few Democratic legislators (31%) sponsored at least one welfare/poverty or *Disadvantaged* bill, but only 6% sponsored more than two.[14] Our final dependent variable, *Any*, is coded as 1 if the legislator engaged in any type of race-gender policy activity defined above, and 0 otherwise. Overall, a little more than a third (35.6%) engaged in *Any* of these forms of race-gender policy leadership.

Race-Gender Identity and Race-Gender Policy Leadership

To test our hypothesis that women of color are the most likely to sponsor legislation addressing the interests of multiple and intersectionally disadvantaged groups, we use logit regression to estimate the relationship between legislator identity and our four dichotomous measures of race-gender policymaking. Our fully specified models classify legislators into six mutually exclusive categories: White man, White woman, Black man, Black woman, Latino, and Latina. Because our theory and hypotheses do not distinguish among minority women (or men), we also employ a set of models in which legislators are grouped into four mutually exclusive categories: White men, White women, men of color (Black and/or Latino), and women of color (Black and/or Latina).[15] In all our regression analyses, the reference category is White men. We control for the same set of district and legislator characteristics employed in our analyses of bill sponsorship in Chapter 3: district racial/ethnic composition and average household income; Democratic vote share in the district's most recent state-house race; legislator seniority and overall bill sponsorship activity; and whether the legislator chaired a policy-relevant committee. To account for differences between states and changes over time, we include state and year fixed effects in all models. For reasons stated above, the bulk of our analysis focuses on Democratic state legislators only.

[14] Supplementary negative binomial regression analysis of the number of welfare/poverty bills sponsored provides very similar results.
[15] In analyses employing these aggregated models, we are able to include three legislators identified as both Black and Latinx who are excluded from the disaggregated analyses.

Taking the most inclusive view, Table 4.1 presents results for a regression of whether Democratic legislators introduced at least one bill or set of bills that fell into *Any* category of race-gender policymaking. These results confirm our general proposition that women of color are more active than any other group

Table 4.1 Sponsorship of Any Type of Race-Gender Bill(s)

	Dependent Variable Bill Sponsorship	
	(1)	(2)
White Woman	.145	.141
	(.189)	(.191)
Man of Color	.327	
	(.236)	
Black Man		.599*
		(.314)
Latino		−.041
		(.326)
Woman of Color	.956***	
	(.279)	
Black Woman		1.212***
		(.369)
Latina		.571
		(.406)
People of Color in District	.012***	
	(.005)	
Blacks in District		.011
		(.006)
Latinxs in District		.011*
		(.006)
Average Income in District	−.001	−.002
	(.006)	(.006)
Democratic Vote-share in District	.005	.005
	(.004)	(.004)
Legislator Seniority	−.014	−.014
	(.011)	(.011)
Chair of Relevant Committee	.543**	.515**
	(.256)	(.258)
Total Bills Introduced (logged)	1.516***	1.538***
	(.124)	(.125)
Constant	−5.289***	−5.096***
	(.612)	(.628)
Observations	1,453	1,450
Log Likelihood	−710.33102	−705.20834
Pseudo R^2	0.2504	0.2543

Logit with state and year fixed effects *p ≤ 0.1; **p ≤ 0.05; ***p ≤ 0.01

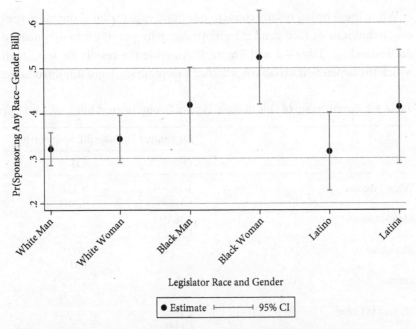

Figure 4.1 Predicted Probability of Sponsoring Any Race-Gender Bill

of lawmakers in sponsoring all kinds of race-gender legislation. Notably, White women and men of color are no more likely than White men to engage in race-gender policy leadership broadly defined. The disaggregated model suggests, however, that Black women are the most engaged. This is seen more clearly in the predicted probabilities for each race-gender group of legislators illustrated in Figure 4.1. The differences between Black women's predicted activity level and those of White men, White women, Black men, and Latinos are all statistically significant (at p ≤ .05). The predicted activity of Black women, while higher, is statistically indistinguishable from that of Latinas (p = .130).

Control variables in this first model behave as expected, and this is generally true throughout our analyses. The percentage of people of color living in a legislative district increases the likelihood of their representative engaging in race-gender policy leadership, usually at traditional levels of statistical significance. Chairs of relevant committees often sponsor bills that are germane to their committees, and the committee chair variables are positive in most models. Also as expected, legislators who sponsor more bills overall are more likely to sponsor at least one race-gender bill or set of bills in all models.[16]

---

[16] Except as noted, district income level and Democratic vote share, along with legislator seniority, have no significant effect on race-gender bill sponsorship.

While these broad results confirm our basic expectations, the more specific definitions of race-gender legislative activity provide a more nuanced understanding. Table 4.2 and Figure 4.2 provide the results for models in which the dependent variable is whether a Democratic legislator introduced

Table 4.2 Sponsorship of One of Each Type of Group Interest Bill

	Dependent Variable Bill Sponsorship	
	(1)	(2)
White Woman	1.175***	1.168***
	(.348)	(.349)
Man of Color	1.165***	
	(.393)	
Black Man		.973*
		(.517)
Latino		1.179**
		(.479)
Woman of Color	2.140***	
	(.443)	
Black Woman		1.583***
		(.592)
Latina		2.543***
		(.538)
People of Color in District	.021***	
	(.008)	
Blacks in District		.029***
		(.011)
Latinxs in District		.016*
		(.009)
Average Income in District	.012	.012
	(.010)	(.010)
Democratic Vote-share in District	.006	.005
	(.008)	(.008)
Legislator Seniority	−.022	−.023
	(.018)	(.019)
Chair of Relevant Committee	.011	−.034
	(.370)	(.377)
Total Bills Introduced (logged)	2.200***	2.199***
	(.251)	(.250)
Constant	−12.086***	−11.893***
	(1.284)	(1.305)
Observations	1,321	1,318
Log Likelihood	−294.36187	−292.84086
Pseudo R^2	0.2883	0.2915

Logit with state and year fixed effects *p ≤ 0.1; **p ≤ 0.05; ***p ≤ 0.01

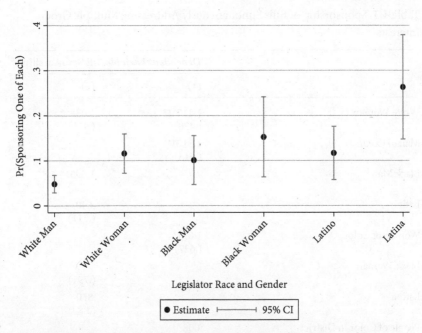

Figure 4.2 Predicted Probability of Sponsoring One of Each Type of Group Interest Bill

One-of-Each, or at least one women-specific bill, and at least one Black- and/ or Latinx-specific bill. As seen in the coefficients in Table 4.2, all historically disadvantaged groups in the model are significantly more likely than White men to introduce separate legislation in each category. The predicted probabilities illustrated by Figure 4.2 suggest Latinas are providing particularly strong leadership in this regard; their likelihood of sponsoring *One-of-Each* is significantly higher than that of every other identity category except Black women (at p ≤ .05). This provides partial support for our expectation that women of color will be on the forefront of race-gender policymaking but signals the possibility that Latinas and Black women may not always choose the same approach.

Table 4.3 shows that, among Democrats, White women and men of color—Black men in particular—are significantly more likely than White men to sponsor bills that we categorize as *Simultaneously* addressing multiple group interests. The predicted probabilities in Figure 4.3 illustrate that Black men are more likely than anyone else to introduce these measures, but only the difference between them and White men is significant (p = .051). This is congruent with our expectation that group differences in this type of race-gender policymaking would be less noticeable and that the leadership

Table 4.3 Sponsorship of Bills Simultaneously Addressing Multiple Group Interests

	Dependent Variable Bill Sponsorship	
	(1)	(2)
White Woman	1.117***	1.038**
	(.420)	(.418)
Man of Color	1.512***	
	(.515)	
Black Man		1.595**
		(.626)
Latino		.640
		(.711)
Woman of Color	1.031*	
	(.627)	
Black Woman		.749
		(.791)
Latina		.850
		(.883)
People of Color in District	.008	
	(.010)	
Blacks in District		.019
		(.014)
Latinxs in District		−.004
		(.013)
Average Income in District	.025**	.020
	(.013)	(.013)
Democratic Vote-share in District	.026**	.021*
	(.011)	(.011)
Legislator Seniority	.011	.008
	(.022)	(.022)
Chair of Relevant Committee	−.170	−.357
	(.488)	(.498)
Total Bills Introduced (logged)	1.037***	1.079***
	(.253)	(.253)
Constant	−8.585***	−7.886***
	(1.484)	(1.503)
Observations	1,360	1,357
Log Likelihood	−207.60214	−201.69656
Pseudo R^2	0.1763	0.1993

Logit with state and year fixed effects *p ≤ 0.1; **p ≤ 0.05; ***p ≤ 0.01

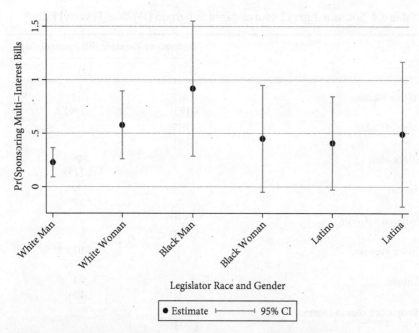

Figure 4.3 Predicted Probability of Sponsoring a Bill Simultaneously Addressing Multiple Interests

of women of color would be least distinctive. The relative activity of Black men on these types of bills also provides additional support for Minta and Brown's (2014) argument that men of color play an important role in calling attention to joint issues of race and gender.

Interestingly, this model is the only one in which control variables for the average income and the Democratic vote-share in the district are significant. Increased income in a legislator's district is found to slightly *increase* the likelihood of sponsoring a *Simultaneous* bill rather than decrease it as we might expect. This may be because many of these bills in our sample promote minority and women-owned businesses in government contracting or non-discrimination in professional settings and are more likely to impact advantaged subgroups of traditionally marginalized groups (Strolovitch 2007). The positive impact of Democratic vote-share may reflect the centrality of these traditional civil rights measures to the party's long-standing agenda.

Table 4.4 presents the results of our final model, which looks at Democratic sponsorship of any welfare/poverty or *Disadvantaged* bill. Here we see Black

Table 4.4 Sponsorship of Disadvantaged Subgroup (Welfare/Poverty) Bills

| | *Dependent Variable* Bill Sponsorship | |
	(1)	(2)
White Woman	−.017	−.017
	(.195)	(.196)
Man of Color	−.017	
	(.240)	
Black Man		.348
		(.325)
Latino		−.378
		(.325)
Woman of Color	.632**	
	(.280)	
Black Woman		1.012***
		(.375)
Latina		.241
		(.406)
People of Color in District	.010**	
	(.005)	
Blacks in District		.004
		(.007)
Latinxs in District		.013**
		(.006)
Average Income in District	−.009	−.009
	(.006)	(.006)
Democratic Vote-share in District	.003	.003
	(.004)	(.004)
Legislator Seniority	−.015	−.015
	(.011)	(.011)
Chair of Relevant Committee	1.240***	1.214***
	(.336)	(.337)
Total Bills Introduced	1.403***	1.411***
	(.125)	(.126)
Constant	−4.368***	−4.351***
	(.605)	(.624)
Observations	1,453	1,450
Log Likelihood	−688.64247	−684.39476
Pseudo R^2	0.2328	0.2359

Logit with state and year fixed effects *p ≤ 0.1; **p ≤ 0.05; ***p ≤ 0.01

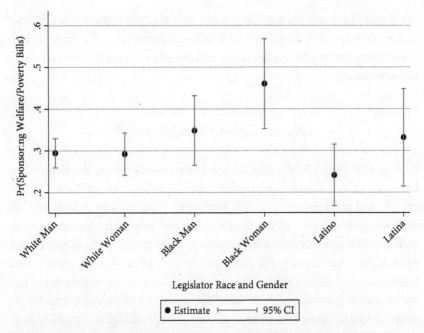

Figure 4.4 Predicted Probability of Sponsoring a Disadvantaged Subgroup (Welfare/Poverty) Bill

women doing the lion's share of the work. The predicted probabilities shown in Figure 4.4 illustrate this point. While all groups have a significant, non-zero probability of introducing at least one *Disadvantaged* bill, Black women are significantly more likely to do so than White men, White women, Black men, and Latinos (p ≤ .05). Black women also appear more likely than Latinas to sponsor bills addressing the needs of *Disadvantaged* subgroups, but the difference is not significant (p = .123). Black men are more likely to sponsor such bills than are Latinos (p ≤ .10), but not more likely than any other group. No other group differences are significant. The relatively low sponsorship rate of Latinas in this model's results is not entirely congruent with our expectation that the leadership of women of color would be most distinct on this measure of intersectional race-gender policymaking. Instead, it is Black women, rather than women of color generally, who take the lead on bills addressing the interests of the poor.[17] Again, our evidence suggests

---

[17] Modeling the number of *Disadvantaged* bills sponsored (rather than the likelihood of sponsoring any such bill) provides very similar results. In the disaggregated model, Black women sponsor

that while Black women and Latinas are strongly committed to race-gender policy advocacy, they may emphasize different pathways—one showing a bit more interest in an additive approach and the other favoring a more intersectional approach.

Generalizable to Republicans?[18]

Race-gender policy leadership is even less frequent among the Republican lawmakers in our sample. Less than 5% sponsor at least *One-of-Each* women-specific and minority-specific bill; hardly any (1%) sponsor at least one bill addressing the specific interests of women and minorities *Simultaneously*; and only 20% sponsor one or more welfare/poverty or *Disadvantaged* bills.[19] All-told, less than a quarter (24%) engage in *Any* form of race-gender policy leadership. As was the case in Chapter 3's analysis of single-axis forms of minority group representation, White GOP men and women are equally inactive across all measures of race-gender policymaking; and participation among GOP legislators of color is highly selective. Nonetheless, over half the Republican legislators of color (55% of women of color, 54% of men of color) participate in at least one form of race-gender policy leadership—rates that rival those of their Democratic counterparts and are significantly higher than those of their White co-partisans (25% of Republican White women, 23% of Republican White men).

Among legislators of color, two Latinos are the only ones who sponsor *One-of-Each*; two other Latinos, along with the one Black man are the only ones who sponsor a *Simultaneous* bill. At the same time, however, substantial portions of GOP Latinx legislators (62% of Latinas, 46% of Latinos) along

---

significantly more bills (on average, 1.3 bills each) than everyone else, except Latinas (.9 bill each). In the aggregate model, however, women of color together sponsor significantly more bills (1.1 each) than everyone else (at p ≤ .01).

[18] Given the very small number of Republican legislators of color, we focus more attention in this section to raw frequencies of race-gender policy activity and less attention to multivariate analysis and tests of statistical significance.

[19] Like the *Simultaneous* bills sponsored by Democrats, those sponsored by Republicans address women/gender and minorities/race-ethnicity in terms of civil rights protections or affirmative action programs for multiple single-axis categories of women and minorities. Unlike the Democrats' bills, however, Republicans' proposals are a mixture of efforts to expand/strengthen and restrict/abolish such laws and programs. None of the three bills sponsored by GOP men of color, however, seems clearly hostile to promoting or protecting civil rights.

with one Black woman (of three) sponsor at least one *Disadvantaged* welfare-poverty bill. Controlling for district and other legislator characteristics does little to change these figures. GOP legislators of color, together, are significantly more likely than their White co-partisans to sponsor welfare/poverty legislation but are just as reticent about engaging in any other form of race-gender policy leadership. Overall, an estimated 55% of women of color and 44% of men of color participate in *Any* form of race-gender policy activity, compared to only 27% and 22% White women and men.[20] Like Democratic Black women, Republican Latinas are more likely than anyone else to sponsor a welfare/poverty bill and thus to participate in any form of race-gender policy leadership, although the differences between them and Latinos and Black women are not statistically significant. This suggests that across party lines, legislative women of color assume distinctive leadership roles in addressing the interests of those who are intersectionally marginalized; but we need more data and analyses before we can be sufficiently confident.

Conclusion

This chapter provides an overview of multiple forms of race-gender policymaking among Democratic and Republican lawmakers in a wide variety of state houses across two decades. Although our conceptions of race-gender policymaking are fairly inclusive, our analysis suggests that relatively few legislators engage in this sort of leadership. Nonetheless, the results here provide additional empirical support for the claim that women of color play an important role in addressing the policy needs of multiple and multiply disadvantaged groups. While other race-gender groups also sponsor such bills, the consistency with which women of color assume leading roles in the promotion of race-gender legislation is notable. On three of four measures of race-gender policy leadership, either Black women or Latinas stand out from their peers, sponsoring more legislation than their minority male, White female, or White male counterparts. In contrast, Black men stand on the forefront of only one type of race-gender advocacy, sponsoring traditional civil rights measures that address multiple group interests simultaneously. White women and Latino men, while occasionally more active than their White

---

[20] All paired differences between legislators of color and White legislators are statistically significant (p ≤ .05) except that between men of color and White women (p = .107).

male colleagues, almost never exert more race-gender policy leadership than their Black or Latina colleagues do.[21]

This chapter demonstrates once again the utility of intersectional theories and tools of analysis for understanding the complexities of gender, race, and representation. By introducing a multidimensional concept of race-gender policy leadership, we are able to test theories of intersectional representation more rigorously and gain new insights into the distinctive, yet varying, contributions women of color make to policy agendas. Limiting ourselves to single-axis conceptions of women's issues or minority issues—especially the more narrow or group-specific ones—fails to fully distinguish the race-gender policy leadership women of color provide, making it seem as if intersectionality rarely matters. As seen in Chapter 3, women advocate for women, regardless of race/ethnicity; Blacks advocate for Blacks, regardless of gender; and Latinas are just as likely as Latinos to advocate for Latinxs, though Latinas sponsor more Latinx-specific bills than Latinos do. Only when we examine overlapping categories of group interests such as health and education bills (especially group-targeted ones) do we see consistent patterns of race-gender intersectionality propelling women of color to the forefront.

Additional intersectional differences come to light when we examine various approaches to race-gender policymaking. Among Democrats (where almost all legislators of color are found), Latina lawmakers are especially active in advancing multiple proposals addressing issues of concern to women or racial/ethnic minorities, as seen in our *One-of-Each* variable analysis. Black women legislators are the most likely sponsors of welfare/poverty bills that address the needs of poor women of color and other intersectionally *Disadvantaged* subgroups. White women's race-gender policy leadership on the other hand falls by the wayside when the interests of poor people are added to the mix—even when controlling for district demographics. Black men, meanwhile, often play particularly important roles in advancing proposals that address multiple gender and racial inequalities *Simultaneously*.

Why these different groups of lawmakers appear to favor different approaches to race-gender policy leadership is an excellent question for future research and theory development. Existing theories of intersectional

---

[21] The only exceptions are the four Republican Latinos who sponsor either *One-of-Each* or at least one *Simultaneous* bill (compared to only one other Republican of color sponsoring one *Simultaneous* bill).

representation cited here may explain why women of color appear no more interested in sponsoring *Simultaneous* bills than their White female and minority male colleagues; but they cannot explain why, among Democrats at least, Latina legislators may be more inclined toward additive approaches to race-gender policy or why Black women may be more partial to intersectional approaches. Further research is needed to verify and explain such divergent approaches to race-gender policy leadership. In addition to expanding the empirical reach of our own quantitative approach, we suspect a more in-depth, qualitative analysis of intersectional variations among women of color (e.g., differences in class background or national origin) and within race-gender policy proposals would be most useful.

Overall, this chapter provides additional evidence that increasing the number of women of color in elected office—from both parties—can have a distinctive effect on substantive representation, increasing the attention paid to issues affecting multiple and multiply disadvantaged populations. It also demonstrates how a more intersectional approach to conceptualizing policy leadership and legislator identity reveals that gender and race interact to distinguish the representational behavior of *all* policymakers—women of color, men of color, White women, and White men alike.

5
Explorations in
Intersectional Policymaking

During her first—and ultimately successful—run for Congress in the summer of 2018, Veronica Escobar was asked in an interview to describe what it is like to live along the Texas-Mexico border and in El Paso in particular.[1] "It's such a beautiful, complex, challenging, infuriating thing," Escobar began.

> It's beautiful because nowhere else do you get an international feel this way. You know what I mean? . . . The connectivity is beautiful. The deep roots that go under and through the Rio Grande are beautiful. Familial roots. Economic roots. All of that.
>
> But, the thing that's so complex is that there's so many different types of immigrants. There's those who can very easily come back and forth and have a visa and can attend the university; who live in Juarez and they make our lives richer and they make their peers' experience richer. They sometimes have no problem. Their biggest problem is the wait times at the border.
>
> Then, you have folks . . . like, I'm mentoring this young woman, who shall remain unnamed, but she's a high school graduate. She's waiting to enroll in one of the local colleges and she is a dreamer. Both her parents are undocumented. Her parents are afraid to go places together because of the fear that they will both be deported at the same time. I can't even imagine growing up like that . . . in fear, that when one of my parents leaves . . . because not both of them are gonna leave at the same time . . . they may not come back. That we may not know where they are or what's happened. That they've been deported. Then, the grueling experience of living in two different countries and not being able to be reunited, then that happens.

---

[1] "An Interview with Veronica Escobar," *frankinterviews* (5 July 2018): http://www.franknews.us/interviews/139/an-interview-with-veronica-escobar.

Race, Gender, and Political Representation. Beth Reingold, Kerry L. Haynie, and Kirsten Widner, Oxford University Press (2021). © Oxford University Press. DOI: 10.1093/oso/9780197502174.001.0001.

She was also the victim of domestic abuse by her boyfriend who knew that she was undocumented and who used it over her. Used it as a weapon. . . . Everybody's experience is different, but living here and knowing people like that. . . . And I'm a citizen! I'm a third generation El Pasoan. My family's been here for well over 100 years, so I had the good fortune of being born on the other side of that skinny little river.

All of these experiences really enrich our humanity and our compassion and it's part of what, I think, has made El Pasoans different. And when people who don't have those experiences, and they don't have someone they care about who's afraid that their parents will be deported, it gives them the excuse to be without that compassion. But having grown up here with those very diverse experiences all around me, has made me a better human being. I think it's made my kids better human beings.

The intersectional qualities of this narrative grab us: the complexities—the beauty and fury—of culture, race, citizenship, class, gender, and kinship; the differences within differences; the commonalities across differences. Escobar's understanding and appreciation of the many-layered problems and intricately tied issues confronting her community and future constituents speaks to the possibilities of intersectional representation. How might such an intersectional perspective find its way into representational activity?

In Chapter 4, we caught a glimpse of what intersectional policy leadership might look like, especially in the welfare/poverty legislation sponsored by women of color and others. Addressing the interests of low-income individuals and communities, we argued, is addressing the problems wreaked by multiple, intersecting systems of marginalization. Yet we were uncertain about the intersectional potential of other types of race-gender bills. How might a women's issue like domestic violence be framed and understood as something more than a single-axis problem of gender relations gone wrong? How might a program promoting government contracts with women- and minority-owned businesses be designed so as to avoid "political intersectionality"—having to make an impossible choice between either race or gender (Crenshaw 1991)?

Such nuances in policy design and problem definition are not likely to be captured by the methodological strategies employed in this book thus far. Quantitative analyses in particular may limit what we can learn and say about intersectional policymaking. In this chapter, we therefore depart from exclusively quantitative depictions of substantive representation as we continue to push beyond single-axis conceptions, to examine and understand the contours of race-gender policy leadership more fully. Drawing from a growing body of intersectional theorizing in law and public policy (e.g., Cho, Crenshaw, and McCall 2013; Crenshaw 1989, 1991; Dill and Zambrana 2009; Hancock 2007, 2011; Hankivsky and Cormier 2011; Lombardo, Meier, and Verloo 2017; Nash 2019; Richie 2012; Roberts 1997; Simien 2007; Verloo 2013; Whittier 2016) and using a qualitative and inductive approach, this chapter investigates the extent to which various women's interest bills, Black interest bills, and Latinx interest bills are re-framed or re-purposed to address the concerns of women of color and others who are "intersectionally marginalized" (Brown and Banks 2014) or "multiply burdened" (Crenshaw 1989). What do such intersectional policy proposals look like and who is more or less likely to introduce them?

What Are Intersectional Policy Proposals?

In general, intersectional policy proposals address issues from more than one perspective, paying attention to multiple and varied forms of inequality, marginalization, deprivation, and oppression. They avoid "a one-size-fits-all approach" or "focusing on single markers" by taking into account diversity among groups and within groups (Hankivsky and Cormier 2011, 218; Strolovitch 2007). Intersectional legislation tends to focus on underserved populations—often "those who are perpetually cast as undeserving" (Spade 2013, 1033)—and is intentional in addressing distinct challenges these groups face by offering culturally or group appropriate specialized programs and services (Whittier 2016). Such "flexibility and customization" are key to intersectionality's distinctive approach to policymaking and its ability to respond to the lived experiences of those who are multiply marginalized (Nash 2019, 127).

It is important to note that intersectionality can be reflected not just in the content of legislation itself but at all stages of policy development and implementation—including who is at the table and who is represented when problems are identified and solutions are proposed, implemented, and evaluated (Hankivsky and Cormier 2011). Some also distinguish intersectional policymaking from more additive approaches, such as adding one more protected category to standard civil rights/anti-discrimination or hate-crime legislation or adding "a multicultural component" to existing anti-violence models "developed largely with the interests of white middle-class women in mind" (INCITE! 2006, 3–4; Brown 2014b; Crenshaw 1991; Hankivsky and Cormier 2011; Spade 2013).

The existing literature also provides some guidance for identifying intersectional proposals in specific policy domains. For example, instead of simply passing tough-on-crime legislation to protect women from sexual and domestic violence, an intersectional response to violence against women recognizes and takes into account how "social, economic, and political forces interact to shape different experiences [e.g., immigrant women vs. African American women vs. White women] and necessary solutions to violence" (Whittier 2016, 791). Thus, recognizing that enhancing the power and reach of law enforcement might lead to increased incidents of police brutality, mass incarceration, and other negative economic and social consequences for their racial/ethnic group (and others), women of color might advocate for anti-crime legislation that repeals or relaxes mandatory arrest policies and expands prevention and rehabilitation programs. In seeking solutions to both interpersonal and state violence, intersectional anti-violence policies might avoid law enforcement and the criminal justice system altogether in favor of more community-based initiatives (Richie 2012; Ritchie 2006).

Intersectional legislation regarding reproductive justice might go beyond ensuring the right to privacy or the right to limit one's reproduction and expressly articulate a positive right to have and parent children (Ross 2006). Similarly, advocates for women of color might propose subsidies that expand access not only to abortion and contraception, but to reproductive healthcare more generally, including expensive reproductive technologies like in vitro fertilization, which are usually out of reach for poor women, who are disproportionately women of color. An intersectional, reproductive justice framework would prioritize preventative pre- and post-natal care in order to reduce infertility and unconscionably high rates of maternal and infant mortality in poor communities of color (Roberts 1997). It also would extend to reforming the child welfare system that too often punishes poor mothers of color deemed "unfit" and relegates disproportionately large numbers of poor children of color to state custody and foster care (Roberts 2002, 2006).

Data, Case Selection, and Methods

Examining how policy proposals might be framed to address the concerns of women of color and others who are intersectionally marginalized requires qualitative analyses and an inductive approach to the study of legislative agendas. We therefore undertake an in-depth content analysis and comparison of the bills sponsored by a small subsample of Democratic state representatives from three states (California, New Jersey, and Texas) during their 1997 and 2005 regular sessions—or, in the case of New Jersey (with odd-year elections), 1998 and 2006. We chose these states for two main reasons. First, they are among the very few states in which White Democrats represented majority-minority districts in the state house. Second, each state legislature provides very informative supplementary documentation of bills as they proceed through the legislative process. New Jersey, for example, requires a statement of purpose at the end of every bill introduced (and of every subsequent version thereafter). The Texas legislature incorporates such statements into their House (and Senate) committee Bill Analyses, along with a detailed outline of bill provisions/sections. The Texas House Research Organization (HRO) also offers bill analyses that summarize supporting and opposing arguments as well as "background" information about existing law. Other documents provide additional information about bill provisions, fiscal impacts, and witnesses who testify in committee for, against, or "on" a particular bill.

To identify legislators for comparison, we used coarsened exact matching (Iacus et al. 2012). Districts represented by women of color were matched to other districts based on state, year, district income, and the minority population of the district. To ensure comparable district income ranges, the 1997–98 sessions and the 2005–6 sessions were matched separately, with district income coarsened into quartiles for each two-year period. For the minority population of the district, we used the combined percentage of Latinx and Black/African American people in the districts and coarsened into four categories: very low (0–20% Latinx and Black), low (20–35%), moderate (35–50%), and majority minority (50+%). Using the MatchIt package in R (Ho et al. 2011), we generated 68 subclasses of districts that had at least one woman of color and at least one legislator of another identity to compare. For this chapter, we selected the subclasses that allowed us to maximize the number of comparisons between the following six race-gender identity types: White man, Black man, White woman, Black woman, Latino, and Latina.

Case Selection

We identified six subclasses or groups of Democratic legislators who are matched on (or share the same) state, year, district racial composition (all majority-minority), and district socioeconomic status (average household income quartiles noted below). Three of the subclasses (or pairs of subclasses) chosen allow for comparisons across all six race-gender groups of Democratic legislators:

- California 2005 (middle income quartiles)
- New Jersey 2006 (upper-middle income quartile)
- Texas 1997 (low-income quartile)

Each of the other three subclasses includes at least one legislator of every identity group *except* White women.

- California 1997 (upper-middle income quartile)
- New Jersey 1998 (upper- and upper-middle income)
- Texas 2005 (lower-middle income quartile)

Within each subclass, there are often multiple legislators who share the same race-gender identity. For example, the TX 97 subclass contains 4 White men (WM), 4 Black men (BM), 16 Latinos (LM) and 5 Latinas (LW). In such instances, we chose to focus our in-depth bill content analysis on one or two legislators who were (a) most similar to the Latina and Black women in the subclass (especially in terms of the districts they served) and (b) most likely to sponsor bills of interest (based on seniority, total number of bills sponsored, other identity characteristics, etc.). To do this, we chose a series of 1-to-1 "most similar" comparisons or pairs of legislators, centered on women of color:

BW—BM	LW—LM
BW—WW	LW—WW
BW—WM	LW—WM
	BW—LW

This means that the best LW-LM pair and the best LW-WW pair may or may not involve the same LW. Nonetheless, when we had the degrees of freedom, we tried to choose the same individual legislators whenever possible. Though not by design, in four cases, one in New Jersey and three in Texas, we chose a legislator for analysis for 2005–6 who was also chosen for analysis as part of the 1997–98 subclass. Table 5.1 lists all legislators, by state, year, and race-gender identity, whose sponsored bills we examined.

Table 5.1 Legislators by Subclass

Subclass	Subclass Members	Race/Gender	Intersectional Bills
1997			
California			
	Grace Napolitano	Latina	Yes
	Edward Vincent	African American Man	No
	Martin Gallegos	Latino	Yes
	Richard Floyd	White Man	No
New Jersey			
	Nia Gill	African American Woman	Yes
	Nellie Pou	Latina	Yes
	Leroy Jones	African American Man	Yes
	Alfred Steele	African American Man	Yes
	Wilfredo Caraballo	Latino	Yes
	Raul Garcia	Latino	Yes
	Neil Cohen	White Man	No
	Louis Romano	White Man	No
Texas			
	Ruth McClendon	African American Woman	Yes
	Jessica Farrar	Latina	Yes
	Leticia Van de Putte	Latina	Yes
	Harold Dutton	African American Man	Yes
	Leo Alvarado, Jr.	Latino	Yes
	Gerard Torres	Latino	No
	Judy Hawley	White Woman	No
	Kevin Bailey	White Man	No
	Tommy Glen Maxey	White Man	Yes

Continued

Table 5.1 Continued

Subclass	Subclass Members	Race/Gender	Intersectional Bills
2005			
California			
	Karen Bass	African American Woman	Yes
	Jenny Oropeza	Latina	Yes
	Mark Ridley-Thomas	African American Man	Yes
	Ronald Calderon	Latino	No
	Jackie Goldberg	White Woman	Yes
	Tom Umberg	White Man	No
New Jersey			
	Oadline Truitt	African American Woman	Yes
	Nellie Pou	Latina	Yes
	Craig Stanley	African American Man	Yes
	Vincent Prieto	Latino	No
	Albio Sires	Latino	No
	Joan Quigly	White Woman	Yes
	Joseph Cryan	White Man	No
	Brian Stack	White Man	No
Texas			
	Senfronia Thompson	African American Woman	Yes
	Norma Chavez	Latina	Yes
	Jessica Farrar	Latina	Yes
	Harold Dutton	African American Man	Yes
	Ismael Flores	Latino	Yes
	Kevin Bailey	White Man	Yes
	Joseph Pickett	White Man	No

Bill Content Analysis Procedure

For each legislator-year chosen, we first gathered a list of all legislation sponsored (as primary sponsor). We then identified the bills included in our quantitative dataset that were coded as women-specific, Black-specific, Latinx-specific, welfare-poverty, health, and/or education bills. Next, we noted the policy/issue area of all other bills (based on readily available synopses or long titles) to see if and when a representative devoted a significant amount of legislative activity to an issue area *not* covered in our dataset. We were particularly attentive to bills related to criminal justice (including policing) and child welfare. Together, these are the types of bills to which we devoted most of our attention.

For each set (subclass) of legislators, we compared sponsored bills within and across the issue areas identified above, noting both similarities and differences. To the extent possible, we paid close attention to any instance in which multiple legislators sponsored "dueling" proposals—that is, alternative (or even duplicate) proposals for addressing the same problem. We analyzed those similarities and differences by addressing the following questions:

- *To what extent and how are women of color addressing these issues/interests differently?*
- *To what extent and how might these differences indicate a more intersectional approach?*
- *To what extent and how is any group of legislators taking a more intersectional approach to policy problems and group interests?*

We also examined each legislator's full "portfolio" of sponsored bills to see whether and how the bills cohered and informed each other. In this way too, we analyzed the content of bills both individually and collectively. We focused our attention primarily on the *introduced* version of each bill, but we noted any significant changes made during the legislative session, especially if that change enhanced or diminished the bill's race, gender, or intersectional qualities.

Our reading of the literature and the theories or concepts of intersectional policymaking it offers gave us a set of coding guidelines with which to identify and distinguish the more likely intersectional proposals and approaches. However, we also very intentionally made room for a significant amount of inductive analysis. Our theoretical expectations were just that; they did not function as hard and fast boundaries or unassailable criteria. Rather, our readings and assessments were intended to be critical and open to different or additional possibilities for what might or might not indicate intersectionality.

Results

Recall that our primary purpose in this chapter is to explore the potential that some legislative policy proposals are written and framed to address some of the distinctive concerns of women of color and others who are intersectionally marginalized. That is, we want to know whether and to what extent legislators employ an intersectional approach to represent various group interests. We are especially interested in knowing whether legislators who are women of color address group interests differently than their male and white female counterparts, and if so, whether they are more likely to exhibit intersectional predispositions in the bills they introduce.

From our examination of more than 1,300 bills introduced in the lower houses of California, New Jersey, and Texas in 1997–98 and 2005–6, we found considerable evidence that intersectional representation does indeed happen via the drafting of public policy proposals. It does not occur often, as most group interest bills we examined appear more congruent with single-axis approaches. Nevertheless, we found numerous examples of bills that simultaneously address multiple and varied forms of inequality, marginalization, and oppression, or that offer group-appropriate programs and services as a targeted response to such conditions. Sixty-eight percent of all the legislators in our sample introduced at least one such bill. When we view these bill introductions through the prism of race, gender, and race-gender identities, a more refined picture emerges. Consistent with the findings and suggestions of previous research (e.g., Brown 2014b; Strolovitch 2007; Bratton, Haynie and Reingold 2006) as well as Chapters 3 and 4, the behavior of the women of color stood out: *all* of the Black women and *all* of the Latina representatives introduced at least one intersectional proposal. By way of comparison, 86% of Black men, 63% of Latino men, 67% of White women, and 20% of White men introduced intersectional legislation.

Our analysis shows that women of color legislators are especially distinctive when we compare the substantive focus and content of their proposals to those of other groups of legislators. That is, we have found meaningful qualitative differences in how women of color address and represent the interests of various marginalized groups. These differences span several policy domains. Here we discuss and provide examples from three areas in which the intersectional pursuits of women of color were especially noticeable: violence against women and criminal justice; healthcare and social welfare; and cross-sector initiatives that reach across multiple policy domains.

Violence Against Women and Criminal Justice

Most of the women of color in our study introduced at least one intersectional bill in the broad area of crime and criminal justice. Many of these proposals address violence against women, some of which eschew law enforcement and /or pay attention to the specialized needs of poor and immigrant women fleeing such violence. For example, Norma Chavez's (LW, TX 05) HB 985 ensures that victims of family violence or stalking (or those trying to protect them) do not lose their eligibility for unemployment compensation—and the bill does not require a police record or protective order to verify such claims. Chavez's attempt (via HB 1561) to allow applicants for state driver's licenses to submit documents issued by foreign governments (e.g., passport, consular identity document) could be particularly beneficial to poor immigrant women fleeing violence who must have a driver's license to obtain much needed jobs and government services while avoiding arrest and deportation for driving without a license. Notably, this bill was supported by the Texas Council on Family Violence as well as the League of United Latin American Citizens (LULAC), Mexican American Legal Defense and Educational Fund (MALDEF), United Farm Workers, American Federation of Labor and Congress of Industrial Organizations (AFI-CIO), and the American Civil Liberties Union (ACLU).

Women of color sometimes venture beyond issues of racial inequities in the criminal justice system, recognizing that at times gender, class, or age are simultaneously linked in triggering problems like police misconduct and mass incarceration. We find instances of this tendency here. A bill sponsored by Nia Gill (BW, NJ 98), AB 3593, requires the Superintendent of the Division of State Police in the Department of Law and Public Safety to establish a database on motor vehicle stops, pursuits, searches, arrests, the use of force, citizen complaints, disciplinary actions, and witnesses. According to the bill, the database must include the race, sex, ethnicity, and age of any subject of a motor vehicle stop, pursuit, search, or arrest; the reason for any vehicle stop, pursuit, search, or arrest, and any charge brought as a result; the identity of all state police troopers or officers and other law enforcement officers involved; a description of any force used; the reason for the use of any force; the disposition of any formal or informal complaint lodged by the subject or others as a result of the traffic stop or arrest; and any disciplinary actions taken against an officer or trooper. Similarly, a proposal by Nellie Pou (LW, NJ 98), AB3590, requires the state police to maintain all logs concerning activity of patrol units; all tape recordings of radio communications between dispatchers and patrol units; and all videotapes recorded by cameras mounted in patrol vehicles for a minimum of 10 years after their creation.

Scholarly research and media exposés have documented the disparities in the rates at which young and urban African American and Latino males are stopped, searched, and arrested as compared to similarly situated Whites, women, or older drivers (Webb 2007; Epp, Maynard-Moody, and Haider-Markel 2014; Baumgartner et al. 2017; Baumgartner et al. 2018). Gill's and Pou's bills are responsive to this problem, as they require the police to be more transparent and accountable, and seemingly are designed to help protect such motorists from undue harm in encounters with public safety officials.

African American and Latina women were especially active in sponsoring legislation aimed at countering or opposing practices and policies that result in the disproportionate arrest and imprisonment of poor people of color, most often young men, but not always. As Jordan-Zachery (2008) reminds us, Black women, because they are over-represented among the poor and among urban dwellers, are also victims of racially biased arrests and sentencing policies. Moreover, the effects of high rates of racialized arrests and mass incarceration are not limited only to the individuals who have direct contact with the justice system. Several studies show there are collateral consequences for entire communities—consequences like family disruption and economic dislocation (Bowers and Preuhs 2009; Burch 2013; Weaver and Lerman 2010). Proposals by women of color in this domain include bills that repeal or relax mandatory arrest policies and those that expand prevention and rehabilitation programs. For example, AB 2182, introduced by Oadline Truitt (BW, NJ06), seeks to reduce the number of repeat arrests for outstanding warrants for not satisfying court-imposed fines when the person does not have the means to pay. The bill allows the court to provide credit for time served, to revoke or suspend the fine, or to order community service. Karen Bass (BW, CA05) proposed a measure (AB 1981) that would fund adult education, vocational training, and rehabilitation programs for prisoners in the interest of reducing the rate of recidivism and increasing the potential for successful re-integration into society. Truitt's AB 929 authorizes, under certain circumstances, the automatic expungement of the criminal record of a person convicted of disorderly conduct and violation of municipal ordinances. All of these bills could help interrupt or even reverse some of the damage done to individuals and communities stemming from biases in the criminal justice system.

Our analysis shows that the women of color, more than any of the other legislative subgroups we examine, demonstrated concern for protecting the rights of the incarcerated. For example, Nellie Pou's AB 1804 requires the chief probation officer in each New Jersey county, the State Parole Board, and the Commissioner of Corrections to assist every person under their jurisdiction completing probation, parole, or a criminal sentence with completing a voter registration form. Karen Bass's (BW CA05) AB 860 and AB 862 require authorities to provide every person who is arrested or incarcerated and has minor children with information about their parental rights and responsibilities, including information about how to modify child support orders. Like Truitt's AB 2182, and Bass's AB 1981 discussed above, these bills would help mitigate the family disruption and economic dislocation associated with raced-gendered incarceration. Jessica Farrar (LW, TX97) proposed a bill, HB 2283, to prohibit correctional officers from having sex with inmates. Unlike many of the other criminal justice policies that disproportionately impact men, Farrar's HB 2283 and Bass's AB 860 and 862 may be just as likely to protect women of color, if not more so.

Health and Social Welfare

We found several examples of the women of color legislators engaging in intersectional representation in the healthcare and social welfare domains. In a series of bills (AB 1982, 2182, 2469 and 2495) Karen Bass (BW, CA 05) sought to make California's Kinship Support Services Program more accessible and more financially secure. Kinship Support is a program that provides non-financial support services to extended family caregivers and the children who have been placed in their homes by juvenile court. The goal of program is to offer a stable, safe alternative living arrangement for children who are unable to live with their biological or adoptive parents. Research shows that kinship care, both formal and informal, is used disproportionately by families of color (Bramlett, Radel, and Chow 2017). Similarly, Gill's (BW, NJ98) AB 327 allocates $20 million for the purpose of providing subsidies to purchase healthcare for low-income uninsured children, who are perhaps the most underserved group in society. A California 2005 bill, AB 2283, introduced by Jenny Oropeza (LW), addresses a health concern of other disadvantaged and sometimes disempowered groups, immigrant and language minorities. The bill makes it easier for immigrants and racial, ethnic, cultural, and language minorities to locate and access medical care. It would require information regarding the cultural background and foreign language proficiency of physicians to be collected annually, aggregated by zip codes, and published on the medical board's website.

Norma Chavez (LW TX05) introduced a bill that would bring public healthcare to "one of the most medically underserved regions in the United States" (HB 2420, HRO Bill Analysis)—the U.S./Mexico border region surrounding her El Paso district. Senfronia Thompson (BW, TX05) introduced three bills (HB 174, 676, 677) seeking to establish a minimum standard of care in the emergency services that hospitals provide for sexual assault survivors. These bills not only attempt to strike a balance between preserving "the chain of evidence" in forensic medical exams and promoting "the dignity [and health] of survivors" (House committee Bill Analysis), but also are careful to define a sexual assault survivor so as not to require the involvement of law enforcement ("regardless of whether a report is made or a conviction is obtained in the incident").

Jessica Farrar's (LW, TX05) HB 1658 incorporates Thompson's provisions for emergency medical services for sexual assault survivors into a more comprehensive effort to promote "sexual health and the prevention of abortion." HB 1658 also reforms abstinence-dominated sex education requirements; expands access to emergency contraception without a prescription (as does Thompson's HB 1637); and, importantly, expands medical assistance (Medicaid) for pregnant women by raising the income eligibility cap and extending eligibility to "qualified aliens" who have lived in the United States for at least five years. As such, HB 1658 is the centerpiece of several measures sponsored by Farrar that address elements of a women-of-color centered *reproductive justice* agenda—one that ensures "the right to have and not to have a child" (Ross 2006, 62-63):

- HB 145 and 146 push back on informed consent requirements for abortion services by providing waivers in cases of sexual assault, incest, and fetal abnormality.
- HB 1216 promotes breast-feeding and the right to do so in the workplace and other public spaces.

- HB 1878 and 1879 call for mercury testing and warning labels for fish in the name of protecting "women considering becoming pregnant, pregnant women, nursing mothers, and [parents of] young children."
- HB 1927 requires those charged with prostitution-related offenses (buyers and sellers alike) be tested for AIDS, HIV, and other sexually transmitted infections (STIs).

Note that just because a bill seeks to remedy an intersectional harm does not mean that it cannot have adverse consequences, however. In its intersectional aim to protect the health of sex workers, HB 1927 could also enable state surveillance in ways that may be problematic for the very people it seeks to help.

Some of Thompson's bills are also congruent with the reproductive justice movement's efforts to address women's reproductive health and choices more holistically. In addition to expanding access to emergency contraception (HB 1637), HB 131 ensures that people who quit their jobs or take a leave of absence to provide "at-home infant care" do not forfeit eligibility for unemployment compensation. By targeting lower-income families (≤ 300% of federal poverty levels) and explicitly recognizing the needs of single and teen parents, HB 131 makes its intersectionality even more apparent.

Chavez and Thompson each introduced a bill (HB 288 and 24, respectively) to raise the personal needs allowance for Medicaid recipients residing in long-term care facilities, most of whom are likely to be poor, elderly women. In an effort to pressure Walmart and others to provide health care benefits and a living wage to its low-level employees (most of whom are likely, especially in Texas, to be low-income women of color), Chavez sponsored a bill (HB 954) requiring applicants for public healthcare assistance to identify their employer. Farrar's HB 260 may also chip away at some of the race-gender violence imposed by the state child welfare system by granting visitation rights to adult siblings of children who are (still) in foster care or otherwise separated from their families.

At the time Karen Bass (BW, CA05) introduced AB 855, persons convicted under federal or California law of a felony that involved the possession, use, or distribution of a controlled substance were ineligible for assistance under any state program funded under provisions of TANF (Temporary Assistance to Needy Families) or the Food Stamp Program. AB 855 creates exceptions so that a person convicted of drug-related felonies could remain eligible for state and federal social welfare benefits. Similarly, her AB 1533 allows an individual or their dependent, who has lost or will lose healthcare benefits under the Healthy Families Program, to be deemed an "exception" and eligible for enrollment in an employer-sponsored health insurance plan after the enrollment period has closed. Healthy Families is California's version of the federal Children's Health Insurance Program (CHIP).[2] Both bills are clearly designed to benefit disadvantaged groups who are marginalized on multiple dimensions.

Cross-Sector Legislation

In several instances we found women of color participating in what Hankivsky and Cormier (2011) refer to as addressing social problems at the intersections of different policy silos. That is, because the problems they are seeking to address often are multifaceted, their policy proposals sometimes do not fit into one policy category. Two New Jersey bills introduced by Nellie Pou (LW), AB 1428 in 1998, and AB 1793 in 2006, are good examples. AB 1793 creates the Office of Women's Research and Policy in the New Jersey Division on Women in the Department of Community Affairs. The purpose of the office is to stimulate and encourage study and review of the status of women and to disseminate information to New Jersey policymakers on a spectrum of issues relevant to women's lives, including but not limited to women's status in the workforce, access to child care and other resources, education equity, violence against women, and economic self-sufficiency. Likewise, AB 1428 appropriates funds to the New Jersey Division of Housing and Community Resources in the Department of Community Affairs to fund the Center for Hispanic Policy, Research and Development. The Center's activities include studying narcotics addiction control, employment, and housing renovation projects. Both bills seem to recognize that finding policy solutions or creating opportunities require addressing multiple problems from multiple perspectives.

The legislative agenda advanced by Norma Chavez (LW TX05) also seems to be guided by this approach. Her policy efforts address a diverse array of issues faced by her constituents and other low-income, immigrant communities of color in the Texas-Mexico border region, including

---

[2] CHIP provides low cost health, dental, and vision insurance coverage to uninsured children.

expanded public healthcare (HB 2420, already mentioned); substandard ("virtually uninhabitable") migrant labor housing (HB 1099, HRO Bill Analysis) and water/sewage infrastructure in "colonias" (HB 3473); predatory and/or discriminatory financial practices (e.g., sub-prime lending) exacerbated by a lack of "financial literacy" (HB 763, 900); cross-border transportation of hazardous waste (HB 1563); substance abuse (HB 3426); and various challenges posed by state/local-tribal relations (HB 179, 1562, 2797, 3333). Individually and collectively, her bills approach these issues from multiple, diverse perspectives—often focusing on the most disadvantaged and marginalized populations. HB 3426, one of four measures establishing a broadly defined border task force or "interagency work group," is a good example. Establishing a Binational Alcohol and Substance Abuse Task Force, it frames the problem of substance abuse as a community health and safety issue, not a law enforcement issue. The Task Force is charged with studying the causes and effects of substance abuse among border residents, especially teens and young adults (i.e. binge drinking and exploitation by drug traffickers); and it is to be composed of local legislators and district attorneys, representatives from the Department of State Health Services, Department of Public Safety, local law enforcement, State Bar of Texas, the Mexican American Bar Association, local nonprofits, physicians, and members of the public with "significant experience working in substance abuse and interventional programs" in border communities.

How Distinctive Are the Women of Color?

The African American and Latina women in our study are disproportionately active in proposing measures that simultaneously address multiple and varied forms of inequality, marginalization, and oppression, or that offer targeted group programs and services as possible remedies to these conditions. However, they were not the only ones to introduce these kinds of bills. As we report above, 86% of Black men, 63% of Latinos, 67% of White women, and 20% of White men sponsored intersectional legislation. The number and percentage differentials address one of the questions that motivated our exploration. We also want to know whether there are substantive differences in how women of color address these issues.

Thus far our examination and discussion has focused mostly on the bills African American and Latina women introduce. Violence against women and criminal justice, healthcare and social welfare, and cross-sector legislation are three areas in which the intersectional pursuits of women of color were especially noticeable. How do the other legislative subgroups, White men, White women, Latinos, and Black men compare to women of color in this regard? Do other policy areas stand out as areas in which members of these groups advanced intersectional policies?

White Men

Only two of the 10 White men in our study introduced intersectional proposals. Both of them, Kevin Bailey and Glen Maxey served in the Texas House, Maxey in 1997 and Bailey in both 1997 and 2005. Maxey is one of two men in our sample who are noticeable outliers when it comes to advancing a wide-ranging intersectional legislative agenda. We discuss his activities separately below.

In general, the White men in our study—all of whom serve majority-minority urban districts similar to those served by the women of color in our sample—rarely sponsored bills that could be characterized, individually or collectively, as intersectional. Like all the other legislators we examine, they were attentive to their districts' distinctive needs; but unlike most of the women (and men) of color, those needs are only occasionally characterized in terms of multiple intersecting disadvantages. For example, Joseph Pickett's (WM, TX05) efforts to serve his El Paso district were limited to two measures authorizing revenue bonds for the local branch of the University of Texas (HB 2141, 2383) and one bill channeling certain "economic development [funding] tools" to local hotel projects. None of these measures seem focused directly or explicitly on the particular needs of his low-income, heavily immigrant, Latinx constituency.

Bailey devoted a significant portion of his 2005 legislative agenda to serving the needs of his Houston district. Yet only three of these bills acknowledge the "economically distressed" nature his district (HB 467) or its experience with "extreme economic decline and social change" (HB 1458, statement of purpose, House committee Bill Analysis). Bailey also sponsored a pair of bills (HB 2713, 3191) aimed at employment practices in the construction industry that deny benefits to their workers, most of whom are likely to be low-income, immigrant and/or Latino men.[3] However, HB 2713 gives priority preference for state construction contracts to companies that provide health benefits to their *full-time* employees. Thus, the legislation would not help part-time and contingent workers, who are disproportionately likely to be low-income Latinos.

Two of his intersectional bills in 2005 focus on increasing school choice, which could be seen as providing more options for kids in failing schools, which are disproportionately located in poor communities of color. One of the bills would require all districts to have a charter school plan. The other would allow students to transfer to any other school in their own district, or, if their home school was consistently not meeting standards, to apply to transfer to a school in a neighboring district. He also had a bill to increase the minimum wage, which would benefit low-wage workers who are slightly more likely to be women (3% of women v. 2% of men) and Black (3% of Black workers v. 2% from other major racial/ethnic categories).[4]

Bailey's approach to criminal justice policy, seeking tougher punishments and a stronger, less encumbered role for law enforcement, is in direct contrast with how the women and men of color engaged this issue. For example, his HB 639, introduced in 2005, seeks to protect public safety officers and firefighters from "baseless accusations" of misconduct by requiring due diligence and "sufficient evidence" before disciplinary measures can be taken (HRO Bill Analysis). It also gives discretion to local police or fire departments to determine what constitutes sufficient evidence. Conversely, the legislators of color introduced several bills that require more transparency and accountability on the part of the police. A significant portion of Bailey's criminal justice bills from both 1997 and 2005 are expressly supportive of police and detention officers (and in some cases, firefighters), except in their efforts to bargain collectively (see HB 429, 586, 1122, 1124, 1125, 1231, 1232, 2186, and 2758 from 1997 and HB 466, 640, 641, 771, 2173, 2216, 2712, 2865 from 2005).

A few of the White men legislators introduced measures that reflect single-axis conceptions of gender, race, or ethnicity. For example, Neil Cohen (NJ 98) introduced a trio of bills (AB 89, 308, and 309) that together prohibit

---

[3] As is true throughout the country, Latinos, many of whom are foreign born, make up a substantial portion of the construction workforce in Texas. See, for example, https://www.dmagazine.com/publications/d-ceo/2018/march/foreign-born-workers-important-to-building-texas/.

[4] Bureau of Labor Statistics Reports, *Characteristics of Minimum Wage Workers 2017*, https://www.bls.gov/opub/reports/minimum-wage/2017/home.htm.

demonstrating or picketing the residence or dwelling of healthcare providers and makes it unlawful to interfere with access to a healthcare facility or physician's office. These bills are aimed at making sure women have unfettered access to family planning and abortion services, which traditionally have been considered women's issues.

As we note above, Glen Maxey (TX 97) is an outlier when it comes to introducing bills that employ intersectional approaches for addressing issues of race, gender, and marginalization. The range and depth of his intersectional engagement makes him unique among the White men and distinguishes him from most of the other legislators in our study, men and women alike. Maxey's intersectional bills cluster in three areas: health, education, and income inequality. Many of his health bills intersectionally target the needs of poor communities. For example, he has a bill, HB 687, that would prevent insurance companies from charging more for diabetes treatment, which disproportionately affects poor people of color, than for other medical conditions. Other proposals seek to increase funding and availability of healthcare for the poor. He also introduced a number of bills that seek to improve the efficiency of the administration of public assistance, both in terms of medical and cash assistance, and to reduce waste and fraud. Maxey, who was the first openly gay legislator in Texas, introduced over 40 bills related to health, an interest likely related to his history as an HIV/AIDS activist. His efforts to assist those living with HIV/AIDS extended to other policy arenas, such as employment discrimination (HB 200) and life insurance (HB 163, 1865).

Most of Maxey's education bills focus on improving equal opportunity for college in an intersectional way. For instance, he introduced HB 2725 to eliminate admissions and financial aid requirements for standardized tests, which are often thought to be biased against Black and Latinx applicants. Another bill, HB 1129, requires state colleges to grant credit for community college classes; Black, Latinx, and low-income students are the most likely to start at community colleges. He also introduced a bill to study how recent policy changes have affected minority student enrollment and success.

Finally, Maxey's bills show a concern with income inequality. He introduced several bills that would make the tax system less regressive. For example, one would give a refund for sales tax paid over 5% of one's total income, and another would put a 4% marginal tax rate on earnings above $89,000 a year. Another bill would regulate check-cashing services and limit the fees that could be charged. These bills could increase economic justice, to the benefit of low-income communities.

White Women

There are three White women in our sample. Two of them introduced inter-sectional legislation. Jackie Goldberg (CA 05) introduced one such bill, and Joan Quigley (NJ 06) introduced two. All three are health and social welfare bills that are similar in substance and intent to bills introduced by women of color. Quigley's AB 1368 would permit a person who is determined ineligible for benefits under the Work First New Jersey (WFNJ) program, because the person was convicted of a felony drug distribution offense, to receive pre-scription drug benefits for a life-saving or sustaining medication. Goldberg's AB 1349 allows narcotic treatment program providers who establish a sliding indigency scale for low-income persons who are not eligible to participate in the Medi-Cal Drug Treatment Program to be deemed in compliance with federal and state law for purposes of reimbursement requirements. Both bills are similar to one proposed by Karen Bass (BW, CA05), AB 855, which creates exceptions so that a person convicted of drug-related felonies could remain eligible for state and federal social welfare benefits. All three bills seek to provide healthcare and social services benefits to disadvantaged groups who are marginalized on multiple dimensions.

Judy Hawley (TX 97), the lone White woman who did not propose any in-tersectional legislation, did, however introduce two bills on school bus safety, a topic that has traditionally been considered a women's issue. Hawley also introduced other education bills having to do with expulsion—HB 824 adds an additional ground for expulsion, and HB 825 prevents another school from enrolling a student who is under expulsion. Given the disproportionate rates at which children of color, particularly boys, are subjected to school dis-cipline, these bills could work against their interests. In contrast, Hawley's African American colleague Ruth McClendon (BW, T05) introduced bills to protect children in juvenile detention centers, who are disproportionately boys of color—HB 1929 would make employees of these facilities manda-tory child abuse reporters, and HB 1928 and 2749 would improve quality standards for the facilities and increase inspections.

There are also stark differences between Hawley and the women of color in our study with respect to criminal justice bills. Hawley had two criminal jus-tice bills, both of which could be construed as anti-criminal defendant. HB 1112, which allows transfer of parole violators to other correctional facilities, was opposed in committee by the criminal defense bar and a prisoners' rights group. The other, HB 1440, limits the circumstances in which a court clerk has to produce a transcript, which could negatively impact a defendant's ability to appeal.

Latinos

There are nine Latinos in our study sample, five of whom introduced at least one proposal that appeared intersectional in content. With regard to intersectional policy pursuits, the Latinos, like the women of color legislators, advanced noteworthy criminal justice measures. Their bills in these areas have the same focus and intent as bills introduced by the women of color. For example, bills sponsored by Wilfredo Caraballo and Raul Garcia (AB 3601 and AB 3598, respectively), both from the 1998 New Jersey subclass, are identical to Nia Gill's (BW, NJ 98) AB 3593, which requires the Superintendent of the Division of State Police in the Department of Law and Public Safety to establish a database on motor vehicle stops, pursuits, searches, arrests, the use of force, citizen complaints, disciplinary actions, and witnesses; and to Nellie Pou's (LW, NJ 98) AB3590, which requires the state police to maintain all logs concerning activity of patrol units. Leo Alvarado Jr.'s (TX 97) HB 1565 is yet another bill that is similar to one introduced by a woman of color Karen Bass (BW, CA05). His bill, like hers, requires rehabilitation, job training, and re-integration services for prisoners. The intent of both bills is to reduce the rate of recidivism and increase the potential for the previously incarcerated to successfully re-integrate into society.

The Latino legislators were also active in proposing welfare and poverty legislation that provided for targeted group programs and services. Leo Alvarado (TX 97) had one bill that would create training centers for public assistance recipients to learn how to work in or run a child care facility, and another that would prevent insurance companies from denying coverage based on someone's credit rating.

Education is another area in which the Latino men utilized intersectional approaches in response to constituent concerns. Proposals by Ismael Flores (TX 05) and Wilfredo Caraballo (NJ 98) are representative of such efforts. Flores introduced five education bills, one of which (HB 1737) was touted as an effort to improve opportunities for his rapidly growing, low-income, poorly educated community (HRO Bill Analysis). Likewise, Caraballo's AB 889 seeks to revise the laws governing the operation of state-operated school districts to require that local boards of education be re-established six months after the creation of the state-operated district. This bill is an attempt to return "Abbott" school districts to local control. Abbott districts were created as a result of the New Jersey Supreme Court ruling that found that the education provided to children in poor urban communities was inadequate and unconstitutional.[5] Abbott districts were identified by the Court as "poorer urban districts" or "special needs" districts, with the lowest socioeconomic status.[6] Participation in local school politics has been a springboard for minority group political power, with school board members going on to serve on city councils or as mayors. Thus, Black and Latinx political power is weakened by state takeovers of urban school districts that disband elected school boards (Morel 2018). This bill would return control of these schools to the communities they serve, empowering those communities to participate in their own self-governance.

Two Latino legislators, Ronald Calderon (CA 05) and Gerald Torres (TX 97), did not introduce a single bill that has clear intersectional implications. In fact, most of their bills do not obviously favor any identity characteristic— they are almost all general interest. The one exception is Torres' HB 2551, which would require employers to pay bilingual employees more if they ask them to use their language skills in a way that is outside their regular job description.

African American Men

With one notable exception, Harold Dutton (TX 97 and 05), the seven African American male legislators, individually and collectively, sponsored only a few bills that can be characterized as intersectional. Most of these bills focus on the criminal justice system. Similar to the women of color and several of the Latino legislators, the African American men attempt to address police misconduct and assist intersectionally marginalized people who come into contact with law enforcement and the criminal justice system. Indeed, Alfred Steele (NJ 98) joined three of his colleagues, Wilfredo Caraballo, Nia Gill, and Nellie Pou, in sponsoring legislation requiring police and state troopers to record and document the details of all traffic stops and arrests. Relatedly, Craig Stanley, also in New Jersey, introduced a measure in 2006

---

[5] *Abbott v. Burke*, 100 N.J. 269, 495 A.2d 376 (1985) (*"Abbott I"*).
[6] *Abbott v. Burke*, 119 N.J. 287, 575 A.2d 359 (1990) (*"Abbott II"*).

that empowers county prosecutors to intervene to assume administrative and operational control of any municipal law enforcement agency in their county for incompetence, malfeasance, corruption, civil rights violations, discriminatory practices, misconduct, and making derogatory racial or ethnic slurs.

A bill introduced by Leroy Jones (NJ, 98) is noteworthy for its attempt to address a social problem that is at the intersection of different policy silos. AB 896 changes the structure and scope of the Commission on Racism, Racial Violence and Religious Violence to equip it to study the various problems of racism, racial violence, and religious violence, including determining the best methods of preventing such violence.

Harold Dutton (TX 97 and 05) is a clear outlier. He stands out for being extraordinarily active in introducing bills that would benefit intersectionally marginalized groups. Over the two legislative sessions we examined, his many bills focus a great deal of attention on three issues: education, the "women's issue" of child support (and a few other related matters of child custody and visitation), and a wide array of criminal justice matters, most notably the death penalty. Across all these bills, evidence suggests these are efforts to confront the multiple, intersecting forces of race, gender, and class that marginalize, penalize, incarcerate, and kill low-income men of color in particular. He introduced more of this legislation than any other legislator, including all of the women.

His intersectional engagement with education was most pronounced in the 1997 legislative session. In that session, one of his education bills, HB 2885, focused on the school-to-prison pipeline—it would improve due process protections for student discipline and would increase educational requirements for alternative schools that serve expelled children. Another bill, HB 1105, would establish remedial reading, writing, and math programs for third- to sixth-graders in low-performing schools, which are disproportionately found in poor communities of color. Still another, HB 509, would require colleges to include whether a student attended a poor performing school as an admissions criterion, presumably to increase the acceptance rate of such students.

Many of Dutton's child support measures tend to favor the non-custodial paying parent over the custodial receiving parent and are supported by the Texas Fathers Alliance and other fathers' rights groups. This could be part and parcel of the men's rights backlash against feminist reform of family law—an effort to preserve traditional, middle-class gender roles and/or ignore, discount, or contest women's claims, needs, and experiences of financial hardship or domestic violence and abuse (Crowley 2008, 2009). Indeed, arguments supporting Dutton's 2005 bill (HB 437) requiring genetic testing to establish paternity in disputes over child support point to problems of "paternity fraud" on the part of mothers (HRO Bill Analysis, House committee Bill Analysis). But this could also reflect an effort to stand up for low-income men of color (especially Black men), often stereotyped as "deadbeat dads," who cannot afford child support, and to counteract the criminalization of child support enforcement that arguably contributes to mass incarceration of low-income men of color (Battle 2018; Dinner 2016; Sparks 2003). Notably, Dutton's 2005 child support legislation includes two measures aiding incarcerated or formerly incarcerated parents who owe child support (HB 425, 440).

An even greater portion of Dutton's sponsored legislation in both 1997 and 2005 tackles multiple dimensions of criminal justice reform, almost all of which is congruent with what is now widely recognized as a racial justice agenda against mass incarceration, police violence, and the criminalization and surveillance of people of color and low-income communities. Like "racial justice organizing" in general, Dutton's legislation "has generally focused on racism as it primarily affects men, and has often ignored the gendered forms of racism that women of color face" (INCITE! 2006, 1; see also Ritchie 2006).

As part of his criminal justice agenda in 1997, he proposed a bill, HB 1001, that eliminated a two-year waiting period after a sentence was served before a person with a felony conviction could be re-enfranchised. Another bill that year, HB 504, would have expanded the circumstance under which criminal records could be expunged. Some of his bills seem to seek to improve the transparency and fairness of the courts; with regard to criminal cases, these bills may disproportionately benefit men of color, but they would do so more indirectly. These bills include measures to improve the impartiality and qualifications of court reporters and one that would clarify the bail bond process.

At the center of his 2005 criminal justice agenda lie 10 bills that seek to abolish or severely constrain the death penalty and death penalty proceedings (HB 408, 431, 432, 434, 450, 452, 454, 456, 458, 696). Also prominent on Dutton's agenda that year are measures aimed at the school-to-prison pipeline (HB 442, 461, 1687, 1688, 1689, 3088) and related matters of juvenile justice reform (HB 1575, 2669), expungement or restriction of criminal records (HB 433, 435, 457, 697), sentence reduction (HB 254, 455, 1824, 2098), and police and/or prosecutorial misconduct (HB 382, 2418).

Relatively few of Dutton's criminal justice bills seem to take on "gendered forms of racism that women of color face" (INCITE! 2006, 1). HB 254 and 2098, proposed in 2005, reduce penalties for possession of small amounts of marijuana and other controlled substances, which are often cited as causes of dramatic increases in the number of incarcerated women of color (Ritchie 2006; Allard 2006; Jordan-Zachery 2008). HB 1177, one of Dutton's two 2005 bills to address violence against women (and children), strengthens domestic violence protective orders by extending their enforcement through an appeal process. No other legislator in our sample comes close to offering the breadth and depth of criminal justice reforms that Dutton's bills present.

Four of Dutton's 2005 bills (HB 383, 384, 1014, 1099) take on the child welfare system, but it is not clear whether or to what extent they are congruent with intersectional reproductive justice and anti-violence agendas that center women of color's interests. For example, much like his child support bills, HB 384 calls for a greater role for the non-custodial parent (or relative) vis-à-vis the best interest of the child—noting that their "financial instability, antiquated criminal history, or lack of home furnishings" too often work against them (statement of purpose, House committee Bill Analysis). Two measures (HB 383 and 1014) appear to rein in over-zealous child protective services by making corporal punishment a parental right and prohibiting interviews or medical/psychological exams of children allegedly abused. At the same time, HB 1014 includes a provision allowing mothers to continue breast-feeding after losing custody of their children.

Conclusions

From a sample of just 41 legislators, across two legislative sessions in only three states, we hesitate to draw any firm conclusions from our analysis. Nonetheless, we can offer some profound, albeit tentative, observations. To begin, our content analysis reveals a wide array of diverse approaches to intersectional policymaking. For just about any general policy area traditionally associated with the interests or expertise of women, racial/ethnic minorities, or poor people, there is a legislator offering a more intersectional alternative. Intersectional legislation also varies in terms of the intersectionally disadvantaged target population. Often intersectional bills address problems that affect women of color, especially poor women of color, disproportionately— including issues of interpersonal violence and reproductive justice. But not always. Many if not most of the intersectional approaches to crime and criminal justice (especially those not specific to domestic violence or sexual assault) are most likely to benefit the low-income men and boys of color who are overwhelmingly over-represented among those stopped, searched, disciplined, arrested, expelled, imprisoned, and paroled. Not surprisingly, many of the legislators examined sponsored bills that address the intersectional needs of the low-income communities of color they serve—and in ways that are not clearly gendered or gender-specific.

It is also the case that intersectional policymaking is not necessarily the province of any particular type of legislator. We found instances of intersectional bill sponsorship among all six race-gender groups of legislators— women and men; Black, Latinx, and White (keeping in mind, these are the most likely candidates: those who serve low- or moderate-income majority-minority districts). Indeed, each group of legislators offered a mix of bills, some more intersectional than others. Nonetheless, we observe some nascent patterns among our three subclasses. Women of color are almost always active in proposing at least some legislation that is intersectional in design or probable effect. But they are not unique or even always the most active among their subclass in this regard. In Texas and New Jersey alike, two of the most intersectionally active legislators were a Black man and a White man. In some, but certainly not all of these cases, the targeted beneficiaries were most likely men or boys of color. In these respects, our findings may call into question some conventional thinking about intersectionality as only or even primarily applicable to women of color or Black women in particular. Nonetheless, our evidence thus far suggests that White legislators—men and women—and Latino men may be less reliable advocates for intersectional interests. Additionally, White women and men (in Texas, at least) were the most likely to sponsor bills that seem to work against those who are intersectionally marginalized. Whether such patterns emerge in other places and times, and what might explain them, are excellent avenues for future research.

6

Welfare Policy Outcomes

Comparing Single-Axis and Intersectional Approaches

As we have learned thus far, one of the most important ways the legislative leadership of women of color stands out is their efforts to place intersectional issues of welfare and poverty—and the interests of poor women of color in particular—on the legislative agenda. But how consequential is that? How far does the influence of legislative women of color reach? Do they have the power to affect what policies are actually enacted? Can they make a difference in that regard—one that undoubtedly affects the lives of those who are intersectionally marginalized and multiply disadvantaged? More generally, how do race, gender, and representation interact to effect policy outcomes? In this, our final empirical chapter, we demonstrate how a more intersectional approach can effectively address these weighty questions in the context of federally mandated state welfare reform in the late 1990s.

Under the guidelines of the Personal Responsibility and Work Opportunity Reconciliation Act of 1996 (PRWORA), every state in the country undertook unprecedented efforts to "end welfare as we know it." Gone was the federal entitlement to means-tested benefits in the form of Aid to Families with Dependent Children (AFDC). Taking its place, Temporary Assistance to Needy Families (TANF) is restricted to a lifetime maximum of five years, contingent upon work-related activity outside the home, and subject to numerous sanctions for uncooperative or unproductive behavior. Its primary goals are to reduce welfare caseloads by instilling or otherwise requiring more "responsible" behavior on the part of recipients. And while the PRWORA imposes a number of goals, limits, and minimal requirements, it grants the states a lot more discretion over welfare policy than they had before.

Yet, despite all these changes in the law, one thing remained constant: race and racial politics had a profound impact on state implementation of welfare policy. As was the case with AFDC (Fording 2003; Hero 1998; Johnson 2001; Plotnick and Winters 1985; Volden 2002), the more racially

Race, Gender, and Political Representation. Beth Reingold, Kerry L. Haynie, and Kirsten Widner, Oxford University Press (2021). © Oxford University Press. DOI: 10.1093/oso/9780197502174.001.0001.

diverse the state welfare rolls (or population), the less generous the TANF benefits and the more rigid the rules and regulations governing eligibility and work requirements (Avery and Peffley 2005; Fellowes and Rowe 2004; Hero and Preuhs 2007; Larimer 2005; Preuhs 2007; Soss et al. 2001).[1] State policymakers, it appears, have responded to or internalized the racial stereotypes, resentments, and fears that shape judgments of welfare recipients and drive the call for less generous, get-tough welfare policy among Whites (Dyck and Hussey 2008; Gilens 1999; Peffley, Hurwitz, and Sniderman 1997; Soss et al. 2003).

There is growing evidence, however, that the presence and power of African Americans and Latinxs in state legislatures can offset this sort of racial backlash (Fording 2003; Owens 2005; Preuhs 2006, 2007). In effect, states with relatively large proportions of Black and Latinx citizens and welfare recipients would have even less generous welfare benefits and rules if they had not managed to elect Black and Latinx representatives—and if those Black and Latinx representatives had not managed to accumulate some modicum of legislative power.

The research thus far contributes greatly to our understanding of the racialization of American welfare policy and politics, as well as the significance of the election and political incorporation of racial/ethnic minorities in the states. Notably missing, however, is sustained attention to the *gendered* nature of American welfare policy and politics, and the role of female policymakers in the states. Our inquiry begins, therefore, with the question of whether the election and incorporation of women into state legislatures has any effect on state welfare policy.

Yet the politics of welfare may not be properly understood in terms of *either* race *or* gender. More likely, welfare policymaking in the states is "raced-gendered" (Hawkesworth 2003)—shaped simultaneously by both racial and gender politics. For that reason, we undertake and compare both an "additive" and an "intersectional" approach to incorporating gender into the study of race, representation, and state welfare policy. The contrast between the two most powerfully demonstrates what intersectionality as a research paradigm (Hancock 2007) or analytic tool (Simien 2007) is and offers. Our additive approach treats gender as a separate, "single-axis" category of analysis, independent of race and ethnicity; highlights the gendered nature of American

---

[1] Larger populations of African Americans and Latinxs are both associated with harsher state welfare policies.

welfare politics; and gauges the impact of all state legislative women (undifferentiated by race/ethnicity) on welfare policy, controlling for the impact of their African American and Latinx colleagues. Our intersectional approach, in contrast, treats gender and race/ethnicity as overlapping, interlocking categories of analysis, highlights the "raced-gendered" nature of welfare politics, and compares the impact of legislative women of color to that of other women and men of color.[2]

We gauge the impact of state legislative women on numerous dimensions of state TANF policy, including benefit levels and the various rules and regulations used to determine eligibility, enforce work requirements, and promote more "responsible" behavior. Our analysis reveals that the impact of legislative women on welfare policy is highly contingent: depending on which women and which policies one examines, the presence and power of legislative women has a liberal effect, a conservative effect, or no effect. Across the policy dimensions, however, legislative women of color have a distinctive effect, one that is more consistent and consistently liberal than that of other legislative women or men of color. We therefore conclude that the study of representation and welfare policymaking must take into account the simultaneous and overlapping nature of race/ethnicity and gender and acknowledge the diversity among women and within racial/ethnic minority groups. We also demonstrate how an intersectional approach can add valuable theoretical and empirical insight to investigations of the policy impact of women and minorities in public office (Simien and Hancock 2011).

Theorizing Gender and Race in Welfare Policy and Politics

An additive approach, as suggested above, examines welfare policy and politics through a gender (-only) lens, adding women (undifferentiated by race or ethnicity) to the theoretical and empirical story. It begins with the observation that the history and politics of welfare in the United States are

---

[2] We use the term "intersectional" to characterize our raced-gendered analytic approach, the hypothesis it tests, and the models it employs. In contrast, our "additive" approach and models test a "single-axis" hypothesis (regarding the impact of legislative women) using three "single-axis" measures of legislative incorporation (one each for women, African Americans, and Latinos). We do not use the same "single-axis" term to refer to the approach and models associated with the single-axis hypothesis and variables because the approach and models are more accurately described as ones that *add* gender (as a singular, unidimensional category of analysis) to the study of race and welfare policymaking in the states.

gendered in many of the same ways they are raced. One can see gender in the demographic composition of welfare recipients and the poor more generally; in the history of social welfare policymaking and implementation; in public opinion; and in the behavior of elected officials. In all of these arenas, gender biases and differences suggest that welfare is very much a "women's issue" and that those who advocate for and actively represent women on this issue will fight to make welfare policy more generous and accessible—in effect, more women friendly.

Researchers have long noted the "feminization of poverty" (McLanahan and Kelly 1999; Pearce 1978). In 2008, at the brink of the Great Recession, the poverty rate for women and girls (14.4%) was approximately 2% higher than that for men and boys (12.0%), which translates into almost 4.5 million more females living in poverty.[3] Because poverty assistance is targeted almost exclusively to poor families with dependent children and most of those families are headed by single women, adult welfare recipients are almost always female. In FY1996, 87% of all adult AFDC recipients were female.[4] Under TANF, little changed. In FY2006, a full 90% of all adult recipients were female.[5]

These figures only begin to capture the myriad ways in which social welfare policy, from colonial times to the present, has been gendered. In its design and implementation, the American welfare state has been quite selective, extending its most generous assistance to those "deserving" women whose morals, marital status, sexuality, and reproductive lives comport with dominant gender and family norms (e.g., widows with small children). For those deemed undeserving (e.g., unmarried mothers), assistance has been either denied altogether or meted out in the most miserly, intrusive, and punitive fashion (Abramovitz 1996; Gordon 1994; Mink 1995, 1998). Women receiving welfare benefits often have been subject to state surveillance and regulation of their personal lives, not simply to prevent waste, fraud, and abuse, but also to ensure morally "suitable" homes and proper parenting (Abramovitz 1996; Mettler 2000; Mink 1995; Roberts 1997; Smith 2007; Williams 2004). PRWORA is certainly not the first attempt to regulate

---

[3] US Census Bureau, Current Population Survey, 2009 Annual Social and Economic Supplement, http://www.census.gov/hhes/www/cpstables/032009/pov/new01_100_01.htm (accessed 25 October 2009).

[4] US Department of Health and Human Services (HHS) 1997, http://www.acf.hhs.gov/programs/ofa/character/FY96/index96.html (accessed 25 October 2009).

[5] HHS 2007, http://www.acf.hhs.gov/programs/ofa/data-reports/annualreport8/chapter10/chap10.htm (accessed 25 October 2009).

women's lives (Abramovitz 1996), police women's sexuality (Smith 2007), restrict poor women's fertility (Roberts 1997), and instill more "personal responsibility" among low-income, single mothers (Mettler 2000). But it may be the most emphatic and explicit (Smith 2007, 89 and 94).

Public opinion on welfare is also gendered. For decades, national surveys have shown women to be significantly more liberal than men on various social welfare issues. Shapiro and Mahajan (1986), for example, show that throughout the 1960s, 1970s, and 1980s, and across hundreds of survey items and multiple survey organizations, women were more supportive of a government role in providing jobs, minimal incomes, health care, and other types of aid to the needy. By the 1990s, such gender gaps in support for a public safety net were well established and widely recognized as a major cause of gender gaps in party preferences and vote choices (CAWP 1997; Chaney, Alvarez, and Nagler 1998; Kaufmann and Petrocik 1999; Schlesinger and Heldman 2001). Extensive analysis of the American National Election Study (ANES) also reveals that since the 1960s, women have been more likely than men to cite poverty as an important national problem and policy priority (O'Brien 2004; see also CAWP 1997). Other research further indicates that "gender specific assumptions about the sexual and reproductive behavior of welfare recipients" (Foster 2008, 173) fuel opposition to welfare spending, as do racially specific assumptions about recipients' work ethic (Dyck and Hussey 2008; Gilens 1999; Peffley, Hurwitz, and Sniderman 1997; Soss et al. 2003). Survey respondents who believe that receiving welfare encourages women to have more children than they otherwise would are more likely than those who do not to oppose any increase in welfare spending (Foster 2008, 172).

Researchers have not examined policymakers' attitudes toward welfare recipients directly, but there is evidence to suggest that gender gaps in the welfare policy preferences and priorities of the electorate are reflected in those of elected officials. Research spanning multiple decades and levels of office shows that, compared to their male counterparts, female officials are more liberal and more likely to take the lead on a variety of women's rights and social welfare issues, including poverty alleviation (Reingold 2008). In a 2000 national survey of state legislators, for example, Poggione found that female lawmakers "hold more liberal preferences on welfare policy than their male colleagues, even after accounting for other factors like constituency demands, party, and ideology" (2004a, 305). Other studies have found that women (again, undifferentiated by race/ethnicity) are more likely than men to introduce welfare or anti-poverty legislation, even after controlling for party, district demographics, and committee assignments (Bratton and Haynie 1999; Bratton, Haynie, and Reingold 2006; but see Reingold 2000; Thomas 1994). In these ways, shared gender identity is thought to motivate (all) female legislators to pursue more liberal welfare policies.

Yet, while evidence suggests female legislators are more likely to act for poor women on or in need of welfare, it is still unclear whether they could, as a group, exert enough influence to impact state policy. When the PRWORA was signed into law in 1996, women had never claimed a majority of the seats in any state legislative chamber. In most states (38, to be exact), women held no more than a quarter of the seats in the legislature (CAWP 1996). Perhaps for this reason, studies that have examined the impact of legislative women on state policy outcomes report mixed results, at best. On some issues, such as abortion and child support, studies show that female legislators can and do make a difference (Berkman and O'Connor 1993; Crowley 2004; Keiser 1997); but on other "women's issues" such as domestic violence and women's health, female lawmakers have no discernible impact (Tolbert and Steurnagel 2000; Weldon 2004, 2006). In the most comprehensive study to date, Cowell-Meyers and Langbein (2009) find that the percentage of women in state legislatures is associated with the adoption of only eight of the 34 women-friendly policies examined; and in three instances, the relationship is in the opposite direction. Likewise, on the seven dimensions of TANF policy examined, the greater presence of female legislators is just as likely to increase the odds of adoption as it is to decrease the odds, as it is to have no effect at all (Cowell-Meyers and Langbein 2009, 508–11; see also Keiser 1997).

Some studies of welfare policymaking are more optimistic about the liberal influence of women in power. In-depth analyses of legislative efforts leading up to the passage of the PRWORA in the Republican-dominated 104th Congress show that some of the more senior, moderate Republican women were able "to temper or moderate some of the harsher effects of the proposed legislation and to expand the legislation to include provisions for child care, child support, and child protection" (Hawkesworth et al. 2001, 46; Dodson 2006). Poggione (2004b) also finds that state legislative women can have an impact on TANF policy, under certain conditions. When the percentage of women in the majority party is high and the majority party holds a slim margin, and when the percentage of women on welfare-related committees is high and the committees are relatively autonomous, TANF policies are significantly more liberal.

As these studies suggest, "sheer numbers" of legislative women may not be enough (Beckwith and Cowell-Meyers 2007; Browning, Marshall, and Tabb 1984; Weldon 2002). The impact of women on state policy outputs may also depend on their incorporation into dominant coalitions and leadership structures. We therefore anticipate that it is the *combination* of women's descriptive representation and legislative incorporation—their presence and positions of power in the legislature (Preuhs 2007)—that enables them to move welfare policy in a more liberal, generous, accommodating, and women-friendly direction.

> *H1 (Single-Axis Hypothesis)*: The greater the incorporation of women in the state legislature, the more generous, accessible, flexible, and lenient the state welfare policy.

An intersectional approach posits that welfare politics in the United States is not simply gendered or raced, or even gendered and raced; it is raced-gendered (Hawkesworth 2003; Neubeck and Cazenave 2001). The raced-gendered nature of welfare is perhaps best understood where it is most powerfully manifested: in the distinctive position—real or imagined—of poor women of color (Simien 2007).[6] It is, after all, not simply women, African Americans, or Latinxs who are overrepresented among welfare recipients; it is women of color. As the histories of social welfare policy (cited above) make clear (when read through an intersectional lens), determinations of which women are more or less deserving of assistance, privacy, and dignity have always been tainted by racial and ethnic biases. As a result, poor women of color have been subject to the most stringent eligibility requirements, the most intense moral scrutiny, and the harshest penalties welfare policy has to offer.

Evidence also suggests that it is not simply racial or gender stereotypes of lazy or overly fecund welfare recipients that have fueled successive waves of disciplinary welfare reform. Rather, it is the "controlling image" of the raced-gendered welfare queen who promiscuously gives birth to multiple children in order to receive more benefits and avoid working that has come to symbolize the typical recipient and all that is wrong with American welfare

---

[6] The bulk of the literature on women of color and welfare politics is specific to the experiences of and assumptions about Black women. However, there are some indications that, as their numbers have increased in recent years, the experiences of and assumptions regarding poor Latinas may be quite similar (Preuhs 2007; Soss et al. 2003; but see Fox 2004).

policy (Collins 2000; Hancock 2004; Neubeck and Cazenave 2001; Roberts 1997; Sparks 2003; Williams 2004). In Foster's (2008) analysis, for example, public support for government welfare spending is contingent upon the predicted reproductive behavior of (hypothetical) *Black* welfare mothers, not that of White welfare mothers.[7] O'Brien (2004) finds that, as the number of Black women on welfare rose and the welfare queen emerged in popular discourse, women no longer spoke in one voice about the need to alleviate poverty. Starting in the late 1970s, African American women became much more likely than other women to consider poverty a major national priority.[8] Perhaps as a result, gender gaps in public support for "welfare" spending in particular were noticeably absent in the 1990s and early 2000s; national samples of (mostly White) women and men were equally opposed (Clark and Clark 2006; Gilens 1999; but see Dyck and Hussey 2008).

The raced-gendered images and assumptions associated with the welfare queen, which featured prominently in congressional debates on welfare reform in the 1990s (Hancock 2004; Hawkesworth 2003; Sparks 2003), may have had similar effects on the behavior of legislators. According to Hawkesworth, "congresswomen of color were among the most outspoken opponents" of the PRWORA precisely because they saw "the Republican focus on out-of-wedlock births, unwed mothers, and single-women heads of households . . . [as] a thinly veiled attack upon poor women of color" (2003, 542–43). But while congresswomen of color were united in their opposition to welfare reform, their White female colleagues were deeply divided; some, in fact, were on the forefront of efforts to frame poverty and welfare reform in terms of deviant behavior and the lack of "personal responsibility" associated with the welfare queen (Hawkesworth 2003; Hawkesworth et al. 2001; Neubeck and Cazenave 2001). Here again, scholars point to collective identities and experiences as motivating factors; only this time, those identities and experiences are intersectional. Hawkesworth argues that it was the "anger and resistance engendered by . . . experiences of racing-gendering in the halls of Congress" (2003, 532) that compelled congresswomen of color to "devote such time and energy to the representation of an unorganized majority-white underclass" (539). Mink (1998, 1–27) and Neubeck and Cazenave (2001, 170–76), on the other hand, attribute the relative indifference of White

[7] The predicted work behavior of welfare mothers also influences attitudes toward welfare spending, but race makes no difference in this case (Foster 2008, 175–77).

[8] The attitudes of other women of color (Latinas, Asian American, and Native American women grouped together) were "indistinguishable" from those of White women (O'Brien 2004, 51).

feminists in Congress and elsewhere to their own positions and experiences of race and class privilege.

For all these reasons, one might expect that at the state legislative level, it is women of color who are the most vocal and active advocates for more generous and less punitive approaches to welfare and who, in the end, have the greatest countervailing influence on welfare policy. It might even be the case that what previous studies (e.g., Preuhs 2006, 2007) have characterized as the ability of (all) Black and Latinx legislators to "mitigate [welfare] policy backlash" is really the doing of Black female and Latina legislators. And, given how racially polarized the experience and politics of welfare have been, White female legislators may be more ambivalent about welfare reform, and—as Chapter 4 suggests—more reluctant to become involved. As a result, they may make little or no distinct impression upon state welfare policy.

H2 (Intersectional Hypothesis): The (liberal) impact of legislative women of color on state welfare policy will be greater than that of other women or of men of color.

But while legislative women of color may be the most committed and active advocates for poor women, they also may be the least influential. The women of color who fought so hard against welfare reform in Congress met with little success. Even when they had a seat at the table (during the Democratically controlled 103rd Congress), their efforts were rebuffed or ignored altogether and their credibility was repeatedly impugned (Hawkesworth 2003). Hawkesworth, in fact, uses welfare reform as a "particularly appropriate case" for examining "racing-gendering" within Congress and the mechanisms by which elected women of color are themselves marginalized and disempowered (2003, 539). As in Congress, state legislative women of color often lacked the "sheer numbers" and positions of power with which to influence the development of TANF policies. In 1997, they were entirely absent from 12 state legislatures, constituted less than 10% of the remaining legislatures, and held positions of leadership (top party positions or committee chairs) in only 19.[9] Furthermore, Smooth's (2008) study of African American women serving in the Georgia, Maryland, and Mississippi legislatures illustrates how women of color can be effectively denied power

---

[9] These figures are based on our own data compiled and analyzed for this study.

and influence even when they possess (relatively) large numbers, seniority, majority party status, and positions of leadership.

Nonetheless, other studies suggest that state legislative women of color can and do have influence, under some circumstances at least. Orey et al. (2006) find that, contrary to their expectations, bills sponsored by African American women in the Mississippi state house in the late 1980s and 1990s were no less likely to pass than those introduced by others. Fraga et al. theorize that Latina state legislators "are uniquely positioned to leverage the intersectionality of their ethnicity and gender" in ways that enable them "to be the most effective long-term advocates on behalf of working-class communities of color" (2008, 158). Their survey of Latinx state legislators shows that Latinas are more likely to forge coalitions across ethnic and gender lines, giving them a "strategic advantage" (162) in the policy-making process. By empirically gauging the distinct impact of state legislative women of color on welfare policy, this study sheds additional light on these debates about the power of intersectional representation in legislative settings.

Models and Measures

To gauge the impact of legislative women on state welfare policy with attention to the intersecting dynamics of race and ethnicity, we compare two models of policy adoption. The first, *additive* model tests the single-axis hypothesis (H1) by gauging the relationship between state welfare policy and the presence and power of all women in the legislature, controlling for the presence and power of (all) Black and Latinx legislators. The second, *intersectional* model tests the intersectional hypothesis (H2) by gauging the impact of the size and power of three potential legislative coalitions, each identified in terms of gender *and* race/ethnicity: women of color, White women, and men of color.

Our empirical analysis relies on data we collected for all 50 states, starting (when possible) with 1996, the last year AFDC was in effect, and ending (when possible) with 2007. For reasons explained below, we focus on the states' initial (pre-1999) reactions to the PRWORA mandate. Data sources and descriptive statistics for all measures are available in Appendix Tables A.10a–c.

Dependent Variables

We gauge the impact of legislative women on multiple dimensions of state TANF policy, including those frequently examined in the existing literature as well as those particularly relevant to the raced-gendered stereotypes and political dynamics discussed above. Together, our dependent variables capture many of the most salient, controversial, and consequential components of TANF policy (Soss et al. 2001, 380) and were all subject to the discretion of state policymakers.

Most studies of state AFDC and/or TANF policy have focused at least in part on the generosity of the cash assistance provided to families on welfare, for this is one of the few areas in which state policymakers have always had discretion (Plotnick and Winters 1985; Preuhs 2006). To build upon this longstanding interest, our first dependent variable gauges the level of *cash benefits*, operationalized as the dollar value of the TANF benefit for a family of three, adjusted for the state-level annual cost of living (Berry, Fording, and Hanson 2000). We expect the real value of TANF cash benefits will be higher in states where legislative women—especially women of color—are more numerous and powerful.

Most of our analysis focuses on "the rules and penalties that condition access to resources and structure the treatment citizens receive in government programs" (Soss et al. 2001, 379). TANF rules and regulations are the tools with which the state attempts to modify the behavior of poor people so that they take more "personal responsibility" for themselves and their children (Mettler 2000; Soss et al. 2001). In exercising discretion over these welfare rules, state policymakers choose just how tough they want to be when granting access to TANF benefits and determining the work-related obligations of those who receive them.

We therefore employ two broad indices of state welfare rules designed by Fellowes and Rowe (2004), one capturing how restrictively the states define initial and continued *eligibility* for TANF benefits and the other capturing how *flexibly* states impose work requirements upon TANF clients. Because the Fellowes and Rowe indices are available only for 1997–99, we replicated their measures as closely as possible for 1996–2007, identifying and coding the same 28 eligibility rules and the same 12 rules governing compliance with work requirements. All rules were coded as more or less restrictive/flexible according to the information available in the Urban Institute's Welfare

Rules Database (WRD).[10] Our expectation is that in states where legislative women—especially women of color—are more numerous and powerful, TANF eligibility rules will be less restrictive (the eligibility index will be lower) and the TANF rules governing work-related activity will be more flexible (the flexibility index will be higher).

Our next set of dependent variables focuses on TANF rules that may be particularly gendered, or salient to women. The first indicates whether a state has a *family cap* provision (as documented in the WRD).[11] States that adopt the so-called family cap rule limit the incremental increase in benefits when an additional child is born to a mother receiving aid. One of the most controversial welfare reforms of the 1990s, family caps address many of the concerns surrounding "welfare queens" who allegedly have more children in order to maximize and fully exploit their "government handouts." Numerous scholars have criticized such policies as racialized violations of poor women's reproductive rights (e.g., Neubeck and Cazenave 2001; Roberts 1997; Smith 2007). Our expectation, therefore, is that family caps will be less prevalent in states where legislative women—especially women of color—are more numerous and powerful.

Another dimension of the PRWORA that may be particularly salient to women is the Family Violence Option (FVO), which permits states to temporarily waive program requirements for survivors of domestic violence. Our final dependent variable indicates whether a state grants time limit extensions or exemptions for TANF recipients fleeing from or receiving treatment for domestic violence (according to the WRD).[12] The FVO may

---

[10] Information needed to code several work requirement rules in 1996–98 was unavailable in the WRD. Thus our own flexibility index scores are available only for 1999–2007. The 28 rules that make up the eligibility index specify "the type and number of people that the state will support with welfare" and for how long (Fellowes and Rowe 2004, 365). They determine who can receive TANF benefits (e.g., childless pregnant women, minor heads of households, immigrants), how long they can continue receiving benefits over their lifetime (e.g., less than the five-year federal maximum or not), and who can receive an exemption from or extension of that time limit (e.g., recipients who are working or caring for a young child). The 12 rules that constitute the flexibility index include various provisions that exempt recipients from work requirements (e.g., to care for an ill or incapacitated family member), expand the definition of allowable, work-related activities (e.g., to include post-secondary education), reduce the number of work hours required (e.g., less than the federal requirement), and sanction noncompliance. Additional information regarding the construction of our indices and how they compare with those of Fellowes and Rowe is included in Reingold and Smith (2012) Supporting Information (SI).

[11] We also created an ordinal scale indicating not only whether a state has a family cap provision, but also whether the state offers exemptions for (a) children conceived due to rape or incest; (b) "capped" children who move to another "child-only" unit; and (c) first births to minor parents. Ordered logit results for the scale were similar to those for the dichotomous family cap indicator.

[12] In addition to waiving time limits, the FVO allows states to waive family caps and other program requirements regarding work/job training, residency, paternity establishment, and child support cooperation (PWRORA 42 U.S.C. section 608 (a) (7) (A); Josephson 2002, 8; Graham 2001–2, 453–54).

very well have been inspired by the Violence Against Women Act of 1994 (VAWA), which "initiated a nationally coordinated effort to study the problem of domestic violence"—including its relationship to poverty and welfare (Josephson 2002, 9). In the context of the VAWA, domestic violence was clearly a "women's issue," both in terms of the bipartisan support it received from congresswomen and in terms of how they chose to frame the issue (Hawkesworth et al. 2001).

Nonetheless, initial uncertainty and apprehension about how the FVO would be implemented in the states may have made even the most liberal, pro-women state legislators hesitate. Indeed, according to the WRD, 12 of the 34 states that made available a time limit waiver for domestic violence survivors under AFDC in 1996, declined to adopt one under TANF in 1997. Battered women's advocates (even some who helped draft the FVO provisions) worried that, without effective guidelines, state discretion in identifying and evaluating the needs of survivors could do more harm than good. It could, for example, put such individuals in greater danger, invade their privacy, and jeopardize the assistance they would otherwise receive (Davies 1997; Raphael 1999). Advocates for poor women more generally were concerned that domestic violence waivers might make it more difficult or even impossible for other vulnerable recipients to receive similar waivers for other hardships (Graham 2001–2, 454–55; Mason 1998, 634). Given the long history of raced-gendered welfare politics, poor women of color and their advocates may have been even more wary of state implementation of domestic violence services (Crenshaw 1991; Josephson 2002).

Our expectations regarding the impact of legislative women on state adoption of domestic violence waivers are somewhat uncertain, given these early misgivings. If female state legislators were aware of the potential problems, say, through their ties to women's advocacy networks, then they may have been more ambivalent about adopting FVO waivers than they were about adopting other measures ostensibly designed to ease the restrictions and sanctions associated with TANF. In that case, we would not expect FVO waivers to be any more prevalent in states where legislative women are more numerous and powerful. For reasons mentioned above, however, it may be

We analyze state adoption of FVO time limit waivers only, for that is the only FVO waiver thoroughly documented in the WRD and it is the most common. Among the 47 states that had adopted at least one type of FVO waiver (or the equivalent thereof) by 2004, only two (AZ and TN) declined to include a time-limit waiver (Legal Momentum 2004).

that legislative women—and women of color especially—were even more wary of state implementation of FVO than their male colleagues, especially before 1999, when most of the implementation issues were resolved (Graham 2001–2, 454–55; Josephson 2002, 8). In that case, we might expect to see, prior to 1999, a *negative* relationship between the incorporation of women—especially women of color—in the state legislature and the likelihood of state adoption of domestic violence waivers.

Although our 1996–2007 data permit time-series cross-sectional analyses, modeling changes in state policy over the entire 12-year time period is not always appropriate (Soss et al. 2006, 802–4). Our own analysis indicates that most of the changes made in state welfare policy occurred between 1996 and 1998. For example, between 1996 and 1998, states made 70 adjustments to their TANF eligibility rules, for an average of 35 adjustments per year. Two-thirds of those adjustments involved more than one rule change. In contrast, between 1998 and 2007, states made 108 adjustments in their eligibility rules, or an average of only 12 adjustments per year. Only 29% of those adjustments involved more than one rule change. Cash benefit levels is the only dimension of state TANF policy (examined here) that does not follow this trend. States made slightly more adjustments per year after 1998 than before (11.25 adjustments per year between 1998 and 2006; seven adjustments per year between 1996 and 1998).

Thus, with the exception of cash benefits, the trends in state welfare policy adoption suggest a sort of punctuated equilibrium (Baumgartner and Jones 1993): a flurry of legislative activity immediately following the 1996 passage of the PRWORA, followed by relative stability. It is in the states' initial reactions to the PRWORA, then, where the influence of state legislative women may be most pronounced and readily observed (Avery and Peffley 2005, 50). We therefore employ cross-sectional analyses of our indicators of TANF policy as they existed in 1998, when the equilibrium likely began.[13] And, while the PRWORA may have offered states the opportunity to start from scratch, we anticipate the more likely possibility that states adopted a more incremental approach to the transition from AFDC to TANF (Preuhs 2007). Controlling for the 1996 status-quo of comparable AFDC policies, we gauge the ability of legislative women to effect more subtle shifts in state welfare policy toward

---

[13] Preliminary pooled time-series analysis of 1997–2006 cash benefit levels, using a mix of observed and imputed data for our independent variables, suggests that the legislative incorporation of women (in the additive and intersectional models) made no difference.

less restrictive, more flexible, and more generous options (with the possible exception of the domestic violence time-limit waivers).[14]

Independent and Control Variables

To test our hypotheses regarding the relationships between state TANF policy and the legislative incorporation of women and women of color, our independent variables measure the size and institutional power of several identity-based coalitions in state legislatures. Given existing knowledge of the significance of African Americans and Latinxs as both welfare recipients and legislators, the lack of research on the relationship between other racial/ethnic minority groups and welfare politics, plus the very small numbers of Asian American and Native American welfare recipients and state legislators (except in Hawaii), we focus on the potentially distinctive impact of Black and Latinx legislators—male and female. For the additive models, we measure the single-axis incorporation, or the numerical presence and institutional power, of all female, all African American, and all Latinx legislators in each state; for the intersectional models, we measure the race-gender incorporation of Black and Latina women ("women of color"), all other ("White") women, and Black and Latino men ("men of color").[15]

Each measure of group *incorporation* is a factor score derived from three component variables: (1) descriptive representation, or the percentage of legislative seats in the upper and lower chambers that are occupied by group members; (2) general institutional incorporation, or the average proportion of weighted leadership positions across the two chambers that are occupied by group members (Preuhs 2006); and (3) specific institutional

[14] Because data for our flexibility index are available only for 1999–2007, we rely on Fellowes and Rowe's 1998 flexibility index scores (available for all states except AK, HI, and NE) for our cross-sectional analysis. But because their data do not cover 1996 ADFC policy, we are unable to control for the pre-TANF flexibility baseline.

[15] We group Black and Latinx legislators together as women and men of color for a number of theoretical and empirical reasons. First, existing research (discussed here) suggests that Black and Latinx legislators (male and female, or just female) will have similar effects on welfare policy. Second, measures of Latino and especially Latina incorporation exhibit very limited variation. Latinas are completely absent from 35 state legislatures and hold leadership positions in only three. Latino men are completely absent from 29 state legislatures and hold leadership positions in only eleven. Third, alternative disaggregated models (like those in Chapters 3 and 4) suggest that, with few exceptions, the effects of Black and Latinx incorporation are similar. In one model, in fact, it is clear that the joint liberalizing impact of women of color on TANF eligibility rules is greater than the separate, additive impact of Black and Latina women. More information about these disaggregated models can be found in Reingold and Smith (2012) SI.

incorporation, or the percentage of social/human services committees in both chambers that are chaired by group members (Preuhs 2006).[16] For each group, the three component variables (especially the first two) are strongly related and load on the same factor. Thus, we are confident these factor scores effectively measure the underlying, unidimensional concept of political incorporation (Browning, Marshall, and Tabb 1984; Preuhs 2007).

Across all models, we control for the possible confounding influence of other state political, socioeconomic, and demographic pressures on welfare policymaking. A voluminous body of research identifies a large number and wide variety of factors that shape state welfare policy. We cull from that literature the factors that are also likely to affect the level of legislative representation and incorporation enjoyed by women (overall) and women of color (specifically) in the states (see Chapter 2).[17]

As noted above, the racial and ethnic composition of state populations (and welfare rolls) is key to understanding both the dynamics of welfare policymaking within and across the states and the election of African American and Latinx men and women to state legislatures (Lublin et al. 2009; Preuhs 2007). The racial/ethnic makeup of the state population is also strongly correlated with every measure of group incorporation we employ. Thus, we control for the racial and ethnic composition of state populations (*percent Black and Latinx*) in our models.[18] For similar reasons, we also control for the ideological leanings of state electorates (*citizen ideology*; Berry et al. 1998); party control of the legislature (*Democratic control of legislature*; Klarner 2003);[19] several measures of statewide demand and capacity for welfare reform and expenditures, which are also related to women's socioeconomic status (*percentage of high school graduates, unemployment rate, unmarried birth rate*); and state political culture (*moralistic*; Elazar 1984).[20] All time-varying group

---

[16] See Reingold and Smith (2012) SI for more information regarding the construction of these component variables as well as our rationale for employing factor scores.

[17] See Reingold and Smith (2012) SI for more detailed information concerning the selection and measurement of our control variables as well as the extensive literature upon which our decisions are based.

[18] Because the racial/ethnic composition of state populations is so strongly correlated with the racial/ethnic composition of state TANF caseloads (r = .92 for Blacks; r = .90 for Latinxs), we are essentially controlling for both. Our rationale for measuring the combined Black and Latinx population is discussed in Reingold and Smith (2012) SI.

[19] Controlling for partisan control of the state legislature necessarily excludes Nebraska, with its uniquely nonpartisan legislature, from our analysis.

[20] Our assumption is that by controlling for these potentially confounding factors, we can estimate the likely causal effects of legislative incorporation on state welfare policy. As we explain in Reingold and Smith (2012) SI, alternative methods for minimizing omitted variable bias and generating

incorporation and control variables are lagged one year prior to the observed dependent variable.[21]

Results

Additive Models

We first assess whether the legislative incorporation of all women, regardless of race and ethnicity, affects states' initial decisions regarding TANF benefits and rules. The key independent variables in these additive models are our factor scores of the political incorporation of all women, all Black, and all Latinx legislators. We include these, along with the control variables, in the five cross-sectional models presented in Table 6.1.[22] In model 1, we regress the index of eligibility restrictions on the three single-axis incorporation factor scores. Although none of the coefficients for the incorporation variables reaches standard significance levels, the estimated effect of female incorporation is close ($p = 0.167$). Thus, the presence and power of women legislators may have a slight, liberal effect on TANF eligibility policies.

The remaining models in Table 6.1 provide even less support for the single-axis hypothesis. According to model 2, female legislative incorporation does not influence the degree to which states adopt more flexible TANF work requirements. This model does suggest, however, that state legislatures with higher degrees of Latinx incorporation opt for more flexible TANF regulations. Holding all dichotomous and categorical variables constant at their medians and all other continuous variables at their means, we estimate that, as Latinx incorporation increases from one standard deviation below the mean to one standard deviation above, the predicted flexibility index score increases from 5.5 to 8.4 (King, Tomz, and Wittenberg

---

unbiased estimates of causal effects in non-experimental data are neither feasible nor appropriate, given our theory, concepts, and research design.

[21] We employ several alternative models and measures to assess the robustness of our results. A full discussion of these robustness tests is included in Reingold and Smith (2012) SI.

[22] Given our overriding interest in the effects of group incorporation, we limit discussion of results for the control variables, noting only the very few instances in which our findings diverge from what previous research would suggest.

Table 6.1 Additive Models: The Impact of Women, Blacks, and Latinxs in State Legislatures on Temporary Assistance for Needy Families (TANF) Policies, 1998

	1. Eligibility Index (OLS)	2. Flexibility Index (OLS)	3. Family Cap (Logit)	4. Domestic Violence Time Limit Waivers (Logit)	5. Cash Benefits (OLS)
Legislative Incorporation					
Women	−0.024 (0.017)	−0.072 (0.427)	−0.224 (0.520)	0.309 (0.435)	−12.878** (6.107)
Blacks	0.022 (0.032)	1.092 (0.787)	−0.301 (0.869)	−0.990 (0.793)	12.240 (11.453)
Latinxs	−0.016 (0.023)	1.407** (0.575)	−0.249 (0.633)	−1.050* (0.590)	9.095 (8.408)
Control Variables					
% Black and Latinx Population	−0.001 (0.003)	−0.142** (0.070)	0.081 (0.089)	0.127* (0.074)	−1.469 (1.014)
Citizen Ideology	−0.003** (0.001)	0.089** (0.027)	−0.021 (0.033)	−0.028 (0.028)	0.814* (0.408)
Democratic Control of Legislature	−0.036 (0.022)	0.154 (0.544)	−0.134 (0.685)	1.386** (0.655)	−2.836 (7.925)
Unemployment Rate	−0.002 (0.018)	−0.279 (0.467)	−0.526 (0.620)	0.476 (0.446)	−6.834 (6.544)
Unmarried Birth Rate	−0.004 (0.004)	−0.066 (0.105)	−0.042 (0.127)	0.006 (0.105)	2.749* (1.546)
% High School Graduates	−0.003 (0.005)	−0.224 (0.137)	−0.014 (0.162)	0.151 (0.126)	1.438 (2.178)
Moralistic Political Culture	−0.067 (0.042)	0.045 (1.056)	−1.718 (1.455)	0.904 (1.177)	6.923 (15.330)
Baseline Dependent Variable (1996)	0.176 (0.119)		3.547** (1.419)	0.057 (0.865)	0.976** (0.046)
Constant	1.078** (0.484)	27.012** (13.133)	3.836 (15.821)	−16.987 (12.094)	−196.042 (199.185)
Number of States	49	47	49	48	49
F-statistic	3.25	2.58			114.66
P-value	0.0035	0.0180			0.0001
LR χ2			30.76	12.28	
P-value			0.0012	0.3432	
Adjusted or Pseudo R²	0.34	0.26	0.46	0.19	0.96

OLS = Ordinary Least Squares

*p < 0.1; **p < 0.05

2000). African American incorporation also has a positive effect on flex-ibility, but it is noticeably weaker and not quite statistically significant (p = 0.172).[23]

In model 3, we estimate the impact of legislative women on the probability of states adopting a family cap policy. Here, none of the group incorporation coefficients achieves standard significance levels. Model 4 gauges the impact of the single-axis group incorporation scores on whether states permitted domestic violence time limit waivers in 1998. Here again, the results indi-cate that the legislative incorporation of women has no discernible impact on state TANF policy. Instead, the incorporation of Latinxs in state legislatures appears to be associated with a lower probability of adopting domestic vio-lence waivers. Also surprising (given previous evidence of racial backlash) is the finding that states with larger Black and Latinx populations are more likely to grant such waivers.[24]

Model 5 indicates that female legislators' incorporation is associated with *lower* cash benefits during the early years of the TANF program. Figure 6.1a illustrates this relationship: as the factor score for women's incorporation increases from one standard deviation below the mean to one standard devi-ation above, the mean predicted cash benefit decreases from $528 to $500.[25] Without accounting for racial/ethnic cleavages, we might conclude that states with more numerous and powerful female legislators were more likely than others to reduce cash benefits in the transition from AFDC to TANF. Our intersectional model will cast doubt on this conclusion.

Overall, the models in Table 6.1 provide lackluster and contradic-tory findings regarding the single-axis hypothesis. In only one instance—eligibility requirements—does the presence and power of (all) women legislators even come close to having a significant, liberal effect on TANF policy. In other areas, namely cash benefit levels, female legislative incorpo-ration may have the reverse effect. For the remaining TANF policies, how-ever, legislative women seem to have no significant impact at all.

---

[23] A Wald equivalence test shows that the impact of African American legislators is not statistically different from that of Latinx legislators (F-test statistic = 0.26, p = 0.613).

[24] Model 4 does not pass the likelihood-ratio χ^2 test for minimum adequacy of fit, so we are some-what wary of drawing steadfast conclusions from it. We get very similar results, though, when we model state domestic violence time limit waivers in 1997 (rather than 1998); and, in this case, the model does pass the goodness of fit test (likelihood-ratio χ^2 = 22.84; p = 0.019).

[25] Here, as elsewhere, we hold all dichotomous and categorical variables constant at their medians and all other continuous variables constant at their means. All figures display predicted probabilities or values for the range of observed data.

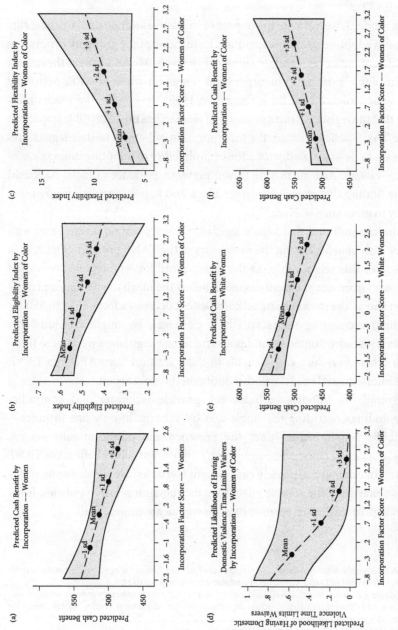

Figure 6.1 Predicted Effects of Group Incorporation

Intersectional Models

In contrast to the additive models, the intersectional models (presented in Table 6.2) distinguish the potential impact of women of color from that of other women and from that of men of color, on the same set of state TANF policies. The key independent variables for the intersectional models are factor scores of the legislative incorporation of women of color, White women, and men of color.

Model 6 considers how well the intersectional model characterizes the relationship between gender, race/ethnicity, legislative incorporation, and state-to-state variation in TANF eligibility policies. From this model, it appears that women of color may have a more pronounced impact on the eligibility index than other legislative women and men of color have. Figure 6.1b shows that as the legislative incorporation of women of color increases from one standard deviation below the mean to one above, the predicted eligibility index falls from 0.60 to 0.52. States where legislative women of color are present and powerful have somewhat more lenient eligibility requirements. The impact of other legislative women is in the same direction, but noticeably weaker; the regression coefficient on the factor score for White women is just slightly above standard significance levels ($p = 0.114$). However, a Wald test reveals that the effect of women of color is not statistically different from that of White women.[26]

In model 7, we find that the legislative incorporation of both women and men of color impacts the flexibility index. The effect of women of color is no different from that of men of color (Wald F-test statistic = 0.02, $p = 0.896$), but it does appear to be greater than that of other women (Wald F-test statistic = 2.71, $p = 0.108$). Figure 6.1c shows that as the presence and power of women of color in the state legislature increases, so too does the flexibility of TANF work requirements. In contrast to the additive model, which indicated that legislative women have no influence over the flexibility of work requirements, the intersectional model shows that *some* legislative women (and some of their male colleagues) can and do have an impact.

Model 8, on the other hand, shows that the intersectional framework is no more helpful than the additive approach in explaining state-level variation

---

[26] A separate Wald F-test shows that the impact of Black female and Latina legislators is not statistically different from that of men of color. Our results do not differ significantly when we disaggregate the legislative incorporation of Democratic and Republican White women. White women, regardless of party, have no significant effect on eligibility requirements; women of color do.

Table 6.2 Intersectional Models: The Impact of White Women, Women of Color, and Men of Color in State Legislatures on Temporary Assistance for Needy Families (TANF) Policies, 1998

	6. Eligibility Index (OLS)	7. Flexibility Index (OLS)	8. Family Cap (Logit)	9. Domestic Violence Time Limit Waivers (Logit)	10. Cash Benefits (OLS)
Legislative Incorporation					
White Women	−0.028	−0.069	−0.228	0.485	−15.762**
	(0.017)	(0.417)	(0.525)	(0.461)	(5.799)
Women of Color	−0.048*	1.208*	0.035	−1.398*	15.164
	(0.028)	(0.683)	(0.796)	(0.722)	(9.723)
Men of Color	−0.002	1.324**	−0.365	−0.505	4.048
	(0.026)	(0.624)	(0.726)	(0.643)	(8.892)
Control Variables					
% Black and Latinx Population	0.001	−0.189**	0.072	0.162**	−2.227**
	(0.003)	(0.076)	(0.094)	(0.080)	(1.070)
Citizen Ideology	−0.003**	0.086**	−0.021	−0.025	0.853**
	(0.001)	(0.027)	(0.033)	(0.029)	(0.390)
Democratic Control of Legislature	−0.024	−0.027	−0.145	1.547**	−3.622
	(0.022)	(0.522)	(0.674)	(0.653)	(7.349)
Unemployment Rate	−0.010	−0.212	−0.558	0.444	−6.020
	(0.017)	(0.434)	(0.605)	(0.416)	(6.107)
Unmarried Birth Rate	−0.005	−0.044	−0.020	−0.062	3.890**
	(0.005)	(0.113)	(0.143)	(0.119)	(1.601)
% High School Graduates	−0.005	−0.204	−0.006	0.130	2.529
	(0.005)	(0.137)	(0.163)	(0.127)	(2.152)
Moralistic Political Culture	−0.072	−0.038	−1.741	0.714	7.473
	(0.043)	(1.045)	(1.438)	(1.147)	(14.802)
Baseline Dependent Variable (1996)	0.214*		3.407**	−0.109	0.953**
	(0.121)		(1.461)	(0.882)	(0.044)
Constant	1.208**	25.582*	2.853	−13.816	−300.521
	(0.498)	(13.279)	(16.078)	(12.515)	(198.693)
Number of States	49	47	49	48	49
F-statistic	3.09	2.75			125.51
P-value	0.0049	0.0125			0.0001
LR χ2			30.81	14.65	
P-value			0.0012	0.1990	
Adjusted or Pseudo R²	0.32	0.28	0.47	0.23	0.97

OLS = Ordinary Least Squares

*p < 0.1; **p < 0.05

in the family cap. The legislative incorporation of women of color (as well as other women and men of color) does not influence whether a state has a family cap policy. Since many states implemented family caps before 1996 through waivers to the AFDC program, our analysis of welfare policy changes that occurred between 1996 and 1998 may not allow for a full investigation of the impact of female legislators on family cap decisions. Indeed, across the additive and intersectional models, the strongest predictor of family caps in 1998 is whether the state had a family cap policy in 1996. The highly salient nature of this policy innovation, so strongly imbued with images of the welfare queen, may also have made it particularly difficult for these legislators to resist or reverse.

The results of model 9 confirm our suspicion that given the uncertainty surrounding the implementation of domestic violence waivers in the early years of TANF, women of color may have been particularly reluctant to entrust such initiatives to the states. Thus, contrary to our general expectations, the presence and power of women of color is negatively associated with having domestic violence time limit waivers in 1998. Equivalence tests show that the coefficient for women of color is significantly different from that of other legislative women (χ^2 statistic = 4.84, p = 0.028), while the impact of women of color is not different from that of men of color (χ^2 statistic = 1.00, p = 0.318).[27] Figure 6.1d illustrates that as the women-of-color factor score increases from one standard deviation below the mean to one above, the predicted likelihood of having domestic violence time limit waivers decreases from 0.78 to 0.28.

Interestingly, in model 10, women of color and White women seem to have opposite effects on the initial adjustment from AFDC to TANF cash benefits; benefits appear to increase when women of color are present and powerful, and they decrease when White women are more fully incorporated. The coefficients for the two factor scores are of nearly equal magnitude, but in opposite directions. The coefficient on Black and Latina women's factor score is just slightly above standard significance levels (p = 0.127), but significantly different from that of other women (Wald F-test statistic = 7.82, p = 0.008). If we were to consider the additive model exclusively, we might conclude that all legislative women have a negative effect on cash benefits.

---

[27] As with model 4, model 9 does not pass a likelihood-ratio χ^2 test for minimum adequacy of fit. Again, we obtain very similar results when we model the presence of domestic violence time limit waivers in 1997; and the 1997 model does pass the goodness-of-fit test (likelihood-ratio χ^2 = 23.98; p = 0.013).

However, our intersectional model demonstrates that only White women's incorporation is negatively associated with cash benefits. This nuanced yet powerful finding is illustrated in Figures 6.1e and 6.1f. As the factor score for White women's incorporation goes from one standard deviation below to one above the mean, the predicted cash benefit decreases from $531 to $497. In contrast, as the presence and power of women of color increases from one standard deviation below the mean to one above, the predicted cash benefit increases from $501 to $527.[28]

In sum, our intersectional analyses indicate that in the formative years of TANF policymaking, legislative women of color did play a distinct role. Our results also demonstrate that the additive model may sometimes obscure the impact of race, ethnicity, and gender as they interact to affect state politics and policymaking. Intersectional models such as ours appear more adept at capturing such complex and contingent relationships (McCall 2005).

Conclusions

At first glance, looking through a single-axis lens, it may seem as if state legislative women failed to move welfare policy in a more liberal, women-friendly direction, even in a period of policy disequilibrium. At best, they may have managed to relax the eligibility criteria a bit; at worst, they may have had a hand in reducing cash benefit levels. But on most policy dimensions examined here, the presence and power of (all) women in state legislatures seems to have made very little difference.

The picture looks quite different, however, when viewed through an intersectional lens. Taking into account the intersecting gender and racial/ ethnic identities of state legislators highlights both the contingent effects of gender and the pivotal role of women of color. In some instances, our analysis suggests that legislative women of all racial/ethnic backgrounds made a difference in state TANF policy. Eligibility restrictions were eased somewhat in states where legislative women of color and White women were more numerous and powerful. In other instances, legislative women of color seem to have acted without their White female counterparts. It was the incorporation of women of color, along with men of color, that pushed some states to adopt

---

[28] Again, our results do not differ significantly when we disaggregate the legislative incorporation of Democratic and Republican White women. White women, Republicans especially, have a negative effect on cash benefits; women of color have a distinctive, positive effect.

more flexible work requirements—not the incorporation of other women. At the same time, the presence and power of women of color (alone) made some states more reluctant to grant time limit waivers to victims of domestic violence. Given the initial uncertainties surrounding state implementation of the Family Violence Option, legislative women of color may have been most wary of the unintended but potentially harmful consequences of this seemingly women-friendly policy. In yet another instance, legislative women of color and other women appear to have worked at cross-purposes. While the presence and power of White women in the legislature is associated with a decrease in cash benefits, the incorporation of women of color is associated with an increase in cash benefits. Across all these divergent patterns, however, one trend is clear: the legislative incorporation of women of color mattered, suggesting they were indeed the most effective advocates for poor women in the era of welfare reform (Fraga et al. 2008).

As our results imply, the impact of women on welfare policy depends on which women and which policies one examines. Nonetheless, it is quite remarkable that women—especially women of color—had any effect whatsoever. Women as a whole were a minority of legislators and legislative leaders in every state, a small minority in most. Women of color enjoyed fewer resources still. During the transition from AFDC to TANF, Black women and Latinas never claimed more than 10% of the votes; they held top leadership positions and chaired social service committees in few states. State welfare policy itself proved resistant to non-incremental change, even in a period of disequilibrium. Overcoming inertia and pushing against the popular mandate of get-tough welfare reform was a tall order, indeed. Yet women of color, when they were able to gain a foothold within their legislative institutions, managed to make a difference.

The implications of our findings are equally notable. They demonstrate, first and foremost, the utility of intersectionality as a concept and an analytic tool, as well as the limitations of more "parsimonious" single-axis or additive approaches to studying the politics of gender, race, and class. The politics of welfare and other cross-cutting issues (Cohen 1999; Htun and Weldon 2010) may *not* be properly understood in terms of only race or gender or class. Nor can we be content with simply adding women (or racial/ethnic minorities or poor people) to the equation, literally or figuratively. Doing so may very well obscure more than it reveals.

Our study also adds an important cautionary note for the study of race, gender, and representation, reinforcing recent calls for more complex theorizing about the descriptive and substantive representation of marginalized groups (Beckwith and Cowell-Meyers 2007; Reingold 2008; Htun and Weldon 2010). Our conclusions about *which* women and *which* policies suggest that questions about group representation and group interests may be better framed and best answered in terms of contingency. "Women's issues" may mean different things to different women, in different places. That such a small but highly motivated group of Black female and Latina state legislators can make a difference in welfare policy also suggests that substantive representation at the aggregate level is not simply a function of large numbers or a critical mass of distinctive individuals (Weldon 2002). Rather, "critical actors" who "put in motion individual and collective campaigns" for policy change (Childs and Krook 2006, 528) may hold the key (see also Preuhs 2005). Here again, intersectionality plays an important role. It not only implores us to think critically about the unity of identity-based, single-axis coalitions and the "vague imperatives of 'sex' or 'gender,'" "race" or "ethnicity" underlying the logic of critical mass theory (Childs and Krook 2006, 528). It also suggests who might be the most likely critical actors: those who, like legislative women of color confronting welfare reform, can best understand and appreciate the complex intersections of inequality and marginalization, power and privilege at work.

7

Conclusion

A great deal of American politics, political commentary, and political science research over the past few decades has been driven by questions about descriptive and substantive representation—who our representatives are and for whom they act (Pitkin 1967). Most often, these conversations, debates, and investigations are about "women," "minorities," or occasionally "women and minorities." We have celebrated various milestones (two Years of the Woman) and firsts (e.g., Barack Obama and Hillary Clinton) yet wondered why more widespread, systemic change is so slow to come (Simien 2015). As discussed in Chapter 1, a great many people—leaders and followers, scholars and everyday observers—care about such matters and what they say about the state of gender and racial equality in politics and society as well as the strength of our democratic institutions.

If we care who elected representatives are in terms of gender or race/ethnicity, then this study provides reason to care about who representatives are in terms of gender, race/ethnicity, and race-gender. Just as the under-representation of women and minorities is of concern, so too should the under-representation of women of color give us pause. Conversely, Year-of-the-Woman surges and other notable gains in minority officeholding—driven in large part by women of color—can be celebrated and evaluated not simply as harbingers of greater gender or racial equality, but as promissory notes for those who are intersectionally marginalized as well. This is what is revealed by our detailed, intersectional analysis of the election, behavior, and impact of American state legislators in the late 20th and early 21st centuries.

Race, Gender, and Political Representation uncovers a wide variety of similarities and differences in the electoral experiences and legislative behavior of Latinas, Latinos, Black women, Black men, White women, and White men in state legislatures across the nation. Our analysis of the political geography of descriptive representation indicates, for example, that women of color, men of color, and White women face similar, different, and unique opportunities and challenges in state legislative elections. The electoral gains of Black men and women, Latinos, and Latinas alike are closely tied to the size and

Race, Gender, and Political Representation. Beth Reingold, Kerry L. Haynie, and Kirsten Widner, Oxford University Press (2021). © Oxford University Press. DOI: 10.1093/oso/9780197502174.001.0001.

prevalence of co-ethnic constituencies. Contrary to expectations and hopes that women of color might capitalize on certain intersectional advantages, we find little evidence to suggest that Latinas and Black women can readily gain significant cross-over support from White women or other racial/ethnic minority groups.

At the same time, women of color candidates (or would-be candidates) may be finding greater opportunities in other electoral institutions besides majority-minority districts. Like White women, Latinas make somewhat greater electoral gains in "multi-member" districts that elect more than one candidate to the state legislature. Unlike any other race-gender group of elected officials, Black women are seeing greater electoral gains in state houses with term limits. Overall, the electoral ambitions of White women and women of color appear to be channeled in different directions. While women of color are finding their greatest opportunities in states and districts with larger shares of co-ethnic voters, White women see their electoral fortunes rising in states and districts with more liberal and fewer minority voters, and where party organizations hold less sway and legislatures are less professionalized. Yet, White women, Black women, and Latinas share one thing in common: no matter what state or district, they are less likely than their male counterparts to run for and win state legislative office.

Once in office, the state legislators we examine exhibit a similarly complex array of race-gender similarities and differences in their representational activity. Among Democrats, where the vast majority of legislators of color are located, White women, Black women, and Latinas are equally likely to take the lead on women's issues, sponsoring more legislation specific to women's interests than any of their male colleagues. Black women sponsor just as many bills specific to Black interests as Black men do; together their policy leadership on such issues surpasses that of any other group of legislators. Latinas sponsor even more Latinx-specific legislation than do Latinos—and much more than anyone else. Women of color, both Latinas and Black women, are also on the forefront of health and education policymaking thought to be of broad, overlapping concern to women, African Americans, and Latinx constituencies alike. Among Democrats, they sponsor more legislation in these arenas than do any other group of lawmakers. Among Democrats and Republicans, women of color are the leading sponsors of health and education bills targeted to address the interests of women or racial/ethnic minorities in particular. This may be one way in which women of color manage to sustain such high levels of representational activity on behalf of multiple group interests.

Indeed, we also find that Black women and Latinas are distinctive in their roles as race-gender policy leaders. More than any other lawmakers, they are the ones to place issues of both race and gender on the legislative agenda. Among Democrats, Latinas stand out as the most likely to sponsor at least one women-specific bill and one Latinx- and/or Black-specific bill. Black women are more likely than any other group of Democrats to sponsor at least one welfare/poverty bill addressing the interests of intersectionally disadvantaged subgroups of women and people of color. Among Republicans, Latinas are the most likely to do the same. The only type of race-gender policy leadership where women of color do not stand out is the sponsorship of bills that address multiple forms of discrimination and inequality simultaneously. Black men are the leading sponsors of such measures (though not by wide margins), almost all of which offer traditional civil rights approaches to remedying discrimination on the basis of sex/gender, race/color, and national origin/ethnicity.

Our exploratory, in-depth analysis of the intersectional content of legislative proposals put forth by a small subset of Democratic state lawmakers (serving similar majority-minority constituencies) unveils even more complex patterns of similarities and differences across race-gender identities. Not surprisingly, most of these lawmakers sponsor a good deal of group-interest legislation that directly or indirectly, explicitly or implicitly, addresses issues of race and gender. On closer examination, the bulk of this legislation appears to approach issues of race and gender (as well as other categories of difference and systems of power) in a single-axis or additive manner—that is, without attention to or recognition of the interests and concerns of individuals or communities subject to multiple, intersecting, and often compounding inequalities and disadvantages. Nonetheless, most of these lawmakers also sponsor bills that do engage in some form of intersectional policy design.

These intersectional policy proposals come in all shapes and sizes, so to speak, addressing many different forms of intersecting marginalization and deprivation. Many appear to address the needs of women of color confronting race-gender violence, economic precarity, little reproductive choice, and other inequities and hardships. But not all. Many other bills address the harms wrought by other intersectional configurations, from those formerly or currently incarcerated, to those fighting the ravages of

HIV/AIDS, to those struggling in poor, immigrant communities with sub-standard housing, plumbing, education, and healthcare. By no means do legislative women of color have a monopoly on intersectional policymaking, especially within this small, select group. But they are among its most reliable practitioners.

Given their distinctive, agenda-setting leadership on behalf of women, minorities, and the poor within the policymaking process, it may come as no surprise that women of color have a distinctive impact on the policies state governments enact. As our research shows, the presence and power of Black women and Latinas in state legislatures mitigated some of the more punitive, restrictive, and potentially intrusive aspects of state welfare reform in the late 1990s—more so than did the presence and power of their White female, Black male, or Latino colleagues. Though incremental, these policy effects are quite remarkable—and surprising—given the very small numbers of women of color elected to state legislatures and the ways in which they have been marginalized within such institutions, especially in raced-gendered debates about "welfare queens" and welfare dependency. Our research highlighting the similarities in the constituencies state legislative women of color and men of color are elected to serve make these and many of the other distinctive roles of Latinas and Black women all the more remarkable.

Our findings and conclusions about race, gender, and political represen-tation are remarkable for another reason. Too few studies before ours have asked questions about how gender and race interact to affect the election, behavior, and impact of raced women and gendered minorities. Too few studies have put women of color at the center of their analysis. And too few studies have taken an intersectional approach to the study of descriptive and substantive representation of marginalized groups. Little of what we dis-cover here would have been revealed otherwise. Without critically evaluating single-axis women-and-politics and race-and-ethnic-politics theories about descriptive representation, we would have little understanding of the com-plex mix of political opportunities and obstacles White women, men of color, and women of color face in and around state legislative elections. Without critically evaluating single-axis concepts of group interests and exploring more intersectional concepts of race-gender policymaking, we would have little understanding of the distinctive policy leadership Latina and Black women legislators offer. The impact of legislative women of color on state welfare reform would remain hidden had we not re-read the literature, theo-rized, and designed our research with an intersectional lens, attentive to the race-gender histories, legacies, and institutional contexts of welfare politics in the United States. None of this would be revealed had we not simply expanded and re-arranged the identity categories in which we place politicians and the politicized groups they ostensibly represent—allowing for multiple unranked or non-linear patterns of race-gender similarities and differences to emerge.

Our hope and intention is not only to demonstrate the power and utility of an intersectional approach to the study of political representation, but also to foster future, additional movements toward a more intersectional approach. Ours is but one small—yet significant—step toward the fuller and more nuanced understandings intersectional research promises. Gender and race are of paramount importance in American politics; Whites, Latinxs, and African Americans, women, and men are the largest groups that constitute the politics of race and gender in the United States—as we know it. Indeed, these are the primary categories of difference that have defined and shaped the study of American politics thus far. They are a good place to begin. Yet intersectionality reminds us that the boundaries, meanings, and salience of these and many other categories are fluid, contingent on political contexts that fluctuate across time, space, and peoples.

We study race, gender, and representation in the wake of the 1992 Year of the Woman as a potential precedent for the politics of race and gender in the wake of the 2018 Year of the Woman. The representational questions, concerns, hopes, and expectations surrounding and even defining each set of events are very similar. But of course, we cannot be sure our findings are generalizable across multiple decades of increasingly polarized and polarizing politics and an increasingly diverse and diversifying population. How are politicized group identities and formations intersecting, expanding, and contracting, coalescing and breaking apart? Which ones are more or less salient—salient enough to elicit calls for descriptive representation? To what extent and how are conceptions of group interests—and, thus, demands for substantive representation—changing? How will campaigns and elections change as voters become more accustomed to seeing the representational work of public officials of increasingly diverse identities and backgrounds?

We examine representational inputs and outputs across a wide variety of legislative institutions and state political cultures, including some of the most diverse and homogeneous, as well as some of the most liberal and conservative. But we have not examined how these various political and institutional contexts shape the dynamics of race, gender, and representation. How, for example, does the race-gender composition of the legislature—and its leadership—shape the recruitment and success of candidates trying to get or remain in office? How does it affect the distribution and fate of race-gender policy proposals? Does a "critical mass" of diverse colleagues promote race-gender policy leadership or engender a backlash against it? A critical mass of whom?

These are all important, productive questions for future, intersectional research on the politics of representation. Yet our work is not simply intended to prompt such questions. Our hope is that it also provides some guidance about how to pursue them—intersectionally. Such intersectional pursuits, if guided by our own example, might begin by critically re-evaluating the analytic choices we have made. What might they conceal or distort? How might we think, read, theorize, design, analyze, and interpret differently? At the same time, we also hope that our use of quantitative, hypothesis-testing methods supplements the intersectional "tool kit" with which others can pursue such critical questions. Every method or methodological tool has strengths and weaknesses, great potential and significant limitations; each should be evaluated accordingly. Intersectionality demands as much. We offer *Race, Gender, and Representation* as a demonstration of the epistemological value of such processes of reflective exploration and evaluation.

APPENDIX

Table A.1 Profile of State House Sample, 1997 and 2005

Year	State	Median Ideology in the House	% Democrats in the House	% Women Legislators in House	% Black Legislators in House	% Latinx Legislators in House
1997	AZ	.45	36.67%	43.33%	3.33%	8.33%
2005	AZ	.57	36.67%	33.33%	1.7%	18.33%
1997	CA	−.84	53.75%	25%	5%	17.5%
2005	CA	−1.26	60%	31.25%	5%	23.75%
1997	FL	.16	49.17%	26.67%	12.50%	9.17%
2005	FL	.43	30%	25%	14.17%	11.67%
1997	MD	−.59	70.92%	34.04%	19.15%	0%
2005	MD	−.74	69.5%	36.88%	22.70%	1.42%
1997	MN	−.52	52.24%	29.85%	.75%	0%
2005	MN	.26	49.25%	27.61%	1.92%	.75%
1997	MS	.23	68.95%	15.57%	28.69%	0%
2005	MS	.25	61.48%	14.75%	29.51%	0%
1997	ND	.60	26.53%	18.37%	0%	0%
2005	ND	.58	28.72%	19.15%	0%	0%
1998	NJ	−.06	40%	20%	13.75%	5%
2006	NJ	−.87	61.25%	20%	13.75%	6.25%
1997	NM	−.56	60%	28.51%	2.86%	32.86%
2005	NM	−.70	60%	34.29%	2.86%	42.86%

(*Continued*)

Table A.1 Continued

Year	State	Median Ideology in the House	% Democrats in the House	% Women Legislators in House	% Black Legislators in House	% Latinx Legislators in House
1997	NV	-.32	59.52%	38.1%	4.76%	0%
2005	NV	-.45	61.90%	35.71%	9.52%	2.38%
1997	OH	.50	39.39%	21.21%	14.14%	1.01%
2005	OH	.68	40.40%	21.21%	14.14%	0%
1997	SC	.57	42.74%	15.32%	20.97%	0%
2005	SC	.72	40.32%	10.48%	20.16%	.81%
1997	TN	-.13	61.61%	15.15%	13.13%	1.01%
2005	TN	-.04	53.53%	16.16%	15.15%	1.01%
1997	TX	.15	54.67%	20%	9.33%	18.67%
2005	TX	.84	42%	20.67%	9.33%	19.33%
1997	UT	.64	26.67%	21.33%	1.33%	1.33%
2005	UT	.74	25.33%	22.67%	1.33%	2.67%
1997/8	Average for Sample	.02	49.52%	24.83%	10.16%	6.33%
1997	National Average	.01	51.95%	22.59%	7.38%	2.59%
2005/6	Average for Sample	.07	48.02%	24.61%	10.74%	8.75%
2005	National Average	.05	49.89%	23.43%	7.98%	3.73%

Sources

Ideology: Shor, Boris and Nolan McCarty. 2011. "The Ideological Mapping of American Legislatures." *American Political Science Review* 105(3):530–551.

Partisanship: Extracted from "Klarner Partisan_Balance_For_Use2011_6_09.dta" (as of 3/10/15), http://www.indstate.edu/polisci/klarnerpolitics.htm. See also Klarner, Carl. 2013. "State Partisan Balance Data, 1937–2011." http://hdl.handle.net/1902.1/20403 IQSS Dataverse Network [Distributor] V1 [Version]. Klarner, Carl E. 2003. "Measurement of the Partisan Balance of State Government." *State Politics & Policy Quarterly* 3 (Fall): 309–19.

Gender Composition: Center for Women in American Politics, Rutgers University. http://www.cawp.rutgers.edu/fast_facts/resources/state_fact_sheet.php#states (10 March 2015).

Racial/Ethnic Composition: Joint Center for Political and Economic Studies, Black Elected Officials Database/Directories; National Association of Latino Elected and Appointed Officials (1997 data); (2005 data) Ramirez, Ricardo. 2006. *The National Latino Legislative Database Project, 1990–2006.* University of Southern California. Personal Communication (9 September 2009).

Table A.2a Descriptive Statistics, State Level Dependent Variables, 2005 (Chapter 2)
(N = 49; Nebraska excluded)

Variable	Description	Mean	Standard Deviation	Min	Max	Sources
% Women (All)	Ratio: percentage of seats in a state legislature's lower chamber held by women, White women, Black women and/or men, Latina women and/or Latino men.	23.30924	7.846616	10.47619	35.71429	Authors' coding (see Chapter 2); Center for Women in American Politics (CAWP); Joint Center for Political and Economic Studies (JCPES) *Black Elected*
% Blacks (All)		7.737424	7.587847	0	28.68852	
% Black Men		5.038272	5.422667	0	22.13115	
% Black Women		2.699152	2.7173	0	8.510638	
% Latinxs (All)		3.834634	7.767636	0	42.85714	
% Latino Men		2.724679	5.62837	0	31.42857	
% Latina Women		1.109955	2.309574	0	11.42857	
% White Women		18.89927	8.188588	3.809524	35.71429	*Officials Roster;* National Latino Legislative Database Project (Ramirez 2006); *National Asian Pacific American Political Almanac* (Nakanishi, Lai, and Kwok 2005–6); and the National Council of State Legislatures' (NCSL's) State Tribal Institute.

Table A.2b Descriptive Statistics, State Level Independent Variables, 2005 (Chapter 2) (N = 49; Nebraska excluded)

Variable	Description	Mean	Std. Dev.	Min	Max	Source
Ideology	Ratio: mean % liberal-% conservative	−13.47347	8.829208	−30.2	8	Erikson, Wright, and McIver (2006)
Moralistic political culture	Dummy: individualistic political culture is excluded category	.3469388	.4809288	0	1	Elazar (1984)
Traditionalistic political culture		.3265306	.4738035	0	1	
% Labor Force that is Professional Women	Ratio: percentage of state civilian labor force who are female,	13.86081	1.597995	10.73654	18.31655	U.S. Census 2000 Special EEO Tabulation Files
% Labor Force that is Professional White Women	White (non-Hispanic) female, African American female, or	11.52149	1.958499	4.64015	15.88978	
% Labor Force that is Professional Black Women	Latina female (EEO-1 Job Codes 01-02)	.9920498	.9980337	.0142955	4.477854	
% Labor Force that is Professional Latinas		.5147311	.6631676	.0720889	3.779268	
Professional Legislature	Dummy: hybrid legislature is excluded category	.2244898	.4215698	0	1	Hamm and Moncrief (2008)/NCSL
Citizen's Legislature		.3469388	.4809288	0	1	
Party Organizational Strength	Interval: state "traditional party organization" (TPO) scores (higher values = greater control over candidate selection process)	2.122449	1.589453	1	5	Mayhew (1986, 197)

		Mean	SD	Min	Max	Source
Multimember districts (any type)	Dummy: =1 if state has any (≥1) multimember state legislative electoral districts of any sort ("free for all" or designated posts)	.2040816	.4072055	0	1	CQ Almanac of State Legislative Elections (Lilley et al. 2008); the State Legislative Election Return Project,[a] state legislative webpages
% Black	Ratio: percentage of state population that is African American	9.936531	9.629884	.26	36.33	U.S. Census 2000 Summary File 3 (Sample)
% Latinx Citizens	Ratio: percentage of state population that is Latino (Hispanic) and native or naturalized citizen	5.747959	7.102491	.59	37.67	U.S. Census 2000 Summary File 3 (Sample)
Term limits	Dummy: =1 if state had legislative term limits (of any length) in effect in 2004	.244898	.434483	0	1	NCSL

[a] State Legislative Election Returns, 1967–2003, Thomas M. Carsey, William D. Berry, Richard G. Niemi, Lynda W. Powell, and James M Snyder, Release Version 5. Codebook and data available at http://www.unc.edu/~carsey/research/datasets/data.htm. Last accessed 3 May 2009.

Table A.2c Descriptive Statistics, District/Seat Level Dependent Variable 2005
(Chapter 2)

(N = 4,685)

Characteristic	Description	Frequency	Percent	Source
White Man	Gender and racial/ethnic identity of legislator holding the seat	3,195	68.20%	Authors' coding (see Chapter 2); Center for Women in American Politics (CAWP); Joint Center for Political and Economic Studies (JCPES) *Black Elected Officials Roster*; National Latino Legislative Database Project (Ramirez 2006); *National Asian Pacific American Political Almanac* (Nakanishi, Lai, and Kwok 2005–6); and the National Council of State Legislatures' (NCSL's) State Tribal Institute.
White Woman		889	18.98%	
Black Man		283	6.04%	
Black Woman		153	3.27%	
Latino Man		118	2.52%	
Latina Woman		47	1.00%	

Table A.2d Descriptive Statistics, District/Seat Level Independent Variables, 2005 (Chapter 2)

(N = 4,685)

Variable	Description	Mean	St. Dev.	Min	Max	Source
Policy Conservatism	Ratio: IRT estimates of district constituency ideology based on responses to surveys conducted by the Annenberg National Election study and the Cooperative Congressional Election Study, 2000–11	−.0045184	.3029494	−1.34547	.7138606	Tausanovitch and Warshaw (2013)
% White College Educated	Ratio: percentage of district population, 25 years and older, that is White, non-Hispanic and has a Bachelor's degree or more	20.55606	12.13761	.1911015	74.19474	U.S. Census 2000 State Legislative District Summary File 4 (Sample)
% Urban	Ratio: percentage of district residents who live in urbanized areas	74.20084	29.69855	0	100	
% Black	Ratio: percentage of district population that is African American	11.99569	18.61508	.02106	98.22356	
% Latinx Citizens	Ratio: percentage of district population that is Latino/a and a native or naturalized citizen	5.419846	9.5611	.1116368	76.14598	
Resources/SES of White Women	Factor Scores: component variables include labor force participation, unemployment rate, educational status (BA degree or above), and median income of each subgroup population in the district. See Reingold and Smith (2012) Supplementary Information for more details.	.0170642	.9022335	−3.502109	4.254256	
Resources/SES of Black Men		−.0172587	.6909106	−3.174719	3.23892	
Resources/SES of Black Women		−.0051554	.6503323	−2.809964	3.542427	

(Continued)

Table A.2d Continued

Variable	Description	Mean	St. Dev.	Min	Max	Source
Resources/SES of Latino Men		-.0065317	.6339225	-3.123655	4.141346	
Resources/SES of Latinas		-.0137066	.6455433	-3.196517	3.796531	
Multimember District	Dummy: =1 if district elects more than one member of the state house (includes both "free for all" and designated post elections)	.1831377	.3868206	0	1	CQ *Almanac of State Legislative Elections* (Lilley et al. 2008); the State Legislative Election Return Project; state legislative webpages

Table A.3 State-Level Descriptive Representation (lower chamber only), 2005 Women-and-Politics Model—Including % White *Democratic* Women Dependent Variable Tobit (robust standard errors)

	% All Women (1)	% White Women (2)	% White Democratic Women	% Black Women (3)	% Latina Women (4)
Ideology	.381* (.151)	.277* (.113)	.323*** (.077)	-.009 (.046)	.044 (.045)
Moralistic Political Culture	1.417 (3.563)	1.913 (3.392)	-.148 (3.898)	.026 (1.202)	1.215 (.952)
Traditionalistic Political Culture	-3.711 (3.521)	-6.116 (3.412)	-4.787 (3.852)	1.481 (1.170)	.783 (.997)
% Labor Force that Is Professional Women	.180 (.963)	NA	NA	NA	NA
% Labor Force that is Professional White Women	NA	.477 (.628)	.418 (.574)	NA	NA
% Labor Force that is Professional Black Women	NA	NA	NA	2.023*** (.315)	NA
% Labor Force that is Professional Latinas	NA	NA	NA	NA	4.046*** (.421)
Professional Legislature	-3.686 (2.159)	-5.016* (2.179)	-4.834** (1.484)	1.731* (.818)	-.430 (.754)
Citizens' Legislature	-.520 (2.349)	.361 (1.952)	.441 (1.785)	.017 (.692)	-1.157 (.805)

(*Continued*)

Table A.3 Continued

	% All Women (1)	% White Women (2)	% White Democratic Women	% Black Women (3)	% Latina Women (4)
Party Organizational Strength	-1.185 (.851)	-1.275 (.774)	-1.038 (.854)	.327 (.304)	.430 (.270)
Multimember Districts (any type)	2.312 (2.715)	3.009 (2.199)	.078 (1.233)	-1.286 (.661)	.631 (.772)
Constant (Intercept)	29.717 (16.654)	21.564* (10.182)	14.735 (10.380)	-1.305 (1.367)	-3.060* (1.260)
No. of States	49	49	49	49	49
	$F_{(8,41)} = 9.59$***	$F_{(8,41)} = 20.44$***	$F_{(8,41)} = 15.33$***	$F_{(8,41)} = 14.40$***	$F_{(8,41)} = 20.49$***
	Pseudo R^2 = 0.0757	Pseudo R^2 = 0.1165	Pseudo R^2 = 0.1085	Pseudo R^2 = 0.2470	Pseudo R^2 = 0.3604
# left-censored observations	0 @ 0	0 @ 0	1 @ 0	15 @ 0	32 @ 0

*$p \leq .05$; **$p \leq .01$; ***$p \leq .001$ (two-tailed tests)

Joint significance of moralistic/traditional political culture:

p(All) = .1323; p(White) = .0037; p(WhiteDem) = .0160; p(Black) = .1747; p(Latina) = .4402.

Joint significance of professional/citizen legislature:

p(All) = .2436; p(White) = .0748; p(WhiteDem)= .0090; p(Black) = .0913; p(Latina) = .3265.

Table A.4 District/Seat-Level Descriptive Representation in State Houses, 2005 Democrats Only
Multinomial Logit (standard errors)

	White Woman/White Man (WM) (1)	Black Man/WM (2)	Black Woman/WM (3)	Latino/WM (4)	Latina/WM (5)
Policy Conservatism	.333 (.274)	.130 (.541)	-.134 (.637)	-.434 (.751)	-.096 (.973)
% White College Educated	.017 (.010)	-.010 (.028)	.011 (.033)	-.057 (.035)	-.015 (.046)
% Urban	.005* (.002)	.022*** (.005)	.034*** (.007)	.007 (.011)	.017 (.016)
% Black	.008 (.005)	.110*** (.009)	.118*** (.011)	.031 (.017)	.020 (.022)
% Latinx Citizens	.012 (.010)	.045** (.017)	.046* (.021)	.144*** (.014)	.152*** (.017)
Multimember District	.573*** (.136)	.307 (.353)	.238 (.410)	.684 (.429)	1.475** (.510)
Resources/Socioeconomic Status (SES) of White Women	.266 (.139)	.025 (.238)	.069 (.259)	.545 (.299)	.486 (.363)
Resources/SES of Black Men	.154 (.112)	.659 (.443)	.226 (.738)	.267 (.442)	.165 (.574)

(Continued)

Table A.4 Continued

	White Woman/White Man (WM) (1)	Black Man/WM (2)	Black Woman/WM (3)	Latino/WM (4)	Latina/WM (5)
Resources/SES of Black Women	.029	-.885*	-.464	.293	.227
	(.111)	(.450)	(.730)	(.383)	(.503)
Resources/SES of Latino Men	-.137	-.445	-.519	.506	-1.737
	(.123)	(.299)	(.347)	(.662)	(1.056)
Resources/SES of Latinas	.129	.066	.131	-.995	.488
	(.110)	(.241)	(.285)	(.603)	(.838)
Constant (Intercept)	-2.053***	-7.117***	-9.580***	-5.318***	-8.401***
	(.331)	(.846)	(1.125)	(1.377)	(2.009)

No. of seats = 2394

LR chi^2(55) = 2264.31***

Pseudo R^2 = 0.3717

*p ≤ .05; **p ≤ .01; ***p ≤ .001 (two-tailed tests)

Table A.5 Bill Content Codes

Interest Area	Groups	Policy Areas
Women-Specific Codes	All General Women Pregnant Women Mothers African American Women Latina Women Native American Women Other Women of Color (e.g., Asian American Women)	**Health:** Reproductive Health, Birth Control: *NOT including abortion* Abortion, Fetal Rights Protection: *including clinic access, emergency contraception* Sex Ed—Abstinence Only: *also available under Education Policy (IF specific to issues of birth control and/or teen pregnancy)* Sex Ed—Other: *also available under Education Policy (IF specific to issues of birth control and/or teen pregnancy)* **Civil Rights and Liberties:** Discrimination, Civil Rights: *including sexual harassment (IF it includes reference to sex/gender/women)* Affirmative action *(IF targeted groups or categories include women)* Hate crimes: *also available under Crime (IF targeted groups or categories include women)* **Family:** Child Custody: *including issues re visitation; NOT including policies re foster care, and/or guardianship* Child Support Other divorce/alimony, Marriage: *NOT including same-sex marriage* Day Care: *including child care and elder care* Family Leave Surrogacy Other family policy *(IF specific to paternity, fathers' "rights," teen pregnancy, abortion, or marriage; NOT including general issues of parental notification or liability)* **Crime:** Harassment, stalking Prostitution, Sex offenses: *NOT including sex offenses against children or trafficking in pornography or prostitution* Domestic Violence: *including shelters and other victim support services* Hate crimes: *also available under Civil Rights and Liberties (IF targeted groups or categories include women)*

(Continued)

Table A.5 Continued

Interest Area	Groups	Policy Areas
Black-Specific Codes	African American Men African American Women All, General Racial/Ethnic Minorities *(in the U.S. context; NOT including White ethnic groups)* African Americans	**Education:** Multicultural Education: *including diversity training, tolerance curricula: in schools or workplace (IF pertinent to African American/Black experience/history in the U.S. and/or issues of race, racism, slavery, etc.)* **Crime:** Harassment, stalking *(IF specific to race or African Americans)* Profiling: *also available under Civil Rights and Liberties (IF pertinent to race/color or African Americans)* Hate crimes: *also available under Civil Rights and Liberties (IF targeted groups or protected categories include African Americans or race/color)* **Civil Rights and Liberties:** Profiling: *also available under Crime (IF pertinent to race/color or African Americans)* Discrimination, Civil Rights *(IF targeted groups or protected categories include African Americans or race/color)* Affirmative action *(IF targeted groups or protected categories include African Americans or race/color)* Hate crimes: *also available under Civil Rights and Liberties (IF targeted groups or protected categories include African Americans or race/color)*
Latinx-Specific Codes	Latino Men Latina Women All, General Racial/Ethnic Minorities *(in the US context; NOT including White ethnic groups)* Latinos	**Education:** Bilingual Education: *including English as a second language (ESL) or limited English proficient (LEP) instruction; for adults and/or children; NOT including foreign language instruction or promotion; NOT including sign language or any measure specific to a language other than Spanish or Portuguese* Multicultural Education: *including diversity training, tolerance curricula; in schools or workplace (IF pertinent to Latinx/Hispanic experience in the United States and/or issues of ethnicity, immigration, migration, etc.)*

Crime:

Harassment, stalking (IF specific to ethnicity/national origin/color, immigration/citizenship status, or Latinxs/Hispanics)

Profiling: also available under Civil Rights and Liberties (IF pertinent to ethnicity/national origin/color, immigration/citizenship status, or Latinxs/Hispanics)

Hate crimes: also available under Civil Rights and Liberties (IF targeted groups or protected categories include Latinxs/Hispanics or ethnicity/national origin/color, immigration/citizenship status)

Civil Rights and Liberties:

Profiling: also available under Crime (IF pertinent to ethnicity/national origin/color, immigration/citizenship status, or Latinxs/Hispanics)

Discrimination, Civil Rights (IF targeted groups or protected categories include Latinxs/Hispanics or ethnicity/national origin/color, immigration/citizenship status)

Affirmative action (IF targeted groups or protected categories include Latinxs/Hispanics or ethnicity/national origin/color, immigration/citizenship status)

Hate crimes: also available under Civil Rights and Liberties (IF targeted groups or protected categories include Latinxs/Hispanics or ethnicity/national origin/color, immigration/citizenship status)

Campaigns, Voting, Elections:

Voter Disenfranchisement: for felony convictions ONLY

Other election or vote fraud measures: voter identification requirements ONLY Redistricting

Immigration, Military, Foreign Affairs:

Immigration: including border control and deportation, employment of undocumented workers, government or public goods and services (e.g., drivers' licenses, rental property) tied to immigration status; NOT including measures specific to non-Latinx/Hispanic groups or countries/regions (e.g., Armenian refugees)

Migrant labor regulations: NOT including measures specific to non-Latinx/Hispanic groups or countries/regions

Other legal immigrant labor regulations: NOT including measures specific to non-Latinx/Hispanic groups or countries/regions

Language politics, English only laws: including bilingual government services/materials, other than bilingual education; NOT including measures specific to non-Latinx/Hispanic groups or countries/regions, or languages other than Spanish or Portuguese

Border relations, trade: IF specific to the US/Mexican border; NOT including general issues re international trade or trade with Mexico, Central or South America

(Continued)

Table A.5 Continued

Interest Area	Groups	Policy Areas
Health Codes		**Health:**
		Mental Health
		Sex Ed—Abstinence Only (also available under Education Policy)
		Sex Ed—Other (also available under Education Policy)
		Reproductive Health, Birth Control: NOT including abortion
		HIV and AIDS
		Occupational Health and Safety
		Disaster Relief: specific to health and public safety; including preparedness measures, emergency procedures, evacuation, shelters, search and rescue
		Drug or alcohol treatment, prevention: including educational efforts (also available under Crime)
		Biomedical ethics, euthanasia, cloning, genetic screening
		Other, General Health: public health and safety; restrictions on smoking in public places; in-home support services; nursing homes; long-term care; general health care reform; medical liability; health promotion and prevention
Education Codes		**Education:**
		Pre-K thru 12, Administration and Management: issues re educational infrastructure (e.g., facilities maintenance, school finance, teacher salary/benefits) or the safety of children and staff at/in schools
		Pre-K thru 12, Curriculum and Programs: issues re the quality and/or equity of education or instruction, including teacher credentials and training
		Higher Ed, Administration and Management: colleges, universities, and vocational schools; including general budget and expenditures, facilities maintenance (including student housing); student loans, financial aid

| Welfare/Poverty Codes | Poor Individuals, Economically Disadvantaged | Higher Ed, Curriculum and Programs: *colleges, universities, and vocational schools; including faculty hiring and promotion, research support/infrastructure* |

Higher Ed, Curriculum and Programs: *colleges, universities, and vocational schools; including faculty hiring and promotion, research support/infrastructure*
Adult literacy
Sex Ed—Abstinence Only *(also available under Health Policy)*
Sex Ed—Other *(also available under Health Policy)*
Bilingual Education: *including ESL instruction; for adults and/or children; NOT including foreign language instruction or promotion*
Multicultural Education: *including diversity training, tolerance curricula; in schools or workplace*
Workforce Training
Other Education: *including anything not related to administration/management or curriculum/programs (in Pre-K thru 12, or Higher Ed)*

Social Welfare Policy:
Homeless: *including restrictions on panhandling; provision, regulation of shelters*
Low-income Housing: *provision and regulation*
Welfare reform: *including "workfare" or work/job training requirements; family caps; time limitations; paternity identification; etc.*
Other, general poverty policy: *aid for the economically disadvantaged; means-tested programs; income support, food subsidies, etc.*

Table A.6 Keyword Search Terms by Interest/Issue Type

Women-Specific	Black/Latinx-Specific	Health	Education	Welfare/Poverty
Abort!	Affirmative action! OR historically OR HBCU	((health AND care) OR healthcare OR health care) OR medic! OR public health OR (health! servic!)	Education	AFDC OR TANF
Abuse AND NOT drug! AND NOT elder!	Afric! OR afro! OR sickle	Anatom! OR (organ AND don!)	Curricul! AND NOT Education	Assistance
Alimony	Black OR negro OR color!	Belt! OR restraint! OR headgear OR helmet!	Teach! OR Faculty OR Tutor! AND NOT Education	At-risk
Birth!	Church AND arson	Birth! AND NOT (marriage OR abortion)	School! OR Colleg! OR University OR Learning AND NOT Education	Beg OR begg!
Breast	(citizen! OR noncitizen) AND NOT senior!	Cancer! OR breast OR mammogra! OR pap smear OR colon! OR prostate	Student! AND NOT Education	Communit! AND invest!
Character!	Confeder! OR civil war	Chiroprac!	Literacy AND NOT Education	Earned income
Child AND care	Cultur! OR intercultur! OR bi-national	Contracep! OR reproduc! OR in vitro OR infertility	Training OR Workforce OR Vocational OR Job skills AND NOT Education	Econ! AND disadvantage!
Child AND custody	Deport! OR border	Department of health OR health! department!	Librar! OR Books OR Bookmobile	Econ! AND distress
Child care OR childcare	Discriminat! OR antidiscrimin!	Disaster! OR Red Cross OR (emergenc! AND NOT declare! PRE/ 2 emergency)		Electronic AND benefit!
Child support	Dispar! OR equitable OR equal! OR disadvan!	Doctor! OR physician! OR nurs! OR midwi! AND NOT (veterinar! OR nurser! OR doctoral)		Food AND aid

Table A.6 Continued

Women-Specific	Black/Latinx-Specific	Health	Education	Welfare/Poverty
Civil right!	Divers! OR tolerance OR civil right!	Earthquake! OR flood! OR (fire! AND NOT firearm!) OR 911 OR 9-1-1 OR school bus!		Food AND program
Contracept!	English OR language	Euthanasia OR suicide AND NOT veterinar!		Food stamp!
Custodia!	Environmental justice	First responder! OR paramedic! OR EMT! OR ambulance!		(Group OR transit!) AND hous!
Day care OR daycare	ESL OR bilingual OR multilingual	Food AND contam! AND NOT (lead OR toxic OR sanita! OR disease!)		Hardship
Dependent! AND care	Farmwork! OR agricult! Worker!	Genetic!		Head OR healthy AND start
Discrimin!	Farm labor!	Geriatric		Healthcare access
Divers!	(felon! OR convict!) AND vot!	Handicap! OR disabled		Homeless! OR panhandl!
Divorce!	Haras! OR bully!	Health! AND access		Housing authority
Domestic violence	Hate OR prejudice	Health! AND counsel!		Human AND service! AND fraud!
Domestic worker!	Immigra!	Health! AND insurance		Income AND eligib!
Early child!	Latin! OR Hispanic OR mexic!	Health! AND reform!		Income-based
Family	Minorit! OR profil!	Health! AND research		Job AND development
Fertilit!	Multicult! OR ethnic!	Health! AND (warning! OR advisor!)		Job AND train!

(Continued)

Table A.6 Continued

Women-Specific	Black/Latinx-Specific	Health	Education	Welfare/Poverty
Fetal OR fetus	Nationality OR country of origin	HIV OR immun!		Legal service!
Gender!	Police AND misconduct	Hospital! OR clinic! OR treatment facilit! OR (health PRE/3 facility)		Low! AND income!
Genital!	Police AND performance	Injur! OR ill OR illn! OR sick OR disease!		Medicaid
Guardian!	Redistricting AND federal	(mental! AND health! AND NOT child!) OR (mental! AND ill!) OR behavioral health		Minimum AND wage
Harass!	Relig! AND fire	Mosquito!		Personal responsibilit!
Head start	Slave! OR middle passage	Nutrition		Pover! OR needy OR need-based
Marriage AND NOT same sex	Undocumented OR migrant OR alien	OSHA OR worker! compensation OR (occupational PRE/4 (health OR care))		Public AND housing
Matern!	Voting right!	Pharm!		Public defen!
Midwi!		(pool! AND NOT wage! AND NOT Poole) OR flotation device		Section 8 OR evict!
Minor! AND consent		Sanita!		Self AND sufficien!
Mother!		Sex! ed! OR abstinence OR (health PRE/3 education)		Underserv!
Obstet!		Smok! OR tobacco OR indoor air		Unemploy!
Ovar!		Steriliz!		Welfare AND benefit
Parent!		Substance OR drug AND abus!		Welfare AND recipient!

Table A.6 Continued

Women-Specific	Black/Latinx-Specific	Health	Education	Welfare/Poverty
Patern!		Tattoo! OR pierc!		Welfare AND reform!
Perinatal OR prenatal OR neonatal		Therap!		WIC
Pregnan!		Toxic! OR noxious OR nuclear OR poison! OR pesticide OR (lead AND paint!) AND NOT (noxious weeds OR energy facilities)		Women AND infant! AND child!
Prostitut!		Wellness		Work! AND development
Public indecency				Cost containment (AZ only)
Rape AND drug!				Calworks (CA only)
Reproduct!				In-home supportive (CA only)
Sex!				Medi-cal (CA only)
Stalk!				Community contribution tax credit
Stay-at-home				Transportation disadvan! (FL only)
Surrog!				WAGES (FL only)
Unborn				Charity care (NJ only)
Wom*n				Family care (NJ only)
				PAAD (NJ only)
				Work first (NJ only)

(Continued)

Table A.6 Continued

Women-Specific	Black/Latinx-Specific	Health	Education	Welfare/Poverty
				YES (NM only)
				Family independence (SC only)
				Families first (TN only)
				Colonias (TX only)
				System benefit fund (TX only)
				Workforce AND investment (TX only)

Table A.7 Average Keyword Capture Rate by Interest/Issue Type

Interest/Issue Type	Average Capture Rate
Black & Latinx	91%
Education	99%
Health	97%
Welfare/Poverty	88%
Women	91%

Table A.8 Average Intercoder Reliability Rates by Interest/Issue Type

Interest/Issue Type	Average Agreement Rate
Black	97%
Education	88%
Health	89%
Latinx	97%
Welfare/Poverty	96%
Women	95%

Table A.9a Descriptive Statistics (Chapters 3–4)

Democrats	N	Mean	St. Dev.	Min	Max
White Men	1,450	.47	.50	0	1
White Women	1,450	.18	.38	0	1
Black Men	1,450	.16	.37	0	1
Black Women	1,450	.07	.26	0	1
Latinos	1,450	.09	.28	0	1
Latinas	1,450	.03	.18	0	1
Blacks in District	1,453	22.67	24.23	0	91.2
Latinx in District	1,453	15.71	22.35	0	95
Average Income in District (in 1000s)	1,453	43.51	18.92	16.61	162.50
Democratic Vote-share in District	1,453	77.32	19.21	0	100
Legislator Seniority	1,453	8.03	7.14	0	39
Chair of Women-Spec Committee	1,453	.04	.19	0	1
Chair of Black-Spec Committee	1,453	.04	.19	0	1
Chair of Latinx-Spec Committee	1,453	.04	.20	0	1
Chair of Health or Educ Committee	1,453	.05	.22	0	1
Bills Introduced (logged)	1,453	2.64	1.08	0	6.14

Table A.9b Descriptive Statistics (Chapters 3–4)

Republicans	N	Mean	St. Dev.	Min	Max
White Men	1,486	.80	.40	0	1
White Women	1,486	.17	.38	0	1
Black Men	1,486	.001	.026	0	1
Black Women	1,486	.002	.045	0	1
Latinos	1,486	.019	.136	0	1
Latinas	1,486	.005	.073	0	1
Blacks in District	1,486	6.46	7.57	0	53
Latinx in District	1,486	8.83	13.06	0	86
Average Income in District (in 1000s)	1,486	53.25	20.97	20.61	150.59
Democratic Vote-share in District	1,486	24.82	19.87	0	100
Legislator Seniority	1,486	6.01	5.12	1	37
Chair of Women-Spec Committee	1,486	.03	.18	0	1
Chair of Black-Spec Committee	1,486	.03	.18	0	1
Chair of Latinx-Spec Committee	1,486	.03	.18	0	1
Chair of Health or Educ Committee	1,486	.06	.23	0	1
Bills Introduced (logged)	1,486	2.50	1.00	0	5.06

Table A.10a Dependent Variables—State Welfare Policy, 1998

Variable	Descriptive Statistics (Mean/St. Dev./Range)	Source
Replicated Eligibility Index	0.53/0.12/0.22-0.71	Welfare Rules Database, http://anfdata. urban.org/wrd/WRDWelcome.cfm
Fellowes & Rowe's Flexibility Index	7/2.77/1-12	Fellowes, Matthew C., and Gretchen Rowe. 2004. "Politics and the New American Welfare State." *American Journal of Political Science* 48(2): 362–73.
Family Cap	0.58/0.50/0-1	Welfare Rules Database, http://anfdata. urban.org/wrd/WRDWelcome.cfm
Domestic Violence Time Limit Waivers	0.61/0.49/0-1	Welfare Rules Database, http://anfdata. urban.org/wrd/WRDWelcome.cfm
Cash Benefits (adjusted for annual state-level cost of living)	515.24/180.19/ 178.17-1208.15	University of Kentucky Center for Poverty Research, http://www.ukcpr. org/AvailableData.aspx; Berry, William D., Richard C. Fording, Russell L. Hanson. 2000. "An Annual Cost of Living Index for the American States, 1960–1995." *Journal of Politics* 62(2): 550–67.

Table A.10b Independent Variables—Determinants of State Welfare Policy, 1997

Variable	Description	Descriptive Statistics (Mean/St. Dev./Range)	Sources
Descriptive Representation— Women (all)	Percentage of total legislative seats held by group members	21.72/8.14/4.29-42.86	Original coding by authors. Center for American Women and Politics, Eagleton Institute of Politics, Rutgers University Joint Center for Political and Economic Studies, *Black Elected Officials Roster* (1997) National Association of Latino Elected and Appointed Officials (NALEO), *National Roster of Hispanic Elected Officials* (1997) *State Yellow Book* (1997 Spring edition) Council of State Governments' *State Leadership Directory* (1997)
Specific Institutional Incorporation— Women (all) (see Preuhs 2006)	Percentage of Social/Human Services committees chaired by group members	32.41/30.14/0-100	
General Institutional Incorporation— Women (all) (see Preuhs 2006)	See description on pages 4–5 of Reingold and Smith (2012) Supporting Information	15.18/9.22/0-38.91	
Legislative Incorporation Factor Score—Women (all)	Factor analysis of group descriptive representation, specific institutional incorporation, and general institutional incorporation	-0.10/1.06/-2.16-2.50	

Table A.10b Continued

Variable	Description	Descriptive Statistics (Mean/St. Dev./Range)	Sources
Descriptive Representation—African Americans (all)	See description for women above	6.94/6.99/0-25.29	
Specific Institutional Incorporation—African Americans (all)		9.05/16.90/0-50	
General Institutional Incorporation—African Americans (all)		4.68/5.96/0-24.43	
Legislative Incorporation Factor Score—African Americans (all)		-0.04/0.90/-0.84-2.34	
Descriptive Representation—Latinxs (all)	See description for women above	2.77/6.39/0-35.71	
Specific Institutional Incorporation—Latinxs (all)		3.67/12.72/0-50	
General Institutional Incorporation—Latinxs (all)		2.81/9.63/0-58.63	
Legislative Incorporation Factor Score—Latinxs (all)		-0.03/1.00/-0.41-5.09	
Descriptive Representation—White Women	See description for women above	18.96/8.68/0.71-41.27	
Specific Institutional Incorporation—White Women		27.97/29.48/0-100	
General Institutional Incorporation—White Women		13.52/9.40/0-38.91	
Legislative Incorporation Factor Score—White Women		-0.05/1.10/-1.95-2.60	

(Continued)

Table A.10b Continued

Variable	Description	Descriptive Statistics (Mean/St. Dev./Range)	Sources
Descriptive Representation—Women of Color	See description for women above	2.81/2.64/0-9.82	
Specific Institutional Incorporation—Women of Color		4.43/12.70/0-50	
General Institutional Incorporation—Women of Color		1.66/2.86/0-12.95	
Legislative Incorporation Factor Score—Women of Color		-0.13/0.86/-0.84-3.09	
Descriptive Representation—Men of Color	See description for women above	6.85/6.89/0-27.68	
Specific Institutional Incorporation—Men of Color		8.28/16.46/0-50	
General Institutional Incorporation—Men of Color		5.87/9.17/0-52.76	
Legislative Incorporation Factor Score—Men of Color		-0.02/1.02/-0.89-4.03	

Table A.10c Control Variables—Modeling State Welfare Policy, 1997

Variable	Description (if necessary)	Descriptive Statistics (Mean/St. Dev./Range)	Source
Percentage Black and Latinx Population	Percentage black population plus percentage Latinx population	16.62/11.78/1.17-42.53	US Census Bureau, "Estimates of the Population by Race and Hispanic or Latino Origin for the United States and States." http://www.census.gov/popest/archives/.
Citizen Ideology		46.40/15.35/13.72-86.19	Berry, William D., Evan J. Ringquist, Richard C. Fording, and Russell L. Hanson. 1998. "Measuring Citizen and Government Ideology in the American States, 1960–93." Revised 1960–2006 citizen and government ideology series. *American Journal of Political Science*, 42(1) (Jan.): 327–48.
Democratic Control of Legislature	Party control of state legislature; 0 = Republican control; 0.5 = one chamber split, other Republican; 1 = split control; 1.5 = one chamber split, other Democratic; 2 = unified Democratic control	1.05/0.89/0-2	Klarner, Carl. 2003. "The Measurement of the Partisan Balance of State Government." *State Politics & Policy Quarterly* 3(3): 309–19.
Unemployment Rate		4.65/1.08/2.4-7.1	University of Kentucky Center for Poverty Research, http://www.ukcpr.org/AvailableData.aspx.

(Continued)

Table A.10c Continued

Variable	Description (if necessary)	Descriptive Statistics (Mean/St. Dev./Range)	Source
Unmarried Birth Rate		31.28/5.42/16.59-45.41	US Department of Health and Human Services, Centers for Disease Control, National Vital Statistics System. "Demographic Characteristics of Mothers by State/County" (1996–2006). http://www.cdc.gov/nchs/nvss.htm.
Percentage High School Graduates		83.13/4.36/74.7-92.1	US Census Bureau, Table 13: Educational Attainment of the Population 25 Years and Over, by State (1996–2006). http://www.census.gov/population/www/socdemo/educ-attn.html.
Moralistic Political Culture		0.34/0.48/0-1	Elazar, Daniel J. 1984. *American Federalism: A View from the States.* 3rd ed. New York: Harper & Row.

References

Abramovitz, Mimi. 1996. *Regulating the Lives of Women: Social Welfare Policy from Colonial Times to the Present*. Rev. ed. Boston: South End Press.

Allard, Patricia. 2006. "Crime, Punishment, and Economic Violence." In *Color of Violence: The INCITE! Anthology*, ed. INCITE! Women of Color Against Violence. Cambridge, MA: South End.

Alexander-Floyd, Nikol. 2012. "Disappearing Acts: Reclaiming Intersectionality in the Social Sciences in a Post-Black Feminist Era." *Feminist Formations* 24(1): 1–25.

Anzaldúa, Gloria. 1987. *Borderlands/La Frontera: The New Mestiza*. San Francisco: Spinsters/Aunt Lute Books.

Arceneaux, Kevin. 2001. "The 'Gender Gap' in State Legislative Representation: New Data to Tackle an Old Question." *Political Research Quarterly* 54(1): 143–60.

Atkeson, Lonna Rae. 2003. "Not All Cues Are Created Equal: The Conditional Impact of Female Candidates on Political Engagement." *Journal of Politics* 65(4): 1040–61.

Atkeson, Lonna Rae, and Nancy Carillo. 2007. "More Is Better: The Influence of Collective Female Descriptive Representation on External Efficacy." *Politics & Gender* 3(1): 79–101.

Avery, James M., and Mark Peffley. 2005. "Voter Registration Requirements, Voter Turnout, and Welfare Eligibility Policy: Class Bias Matters." *State Politics & Policy Quarterly* 5(1): 47–67.

Baca Zinn, Maxine, and Bonnie Thornton Dill. 1996. "Theorizing Difference from Multiracial Feminism." *Feminist Studies* 22: 321–31.

Baca Zinn, Maxine, and Ruth Enid Zambrana. 2019. "Chicana/Latinas Advance Intersectional Thought and Practice." *Gender & Society* 33(5): 677–701.

Bachrach, Peter, and Morton Baratz. 1963. "Decisions and Nondecisions: An Analytical Framework." *American Political Science Review* 57(3): 632–42.

Baker, Andy, and Corey Cook. 2005. "Representing Black Interests and Promoting Black Culture: The Importance of African American Descriptive Representation in the U.S. House." *DuBois Review* 2(2): 227–46.

Barone, Michael, William Lilley III, and Laurence J. DeFranco. 1998. *State Legislative Elections: Voting Patterns and Demographics*. Washington, DC: CQ Press.

Barrett, Edith J. 1995. "The Policy Priorities of African American Women in State Legislatures." *Legislative Studies Quarterly* 20: 223–47.

Barreto, Matt A. 2010. *Ethnic Cues: The Role of Shared Ethnicity in Latino Political Participation*. Ann Arbor: University of Michigan Press.

Barreto, Matt A., Gary M. Segura, and Nathan D. Woods. 2004. "The Mobilizing Effect of Majority-Minority Districts on Latino Turnout." *American Political Science Review* 98(1): 65–75.

Baumgartner, Frank R., Derek A. Epp, Kelsey Shoub, and Bayard Love. 2018. *Suspect Citizens: What 20 Million Traffic Stops Tell Us About Policing and Race*. New York: Cambridge University Press.

Baumgartner, Frank R., Derek A. Epp, Kelsey Shoub, and Bayard Love. 2017. "Targeting Young Men of Color for Search and Arrest During Traffic Stops: Evidence from North Carolina, 2002–2013." *Politics, Groups, and Identities* 5(1): 107–31.

Baumgartner, Frank, and Bryan D. Jones. 1993. *Agendas and Instability in American Politics*. Chicago: University of Chicago Press.

Battle, Brittany Pearl. 2018. "Deservingness, Deadbeat Dads, and Responsible Fatherhood: Child Support Policy and Rhetorical Conceptualizations of Poverty, Welfare, and the Family." *Symbolic Interaction* 41(4): 443–64.

Beale, Frances. 1970. "To Be Black and Female." In *The Black Woman: An Anthology*, ed. Toni Cade. New York: New American Library.

Beckwith, Karen, and Kimberly Cowell-Meyers. 2007. "Sheer Numbers: Critical Representation Thresholds and Women's Political Representation." *Perspectives on Politics* 5(3): 553–65.

Bejarano, Christina E. 2013. *The Latina Advantage*. Austin: University of Texas Press.

Berkman, Michael B., and Robert E. O'Connor. 1993. "Do Women Legislators Matter?" *American Politics Research* 21(1): 102–24.

Berry, William D., Richard C. Fording, and Russell L. Hanson. 2000. "An Annual Cost of Living Index for the American States, 1960–1995." *Journal of Politics* 62(2): 550–67.

Berry, William D., Evan J. Ringquist, Richard C. Fording, and Russell L. Hanson. 1998. "Measuring Citizen and Government Ideology in the American States, 1960–93." *American Journal of Political Science* 42(1): 327–48.

Bledsoe, Timothy, and Mary Herring. 1990. "Victims of Circumstances: Women in Pursuit of Political Office." *American Political Science Review* 84(1): 213–23.

Bobo, Lawrence, and Franklin D. Gilliam Jr. 1990. "Race, Sociopolitical Participation and Black Empowerment." *American Political Science Review* 84(2): 377–93.

Bolsen, Toby, and Judd R. Thornton. 2014. "Overlapping Confidence Intervals and Null Hypothesis Testing." *The Experimental Political Scientist* 4(1): 12–16.

Bowers, Melanie, and Robert R. Preuhs. 2009. "Collateral Consequences of a Collateral Penalty: The Negative Effect of Felon Disenfranchisement Laws on Political Participation of Nonfelons." *Social Science Quarterly* 90(3): 722–43.

Bowleg, Lisa. 2008. "When Black + Lesbian + Woman ≠ Black Lesbian Woman: The Methodological Challenges of Qualitative and Quantitative Intersectionality Research." *Sex Roles* 59: 312–25.

Bowleg, Lisa, and Greta Bauer. 2016. "Invited Reflection: Quantifying Intersectionality." *Psychology of Women Quarterly* 40(3): 337–41.

Bramlett, Matthew D., Laura F. Radel, and Kirby Chow. 2017. "Health and Well-Being of Children in Kinship Care: Findings from the National Survey of Children in Nonparental Care." *Child Welfare* 95(3): 41–60.

Bratton, Kathleen A. 2002. "The Effect of Legislative Diversity on Agenda Setting: Evidence from Six State Legislatures." *American Politics Research* 30: 115–42.

Bratton, Kathleen A. 2005. "Critical Mass Theory Revisited: The Behavior and Success of Token Women in State Legislatures." *Politics & Gender* 1(1): 97–125.

Bratton, Kathleen A. 2006. "The Behavior and Success of Latino Legislators: Evidence from the States." *Social Science Quarterly* 87(5): 1136–57.

Bratton, Kathleen A., and Kerry L. Haynie. 1999. "Agenda Setting and Legislative Success in State Legislatures: The Effects of Gender and Race." *Journal of Politics* 61(3): 658–79.

Bratton, Kathleen A., Kerry L. Haynie, and Beth Reingold. 2006. "Agenda Setting and African American Women in State Legislatures." *Journal of Women, Politics & Policy* 28: 71–96.

Broockman, David E. 2013. "Black Politicians Are More Intrinsically Motivated to Advance Blacks' Interests: A Field Experiment Manipulating Political Incentives." *American Journal of Political Science 57*(3): 521–36.

Brown, Nadia E. 2014a. "Black Women's Pathways to the Statehouse: The Impact of Race/ Gender Identities." In *Black Women in Politics: Identity, Power, and Justice in the New Millennium*, ed. Michael Mitchell and David Covin. New Brunswick: Transaction.

Brown, Nadia E. 2014b. *Sisters in the Statehouse: Black Women and Legislative Decision Making*. New York: Oxford University Press.

Brown, Nadia, and Kira Hudson Banks. 2014. "Black Women's Agenda Setting in the Maryland State Legislature." *Journal of African American Studies 18*: 164–80.

Brown, Nadia E., and Sarah Allen Gershon. 2016. "Intersectional Presentations: An Exploratory Study of Minority Congresswomen's Websites' Biographies." *Du Bois Review 13*(1): 85–108.

Browning, Rufus P., Dale Rogers Marshall, and David H. Tabb. 1984. *Protest Is Not Enough: The Struggle of Blacks and Hispanics for Equality in Urban Politics*. Berkeley: University of California Press.

Bryce, Herrington J., and Alan E. Warrick. 1977. "Black Women in Electoral Politics." In *A Portrait of Marginality: The Political Behavior of the American Woman*, ed. Marianne Githens and Jewel L. Prestage. New York: Longman.

Bühlmann, Marc, Wolfgang Merkel, Lisa Müller, and Bernhard Weßels. 2012. "The Democracy Barometer: A New Instrument to Measure the Quality of Democracy and Its Potential for Comparative Research." *European Political Science 11*(4): 519–36.

Burch, Traci. 2013. *Trading Democracy for Justice*. Chicago: University of Chicago Press.

Burns, Nancy, Kay Lehman Schlozman, and Sidney Verba. 2001. *The Private Roots of Public Action: Gender, Equality, and Political Participation*. Cambridge, MA: Harvard University Press.

Camobreco, John F., and Michelle A. Barnello. 2003. "Postmaterialism and Post-Industrialism: Cultural Influences on Female Representation in State Legislatures." *State Politics & Policy Quarterly 3*(2): 117–38.

Campbell, David, and Christina Wolbrecht. 2006. "See Jane Run: Women Politicians as Role Models for Adolescents." *Journal of Politics 68*(2): 233–47.

Canon, David T. 1999. *Race, Redistricting, and Representation: The Unintended Consequences of Black Majority Districts*. Chicago: University of Chicago Press.

Carbado, Devon W., Kimberlé Williams Crenshaw, Vickie M. Mays, and Barbara Tomlinson. 2013. "Intersectionality: Mapping the Movements of a Theory." *Du Bois Review 10*(2): 303–12.

Carey, John M., Richard G. Niemi, Lynda W. Powell, and Gary F. Moncrief. 2006. "The Effects of Term Limits on State Legislatures: A New Survey of the 50 States." *Legislative Studies Quarterly 31*(1): 105–34.

Carroll, Susan J. 2002. "Representing Women: Congresswomen's Perceptions of Their Representational Roles." In *Women Transforming Congress*, ed. Cindy Simon Rosenthal. Norman: University of Oklahoma Press.

Carroll, Susan J. 2008. "Committee Assignments and Policy Impact." In *Legislating Women: Getting Elected, Getting Ahead*, ed. Beth Reingold. Boulder, CO: Lynne Rienner.

Carroll, Susan J., and Krista Jenkins. 2001a. "Do Term Limits Help Women Get Elected?" *Social Science Quarterly* 82(1): 197–201.

Carroll, Susan J., and Krista Jenkins. 2001b. "Increasing Diversity or More of the Same? Term Limits and the Representation of Women, Minorities, and Minority Women in State Legislatures." Paper presented at the Annual Meeting of the American Political Science Association, San Francisco.

Carroll, Susan J., and Kira Sanbonmatsu. 2013. *More Women Can Run: Gender and Pathways to the State Legislatures.* New York: Oxford University Press.

Casellas, Jason P. 2009. "Coalitions in the House?" *Political Research Quarterly* 62: 120–31.

Casellas, Jason P. 2011. *Latino Representation in State Houses and Congress.* New York: Cambridge University Press.

Center for American Women and Politics (CAWP). 1996. "Women in State Legislatures 1996." National Information Bank on Women in Public Office, Eagleton Institute of Politics, Rutgers University.

Center for American Women and Politics (CAWP). 1997. "The Gender Gap: Attitudes on Public Policy Issues." National Information Bank on Women in Public Office, Eagleton Institute of Politics, Rutgers University.

Chaney, Carole K., R. Michael Alvarez, and Jonathan Nagler. 1998. "Explaining the Gender Gap in U.S. Presidential Elections, 1980–1992." *Political Research Quarterly* 51(2): 311–40.

Childs, Sarah, and Mona Lena Krook. 2006. "Should Feminists Give Up on Critical Mass? A Contingent Yes." *Politics & Gender* 2(4): 522–30.

Cho, Sumi, Kimberlé W. Crenshaw, and Leslie McCall. 2013. "Toward a Field of Intersectionality Studies: Theory, Applications, and Praxis." *Signs* 38(4): 785–810.

Clark, Cal, and Janet Clark. 2006. "The Gender Gap in the Early 21st Century: Volatility from Security Concerns." In *Women in Politics: Outsiders or Insiders?* 4th ed., ed. Lois Duke Whitaker. Upper Saddle River, NJ: Prentice Hall, 45–64.

Cobb, Roger W., and Charles D. Elder. 1983. *Participation in American Politics: The Dynamics of Agenda Building.* 2nd ed. Baltimore: Johns Hopkins University Press.

Cohen, Cathy J. 1999. *The Boundaries of Blackness: AIDS and the Breakdown of Black Politics.* Chicago: University of Chicago Press.

Cohen, Cathy J. 2003. "A Portrait of Continuing Marginality: Studying Women of Color in American Politics." In *Women and American Politics: New Questions, New Directions,* ed. Susan J. Carroll. New York: Oxford University Press, 190–213.

Cole, Elizabeth R. 2009. "Intersectionality and Research in Psychology." *American Psychologist* 64(3): 170–80.

Collins, Patricia Hill. 2000. *Black Feminist Thought: Knowledge, Consciousness, and the Politics of Empowerment.* 2nd ed. New York: Routledge.

Cooper, Anna Julia. 1892. *A Voice from the South by a Black Woman from the South.* Xenia, OH: Aldine.

Cornell, Stephen, and Douglas Hartmann. 2004. "Conceptual Confusions and Divides: Race, Ethnicity, and the Study of Immigration." In *Not Just Black and White,* ed. Nancy Foner and George Fredrickson. New York: Russell Sage Foundation.

Cotter, Cornelius P., James L. Gibson, John F. Bibby, and Robert J. Huckshorn. 1984. *Party Organization in American Politics.* New York: Praeger.

Cowell-Meyers, Kimberly, and Laura Langbein. 2009. "Linking Women's Descriptive and Substantive Representation in the United States." *Politics & Gender* 5(4): 491–518.

Crenshaw, Kimberlé. 1989. "Demarginalizing the Intersection of Race and Sex: A Black Feminist Critique of Antidiscrimination Doctrine, Feminist Theory, and Antiracist Politics." *University of Chicago Legal Forum 139*: 139–67.

Crenshaw, Kimberlé. 1991. "Mapping the Margins: Intersectionality, Identity Politics, and Violence Against Women of Color." *Stanford Law Review 43*: 1241–99.

Crowder-Meyer, Melody. 2013. "Gendered Recruitment Without Trying: How Local Party Recruiters Affect Women's Representation." *Politics & Gender 9*(4): 608–30.

Crowley, Jocelyn Elise. 2004. "When Tokens Matter." *Legislative Studies Quarterly 29*(1): 109–36.

Crowley, Jocelyn Elise. 2008. *Defiant Dads: Fathers' Rights Activists in America*. Ithaca, NY: Cornell University Press.

Crowley, Jocelyn Elise. 2009. "Fathers' Rights Groups, Domestic Violence, and Political Countermobilization." *Social Forces 88*(2): 723–56.

Darcy, R., and Charles D. Hadley. 1988. "Black Women in Politics: The Puzzle of Success." *Social Science Quarterly 69*: 629–45.

Darcy, R., Charles D. Hadley, and Jason F. Kirksey. 1997. "Election Systems and the Representation of Black Women in American State Legislatures." In *Women Transforming Politics: An Alternative Reader*, ed. Cathy J. Cohen, Kathleen B. Jones, and Joan C. Tronto. New York: New York University Press.

Darcy, R., Susan Welch, and Janet Clark. 1994. *Women, Elections, and Representation*. 2nd ed. Lincoln: University of Nebraska Press.

Darling, Marsha J. 1998. "African-American Women in State Elective Office in the South." In *Women and Elective Office: Past, Present, and Future*, ed. Sue Thomas and Clyde Wilcox. New York: Oxford University Press.

Davidson, Chandler, and Bernard Grofman, eds. 1994. *Quiet Revolution in the South: The Impact of the Voting Rights Act, 1965–1990*. Princeton, NJ: Princeton University Press.

Davies, Jill. 1997. "The New Welfare Law: State Implementation and Use of the Family Violence Option." National Resource Center on Domestic Violence and the National Network to End Domestic Violence. http://new.vawnet.org/category/index_pages.php?category_id=190. Accessed 20 May 2010.

Davis, Kathy. 2008. "Intersectionality as Buzzword: A Sociology of Science Perspective on What Makes a Feminist Theory Successful." *Feminist Theory 9*(1): 67–85.

Dill, Bonnie Thornton, and Ruth Enid Zambrana, eds. 2009. *Emerging Intersections: Race, Class, and Gender in Theory, Policy, and Practice*. New Brunswick, NJ: Rutgers University Press.

Dinner, Deborah. 2016. "The Divorce Bargain: The Fathers' Rights Movement and Family Inequality." *Virginia Law Review 102*(1): 79–152.

Dittmar, Kelly, Kira Sanbonmatsu, Susan J. Carroll, and Catherine Wineinger. 2017. *Representation Matters: Women in the U.S. Congress*. New Brunswick, NJ: Center for American Women and Politics, Eagleton Institute of Politics, Rutgers University.

Dittmar, Kelly. 2019. *Unfinished Business: Women Running in 2018 and Beyond*. New Brunswick, NJ: Center for American Women and Politics, Eagleton Institute of Politics, Rutgers University.

Dodson, Debra L. 1998. "Representing Women's Interests in the U.S. House of Representatives." In *Women and Elective Office: Past, Present, and Future*, ed. Sue Thomas and Clyde Wilcox. New York: Oxford University Press.

Dodson, Debra L. 2006. *The Impact of Women in Congress*. New York: Oxford University Press.

Dodson, Debra L., and Susan J. Carroll. 1991. *Reshaping the Agenda: Women in State Legislatures*. New Brunswick, NJ: Center for the American Woman and Politics.

Doherty, David, Conor M. Dowling, and Michael G. Miller. 2019. "Do Local Party Chairs Think Women and Minority Candidates Can Win? Evidence from a Conjoint Experiment." *Journal of Politics 81*(4): 1282–97.

Dolan, Julie, and Jonathan S. Kropf. 2004. "Credit Claiming from the U.S. House: Gendered Communication Styles?" *Harvard International Journal of Press/Politics 9*(1): 41–59.

Dovi, Suzanne. 2002. "Preferable Descriptive Representatives: Will Just Any Woman, Black, or Latino Do?" *American Political Science Review 96*: 729–44.

Dyck, Joshua J., and Laura S. Hussey. 2008. "The End of Welfare as We Know It? Durable Attitudes in a Changing Information Environment." *Public Opinion Quarterly 72*(4): 589–618.

Elazar, Daniel J. 1984. *American Federalism: A View from the States*. 3rd ed. New York: Harper.

Else-Quest, Nicole M., and Janet Shibley Hyde. 2016a. "Intersectionality in Quantitative Psychological Research: I. Theoretical and Epistemological Issues." *Psychology of Women Quarterly 40*(2): 155–70.

Else-Quest, Nicole M., and Janet Shibley Hyde. 2016b. "Intersectionality in Quantitative Psychological Research: II. Methods and Techniques." *Psychology of Women Quarterly 40*(3): 319–36.

Engstrom, Richard L., and Michael D. McDonald. 1981. "The Election of Blacks to City Councils: Clarifying the Impact of Electoral Arrangements on the Seats/Population Relationship." *American Political Science Review 75*: 344–54.

Enns, Peter K., and Julianna Koch. 2013. "Public Opinion in the U.S. States: 1956 to 2010." *State Politics & Policy Quarterly 13*(3): 349–72.

Epp, Charles R., Steven Maynard-Moody, and Donald Haider-Markel. 2014. *Pulled Over: How Police Stops Define Race and Citizenship*. Chicago: University of Chicago Press.

Erikson, Robert S., Gerald C. Wright, and John P. McIver. 2006. "Public Opinion in the States: A Quarter Century of Change and Stability." In *Public Opinion in the States*, ed. Jeffrey Cohen. Stanford, CA: Stanford University Press.

Fellowes, Matthew C., and Gretchen Rowe. 2004. "Politics and the New American Welfare State." *American Journal of Political Science 48*(2): 362–73.

Fording, Richard C. 2003. "'Laboratories of Democracy' or Symbolic Politics? The Racial Origins of Welfare Reform." In *Race and the Politics of Welfare Reform*, ed. Sanford E. Schram, Joe Soss, and Richard C. Fording. Ann Arbor: University of Michigan Press, 72–97.

Foster, Carly Hayden. 2008. "The Welfare Queen: Race, Gender, Class and Public Opinion." *Race, Gender and Class 15*(3/4): 162–79.

Fox, Cybelle. 2004. "The Changing Color of Welfare? How Whites' Attitudes toward Latinos Influence Support for Welfare." *American Journal of Sociology 110*(3): 580–625.

Fraga, Luis Ricardo, Valerie Martinez-Ebers, Linda Lopez, and Ricardo Ramírez. 2006. "Gender and Ethnicity: Patterns of Electoral Success and Legislative Advocacy among Latina and Latino State Officials in Four States." *Journal of Women, Politics & Policy 28*(3/4): 121–45.

Fraga, Lius Ricardo, Valerie Martinez-Ebers, Linda Lopez, and Ricardo Ramírez. 2008. "Representing Gender *and* Ethnicity: Strategic Intersectionality." In *Legislative Women: Getting Elected, Getting Ahead*, ed. Beth Reingold. Boulder, CO: Lynne Rienner, 157–74.

Frederick, Angela H. 2010. "'Practicing Electoral Politics in the Cracks': Intersectional Consciousness in a Latina Candidate's City Council Campaign." *Gender & Society* 24(4): 475–98.

Frederick, Angela. 2013. "Bringing Narrative In: Race–Gender Storytelling, Political Ambition, and Women's Paths to Public Office." *Journal of Women, Politics & Policy* 34(2): 113–37.

Frederick, Brian. 2009. "Are Female House Members Still More Liberal in a Polarized Era? *Congress & the Presidency* 36: 181–202.

Fridkin, Kim L., and Gina Serignese Woodall. 2005. "Different Portraits, Different Leaders? Gender Differences in U.S. Senators' Presentation of Self." In *Women and Elective Office: Past, Present, and Future.* 2nd ed., ed. Sue Thomas and Clyde Wilcox. New York: Oxford University Press.

Gamble, Katrina L. 2007. "Black Political Representation: An Examination of Legislative Activity within U.S. House Committees." *Legislative Studies Quarterly* 32: 421–47.

García, Sonia R., Valerie Martinez-Ebers, Irasema Coronado, Sharon A. Navarro, and Patricia A. Jaramillo. 2008. *Políticas: Latina Public Officials in Texas.* Austin: University of Texas Press.

Garcia Bedolla, Lisa, Katherine Tate, and Janelle Wong. 2005. "Indelible Effects: The Impact of Women of Color in the U.S. Congress." In *Women and Elective Office: Past, Present, and Future.* 2nd ed., ed. Sue Thomas and Clyde Wilcox. New York: Oxford University Press.

Gaventa, John. 1980. *Power and Powerlessness: Quiescence and Rebellion in an Appalachian Valley.* Urbana: University of Illinois Press.

Gay, Claudine, and Katherine Tate. 1998. "Doubly Bound: The Impact of Gender and Race on the Politics of Black Women." *Political Psychology* 19(1): 169–84.

Gerrity, Jessica, Tracy Osborn, and Jeanette Morehouse Mendez. 2007. "Women and Representation: A Different View of the District?" *Politics & Gender* 3: 179–200.

Gershon, Sarah Allen, Celeste Montoya, Christina Bejarano, and Nadia Brown. 2019. "Intersectional Linked Fate and Political Representation." *Politics, Groups, and Identities* 7(3): 642–53.

Giddings, Paula. 1984. *When and Where I Enter: The Impact of Black Women on Race and Sex in America.* New York: Bantam Books.

Gilens, Martin. 1999. *Why Americans Hate Welfare: Race, Media, and the Politics of Antipoverty Policy.* Chicago: University of Chicago Press.

Githens, Marianne, and Jewel L. Prestage. 1977. *A Portrait of Marginality: The Political Behavior of the American Woman.* New York: Longman.

Glenn, Evelyn Nakano. 1992. "From Servitude to Service Work: Historical Continuities in the Racial Division of Paid Reproductive Labor." *Signs* 18(1): 1–43.

Gordon, Linda. 1994. *Pitied But Not Entitled: Single Mothers and the History of Welfare, 1890–1935.* New York: Free Press.

Graham, Mark Matthew. 2001–2. "Domestic Violence and Welfare 'Reform': The Family Violence Option in Illinois." *Journal of Gender, Race, and Justice* 5(2): 433–86.

Griffin, John D. 2014. "When and Why Minority Legislators Matter." *Annual Review of Political Science* 17: 327–36.

Griffin, John. D., and Brian Newman. 2008. *Minority Report: Evaluating Political Equality in America.* Chicago: University of Chicago Press.

Grofman, Bernard, and Lisa Handley. 1989. "Black Representation: Making Sense of Electoral Geography at Different Levels of Government." *Legislative Studies Quarterly* 14: 265–79.

Grofman, Bernard, and Lisa Handley. 1991. "The Impact of the Voting Rights Act on Black Representation in Southern State Legislatures." *Legislative Studies Quarterly* 16(1): 111–28.

Grofman, Bernard, Michael Migalski, and Nicholas Noviello. 1986. "Effects of Multimember Districts on Black Representation in State Legislatures." *Review of Black Political Economy* 14: 65–78.

Grose, Christian R. 2011. *Congress in Black and White: Race and Representation in Washington and at Home*. New York: Cambridge University Press.

Guy-Sheftall, Beverly. 1995. *Words of Fire: An Anthology of African-American Feminist Thought*. New York: New Press/W.W. Norton.

Haider-Markel, Donald P. 2010. *Out and Running: Gay and Lesbian Candidates, Elections, and Policy Representation*. Washington, DC: Georgetown University Press.

Hamm, Keith E., and Gary F. Moncrief. 2008. "Legislative Politics in the States." In *Politics in the American States: A Comparative Analysis*. 9th ed., ed. Virginia Gray and Russell L. Hanson. Washington, DC: CQ Press.

Hancock, Ange-Marie. 2004. *The Politics of Disgust: The Public Identity of the Welfare Queen*. New York: New York University Press.

Hancock, Ange-Marie. 2007. "When Multiplication Doesn't Equal Quick Addition: Examining Intersectionality as a Research Paradigm." *Perspectives on Politics* 5(1): 63–79.

Hancock, Ange-Marie. 2011. *Solidarity Politics for Millennials: A Guide to Ending the Oppression Olympics*. New York: Palgrave Macmillan.

Hancock, Ange-Marie. 2013. "Empirical Intersectionality: A Tale of Two Approaches." *UC Irvine Law Review* 3: 259–96.

Hancock, Ange-Marie. 2016. *Intersectionality: An Intellectual History*. New York: Oxford University Press.

Hankivsky, Olena, and Renee Cormier. 2011. "Intersectionality and Public Policy: Some Lessons from Existing Models." *Political Research Quarterly* 64(1): 217–29.

Harding, Sandra. 1987. "The Method Question." *Hypatia* 2(3): 19–35.

Hardy-Fanta, Carol, Pei-te Lien, Dianne M. Pinderhughes, and Christine Marie Sierra. 2006. "Gender, Race, and Descriptive Representation in the United States: Findings from the Gender and Multicultural Leadership Project." *Journal of Women, Politics & Policy* 28(3/4): 7–41.

Hardy-Fanta, Carol, Pei-te Lien, Christine Marie Sierra, and Dianne M. Pinderhughes. 2007. "A New Look at Paths to Political Office: Moving Women of Color from the Margins to the Center." Paper presented at the Annual Meeting of the American Political Science Association, Chicago.

Hardy-Fanta, Carol, Pei-te Lien, Dianne M. Pinderhughes, and Christine Marie Sierra. 2016. *Contested Transformation: Race, Gender, and Political Leadership in 21st Century America*. New York: Cambridge University Press.

Hawkesworth, Mary E. 2003. "Congressional Enactments of Race-Gender: Toward a Theory of Raced-Gendered Institutions." *American Political Science Review* 97(4): 529–50.

Hawkesworth, Mary, Kathleen J. Casey, Krista Jenkins, and Katherine E. Kleeman. 2001. "Legislating By and For Women: A Comparison of the 103rd and 104th Congresses." Center for American Women and Politics (CAWP), Rutgers University. https://cawp.rutgers.edu/legislating-and-women-comparison-103rd-and-104th-congresses (Accessed 26 July 2020).

Hayes, Matthew, and Matthew V. Hibbing. 2017. "The Symbolic Benefits of Descriptive and Substantive Representation. *Political Behavior 39*(1): 31–50.

Haynie, Kerry L. 2001. *African American Legislators in the American States.* New York: Columbia University Press.

Haynie, Kerry L. 2011. "Comprendre les minorities visibles en politiqu au-dela des axes unique de la race et du genre." In *Minorities visible en politique*, ed. Estjer Benbassa. Paris, France: CNRS Editions.

Hero, Rodney E. 1998. *Faces of Inequality: Social Diversity in American Politics.* New York: Oxford University Press.

Hero, Rodney E., and Robert R. Preuhs. 2007. "Immigration and the Evolving American Welfare State: Examining Policies in the U.S. States." *American Journal of Political Science 51*(3): 498–517.

Hero, Rodney E., and Caroline J. Tolbert. 1995. "Latinos and Substantive Representation in the U.S. House of Representatives: Direct, Indirect or Nonexistent?" *American Journal of Political Science 39*: 640–52.

Higginbotham, Evelyn Brooks. 1992. "African-American Women's History and the Metalanguage of Race." *Signs 17*: 251–74.

Hill, David B. 1981. "Political Culture and Female Political Representation." *Journal of Politics 43*(1): 159–68.

Ho, Daniel E., Kosuke Imai, Gary King and Elizabeth A. Stuart. 2011. "MatchIt: Nonparametric Preprocessing for Parametric Causal Inference." *Journal of Statistical Software 42*(8): 1–28. http://www.jstatsoft.org/v42/i08/.

Hogan, Robert E. 2001. "The Influence of State and District Conditions on the Representation of Women in U.S. State Legislatures." *American Politics Research 29*(4): 4–24.

Holman, Mirya R. 2015. *Women in Politics in the American City.* Philadelphia, PA: Temple University Press.

hooks, bell. 1981. *Ain't I a Woman? Black Women and Feminism.* Boston: South End Press.

hooks, bell. 2000. *Feminist Theory: From Margin to Center.* 2nd ed. Boston: South End Press.

Hull, Gloria T., Patricia Bell Scott, and Barbara Smith, eds. 1982. *All the Women Are White, All the Blacks Are Men, But Some of Us Are Brave.* Old Westbury, NY: Feminist Press.

Htun, Mala, and S. Laurel Weldon. 2010. "When Do Governments Promote Women's Rights? A Framework for the Comparative Analysis of Sex Equality Policy." *Perspectives on Politics 8*(1): 207–16.

Iacus, Stefano M., Gary King, and Giuseppe Porro. 2012. "Causal Inference Without Balance Checking: Coarsened Exact Matching." *Political Analysis, 20*(1): 1–24. http://j.mp/2nRpUHQ.

INCITE! Women of Color Against Violence. 2006. *Color of Violence: The INCITE! Anthology.* Cambridge, MA: South End.

Jewell, Malcolm. 1982. "The Consequences of Single- and Multi-Member Districts." In *Representation and Redistricting Issues*, ed. Bernard Grofman, Arend Lijphart, Robert McKay, and Howard Scarrow. Lexington, MA: Lexington Books.

Johnson, Martin. 2001. "The Impact of Social Diversity and Racial Attitudes on Social Welfare Policy." *State Politics & Policy Quarterly 1*(1): 27–49.

Jordan-Zachery, Julia S. 2007. "Am I a Black Woman or a Woman Who Is Black? A Few Thoughts on the Meaning of Intersectionality." *Politics & Gender 3*(2): 254–63.

Jordan-Zachery, Julia S. 2008. "A Declaration of War: An Analysis of How the Invisibility of Black Women Makes Them Targets of the War on Drugs." *Journal of Women, Politics & Policy* 29(2): 231–59.

Josephson, Jyl J. 2002. "The Intersectionality of Domestic Violence and Welfare in the Lives of Poor Women." *Journal of Poverty* 6(1): 1–20.

Juenke, Eric Gonzalez, and Robert R. Preuhs. 2012. "Irreplaceable Legislators? Rethinking Minority Representatives in the New Century." *American Journal of Political Science* 56(3): 705–15.

Juenke, Eric Gonzalez, and Paru Shah. 2015. "Not the Usual Story: The Effect of Candidate Supply on Models of Latino Descriptive Representation." *Politics, Groups, and Identities* 3(3): 438–53.

Junn, Jane, and Nadia Brown. 2008. "What Revolution? Incorporating Intersectionality in Women and Politics." In *Political Women and American Democracy*, ed. Christina Wolbrecht, Karen Beckwith, and Lisa Baldez. New York: Cambridge University Press, 64–78.

Karnig, Albert K. 1979. "Black Resources and City Council Representation." *Journal of Politics* 41(1): 134–49.

Karpowitz, Christopher F., J. Quin Monson, and Jessica Robinson Preece. 2017. "How to Elect More Women: Gender and Candidate Success in a Field Experiment." *American Journal of Political Science* 61(4): 927–43.

Kaufmann, Karen M., and John R. Petrocik. 1999. "The Changing Politics of American Men: Understanding the Sources of the Gender Gap." *American Journal of Political Science* 43(3): 864–87.

Keiser, Lael. 1997. "The Influence of Women's Political Power on Bureaucratic Output: The Case of Child Support Enforcement." *British Journal of Political Science* 27(1): 136–48.

Kinder, Donald R., and Lynn M. Sanders. 1996. *Divided by Color: Racial Politics & Democratic Ideals*. Chicago: University of Chicago Press.

King, Deborah K. 1988. "Multiple Jeopardy, Multiple Consciousness: The Context of a Black Feminist Ideology." *Signs* 14(1): 42–72.

King, Gary. 1988. "Statistical Models for Political Science Even Counts: Bias in Conventional Procedures and Evidence for the Exponential Poisson Regression Model." *American Journal of Political Science* 32(3): 838–863.

King, Gary, Michael Tomz, and Jason Wittenberg. 2000. "Making the Most of Statistical Analyses: Improving Interpretation and Presentation." *American Journal of Political Science* 44(2): 347–61.

King, James D. 2002. "Single-Member Districts and the Representation of Women in American State Legislatures: The Effects of Electoral System Change." *State Politics & Policy Quarterly* 2: 161–75.

King-Meadows, Tyson, and Thomas F. Schaller. 2006. *Devolution and Black State Legislators*. Albany: State University of New York Press.

Kingdon, John W. 1984. *Agendas, Alternatives, and Public Policies*. Boston: Little, Brown.

Klarner, Carl. 2003. "The Measurement of the Partisan Balance of State Government." *State Politics & Policy Quarterly* 3(3): 309–19.

Klarner, Carl. 2018. "102slersuoacontest20181024–1.tab." *State Legislative Election Returns, 1967–2016: Restructured for Use*. https://doi.org/10.7910/DVN/DRSACA/HJFG1K, Harvard Dataverse, V1, UNF:6:eqlEaHuLdph00pTX/7yCrw== [fileUNF].

Klarner, Carl, William Berry, Thomas Carsey, Malcolm Jewell, Richard Niemi, Lynda Powell, and James Snyder. 2013. *State Legislative Election Returns (1967–2010)*. [Computer file] ICPSR34297-v1. Ann Arbor, MI: Inter-university Consortium for Political and Social Research [distributor]. doi:10.3886/ICPSR34297.v1.

Larimer, Christopher W. 2005. "The Impact of Multimember State Legislative Districts on Welfare Policy." *State Politics & Policy Quarterly* 5(3): 265–82.

Lavariega Monforti, Jessica L., Byron D'Andra Orey, and Andrew J. Conroy. 2009. "The Politics of Race, Gender, Ethnicity and Representation in the Texas Legislature." *Journal of Race & Policy* 5(1): 35–53.

Lawless, Jennifer L. 2012. *Becoming a Candidate: Political Ambition and the Decision to Run for Office*. New York: Cambridge University Press.

Legal Momentum. 2004. "Family Violence Option: State by State Summary." Washington, DC. http://www.legalmomentum.org/assets/pdfs/www6-6_appendix_d_family_violence_option.pdf. Accessed 20 May 2010.

Lien, Pei-te. 2006. "The Voting Rights Act and Its Implications for Three Non-Black Minorities." In *The Voting Rights Act: Securing the Ballot*, ed. Richard M. Valelly. Washington, DC: CQ Press.

Lien, Pei-te, and Katie E.O. Swain. 2013. "Local Executive Leaders: At the Intersection of Race and Gender." In *Women & Executive Office: Pathways & Performance*, ed. Melody Rose. Boulder, CO: Lynne Rienner.

Lilley III, William, Laurence J. DeFranco, Mark F. Bernstein, and Kari L. Ramsby. 2008. *The Almanac of State Legislative Elections: Voting and Demographics 2000–2006*. 3rd ed. Washington, DC: CQ Press.

Lombardo, Emanuela, Petra Meier, and Mieke Verloo. 2017. "Policymaking from a Gender+ Equality Perspective." *Journal of Women, Politics & Policy* 38(1): 1–19.

Long, J. Scott, and Jeremy Freese. 2006. *Regression Models for Categorical Dependent Variables Using Stata*. 2nd ed. College Station, TX: Stata Press.

Long, J. Scott, and Jeremy Freese. 2014. *Regression Models for Categorical Dependent Variables Using Stata*. 3rd ed. College Station, TX: Stata Press.

Lublin, David. 1997. *The Paradox of Representation: Racial Gerrymandering and Minority Interests in Congress*. Princeton, NJ: Princeton University Press.

Lublin, David, Thomas L. Brunell, Bernard Grofman, and Lisa Handley. 2009. "Has the Voting Rights Act Outlived Its Usefulness? In a Word, 'No.'" *Legislative Studies Quarterly* 34(4): 525–53.

MacDonald, Jason, and Erin O'Brien. 2011. "Quasi-Experimental Design, Constituency, and Advancing Women's Interests: Reexamining the Influence of Gender on Substantive Representation." *Political Research Quarterly* 64(2): 472–86.

Mansbridge, Jane. 1999. "Should African-Americans Represent African-Americans and Women Represent Women? A Contingent 'Yes.'" *Journal of Politics* 61: 628–57.

Marschall, Melissa J., and Anirudh V.S. Ruhil. 2006. "The Pomp of Power: Black Mayoralties in Urban America." *Social Science Quarterly* 87(4): 828–50.

Marschall, Melissa J., Anirudh V. S. Ruhil, and Paru R. Shah. 2010. "The New Racial Calculus: Electoral Institutions and Black Representation in Local Legislatures." *American Journal of Political Science* 54(1): 107–24.

Mason, Jennifer M. 1998. "Buying Time for Survivors of Domestic Violence: A Proposal for Implementing an Exception to Welfare Time Limits." *New York University Law Review* 73(2): 621–66.

Masuoka, Natalie. 2008. "Defining the Group: Latino Identity and Political Participation." *American Politics Research* 36(1): 33–61.

May, Vivian M. 2007. *Anna Julia Cooper, Visionary Black Feminist: A Critical Introduction*. New York: Routledge.

May, Vivian M. 2015. *Pursuing Intersectionality, Unsettling Dominant Imaginaries*. New York: Routledge.

Mayhew, David R. 1974. *Congress: The Electoral Connection*. New Haven, CT: Yale University Press.

Mayhew, David R. 1986. *Placing Parties in American Politics: Organization, Electoral Settings, and Government Activity in the Twentieth Century*. Princeton, NJ: Princeton University Press.

McCall, Leslie. 2005. "The Complexity of Intersectionality." *Signs: Journal of Women in Culture and Society* 30(3): 1771–800.

McClain, Paula D., Niambi M. Carter, and Michael C. Brady. 2005. "Gender and Black Presidential Politics: From Chisholm to Moseley Braun." *Journal of Women, Politics & Policy* 27(1/2): 51–68.

McLanahan, Sara, and Erin Kelly. 2001. "The Feminization of Poverty: Past and Future." In *Handbook of the Sociology of Gender*, ed. J. Chafetz. New York: Plenum, 127–45.

Meier, Kenneth J., Eric Gonzalez Juenke, Robert D. Wrinkle, and J. L. Polinard. 2005. "Structural Choices and Representational Biases: The Post-Election Color of Representation." *American Journal of Political Science* 49(4): 758–68.

Merolla, Jennifer, Abbylin H. Sellers, and Derek J. Fowler. 2013. "Descriptive Representation, Political Efficacy, and African Americans in the 2008 Presidential Election." *Political Psychology* 34(6): 863–75.

Mettler, Suzanne. 2000. "States' Rights, Women's Obligations: Contemporary Welfare Reform in Historical Perspective." *Women and Politics* 21: 1–34.

Mink, Gwendolyn. 1995. *The Wages of Motherhood: Inequality in the Welfare State, 1917–1942*. Ithaca, NY: Cornell University Press.

Mink, Gwendolyn. 1998. *Welfare's End*. Ithaca, NY: Cornell University Press.

Minta, Michael D. 2011. *Oversight: Representing the Interests of Blacks and Latinos in Congress*. Princeton, NJ: Princeton University Press.

Minta, Michael D., and Nadia E. Brown. 2014. "Intersecting Interests: Gender, Race, and Congressional Attention to Women's Issues." *Du Bois Review* 11(2): 253–72.

Mohanty, Chandra Talpade. 1991. "Under Western Eyes: Feminist Scholarship and Colonial Discourse." In *Third World Women and the Politics of Feminism*, ed. Chandra Talpade Mohanty, Ann Russo, and Lourdes Torres. Bloomington: Indiana University Press.

Moncrief, Gary, Lynda W. Powell, and Tim Storey. 2007. "Composition of Legislatures." In *Institutional Change in American Politics: The Case of Term Limits*, ed. Karl T. Kurtz, Bruce Cain, and Richard G. Niemi. Ann Arbor: University of Michigan Press.

Moncrief, Gary F., and Joel A. Thompson. 1992. "Electoral Structure and State Legislative Representation: A Research Note." *Journal of Politics* 54(1): 246–56.

Moncrief, Gary, Joel Thompson, and Robert Schuhmann. 1991. "Gender, Race, and the State Legislature: A Research Note on the Double Disadvantage Hypothesis." *Social Science Journal* 28(4): 481–87.

Montoya, Lisa J., Carol Hardy-Fanta, and Sonia Garcia. 2000. "Latina Politics: Gender, Participation, and Leadership." *PS: Political Science and Politics* 33(3): 555–61.

Moraga, Cherríe, and Gloria Anzaldúa, eds. 1983. *This Bridge Called My Back: Writings by Radical Women of Color.* New York: Kitchen Table, Women of Color Press.

Morel, Domingo. 2018. *Takeover: Race, Education and American Democracy.* New York: Oxford University Press.

Nakanishi, Don T., James S. Lai, and Daphne Kwok, eds. 2005–6. *National Asian Pacific American Political Almanac.* 12th ed. Los Angeles: UCLA Asian American Studies Center and the Asian Pacific American Institute for Congressional Studies.

Nash, Jennifer C. 2019. *Black Feminism Reimagined: After Intersectionality.* Durham, NC: Duke University Press.

Neubeck, Kenneth J., and Noel A. Cazenave. 2001. *Welfare Racism: Playing the Race Card Against America's Poor.* New York: Routledge.

Niven, David. 1998. *The Missing Majority: The Recruitment of Women as State Legislative Candidates.* Westport, CT: Praeger.

Norrander, Barbara, and Clyde Wilcox. 2005. "Change and Continuity in the Geography of Women State Legislators." In *Women and Elective Office: Past, Present, and Future.* 2nd ed., ed. Sue Thomas and Clyde Wilcox. New York: Oxford University Press.

O'Brien, Erin. 2004. "The Double-Edged Sword of Women's Organizing: Poverty and the Emergence of Racial and Class Differences in Women's Policy Priorities." *Women and Politics* 26(3): 25–56.

Omi, Michael, and Howard Winant. 1994. *Racial Formation in the United States: From the 1960s to the 1990s.* 2nd ed. New York: Routledge.

Orey, Byron D'Andra, Wendy Smooth, Kimberly Adams, Kish Harris-Clark. 2006. "Race and Gender Matter: Refining Models of Legislative Policy Making in State Legislatures." *Journal of Women, Politics & Policy* 28(3/4): 97–119.

Osborn, Tracy L. 2012. *How Women Represent Women: Political Parties, Gender, and Representation in the State Legislatures.* New York: Oxford University Press.

Osborn, Tracy, and Jeanette Morehouse Mendez. 2010. "Speaking as Women: Women and Floor Speeches in the Senate." *Journal of Women, Politics & Policy* 31: 1–21.

Owens, Chris T. 2005. "Black Substantive Representation in State Legislatures from 1971–1994." *Social Science Quarterly* 86(4): 779–91.

Palmer, Barbara, and Dennis Simon. 2008. *Breaking the Political Glass Ceiling: Women and Congressional Elections.* 2nd ed. New York: Routledge.

Palmer, Barbara, and Dennis Simon. 2012. *Women and Congressional Elections: A Century of Change.* Boulder, CO: Lynne Rienner.

Pantoja, Adrian D., and Gary M. Segura. 2003. "Does Ethnicity Matter? Descriptive Representation in the Statehouse and Political Alienation among Latinos." *Social Science Quarterly* 84: 441–60.

Pearce, Diana M. 1978. "The Feminization of Poverty: Women, Work, and Welfare." *Urban and Social Change Review* 11(1–2): 28–36.

Pearson, Kathryn, and Logan Dancey. 2011. "Speaking for the Underrepresented in the House of Representatives: Voicing Women's Interests in a Partisan Era." *Politics & Gender* 7(4): 493–519.

Pearson, Kathryn, and Eric McGhee. 2013. "What It Takes to Win: Questioning 'Gender Neutral' Outcomes in U.S. House Elections." *Politics & Gender* 9: 439–62.

Peffley, Mark, Jon Hurwitz, and Paul Sniderman. 1997. "Racial Stereotypes and Whites' Political Views of Blacks in the Context of Welfare and Crime." *American Journal of Political Science* 41(1): 30–60.

Phillips, Anne. 1995. *The Politics of Presence*. Oxford: Clarendon Press.

Philpot, Tasha S., and Hanes Walton Jr. 2007. "One of Our Own: Black Female Candidates and the Voters Who Support Them." *American Journal of Political Science* 51(1): 49–62.

Pitkin, Hanna Fenichel. 1967. *The Concept of Representation*. Berkeley: University of California Press.

Plotnick, Robert D., and Richard F. Winters. 1985. "A Politico-Economic Theory of Income Redistribution." *American Political Science Review* 79(2): 458–73.

Poggione, Sarah. 2004a. "Exploring Gender Differences in State Legislators' Policy Preferences." *Political Research Quarterly* 57(2): 305–14.

Poggione, Sarah. 2004b. "Legislative Organization and the Policymaking Process: The Impact of Women State Legislators on Welfare Policy." Presented at the annual meeting of the Southern Political Science Association, New Orleans.

Preuhs, Robert R. 2005. "Descriptive Representation, Legislative Leadership, and Direct Democracy: Latino Influence on English Only Laws in the States, 1984–2002." *State Politics & Policy Quarterly* 5(3): 203–24.

Preuhs, Robert R. 2006. "The Conditional Effects of Minority Descriptive Representation: Black Legislators and Policy Influence in the American States." *Journal of Politics* 68(3): 585–99.

Preuhs, Robert R. 2007. "Descriptive Representation as a Mechanism to Mitigate Policy Backlash: Latino Incorporation and Welfare Policy in the American States." *Political Research Quarterly* 69(2): 277–92.

Preuhs, Robert R., and Eric Gonzalez Juenke. 2011. "Latino U.S. State Legislators in the 1990s: Majority-Minority Districts, Minority Incorporation, and Institutional Position." *State Politics & Policy Quarterly* 11(1): 48–75.

Pyeatt, Nicholas, and Alixandra B. Yanus. 2016. "Shattering the Marble Ceiling: A Research Note on Women-Friendly State Legislative Districts." *Social Science Quarterly* 97(5): 1108–18.

Ramirez, Ricardo. 2006. *The National Latino Legislative Database Project, 1990–2006*. University of Southern California. Personal Communication (9 September 2009).

Raphael, Jody. 1999. "The Family Violence Option: An Early Assessment." *Violence against Women* 5(4): 449–66.

Reingold, Beth. 2000. *Representing Women: Sex, Gender and Legislative Behavior in Arizona and California*. Chapel Hill: University of North Carolina Press.

Reingold, Beth. 2008. "Women as Office Holders: Linking Descriptive and Substantive Representation." In *Political Women and American Democracy*, ed. Christina Wolbrecht, Karen Beckwith, and Lisa Baldez. New York: Cambridge University Press, 128–47.

Reingold, Beth. 2014. "Legislative Diversity." In *CQ Press Guide to State Politics & Policy*, ed. Richard G. Niemi and Joshua J. Dyck. Thousand Oaks, CA: CQ/Sage.

Reingold, Beth, and Jessica Harrell. 2010. "The Impact of Descriptive Representation on Women's Political Engagement: Does Party Matter?" *Political Research Quarterly* 63(2): 280–94.

Reingold, Beth, Rebecca J. Kreitzer, Tracy Osborn, and Michele L. Swers. Forthcoming. "Anti-Abortion Policymaking and Women's Representation." *Political Research Quarterly*. https://doi.org/10.1177%2F1065912920903381.

Reingold, Beth, and Adrienne R. Smith. 2012. "Welfare Policymaking and Intersections of Race, Ethnicity, and Gender in U.S. State Legislatures." *American Journal of Political Science* 56(1): 131–47.

Reingold, Beth, and Michele Swers. 2011. "An Endogenous Approach to Women's Interests: When Interests Are Interesting in and of Themselves." *Politics & Gender* 7(3): 429–35.

Richardson, Lilliard E. Jr., and Christopher A. Cooper. 2003. "The Mismeasure of MMD: Reassessing the Impact of Multi Member Districts on Descriptive Representation in U.S. State Legislatures." University of Missouri. Unpublished paper.

Richie, Beth. 2012. *Arrested Justice: Black Women, Violence, and America's Prison Nation.* New York: New York University Press.

Ritchie, Andrea J. 2006. "Law Enforcement Violence Against Women of Color" In *Color of Violence: The INCITE! Anthology*, ed. INCITE! Women of Color Against Violence. Cambridge, MA: South End.

Roberts, Dorothy E. 1997. *Killing the Black Body: Race, Reproduction, and the Meaning of Liberty.* New York: Pantheon Books.

Roberts, Dorothy E. 2002. *Shattered Bonds: The Color of Child Welfare.* New York: Basic Books.

Roberts, Dorothy E. 2006. "Feminism, Race, and Adoption Policy." In *Color of Violence: The INCITE! Anthology*, ed. INCITE! Women of Color Against Violence. Cambridge, MA: South End.

Rocca, Michael S., and Stacy B. Gordon. 2010. "The Position-taking Value of Bill Sponsorship in Congress." *Political Research Quarterly* 63(2): 387–97.

Rocca, Michael S., and Gabriel R. Sanchez. 2008. "The Effect of Race and Ethnicity on Bill Sponsorship and Cosponsorship in Congress." *American Politics Research* 36(1): 130–52.

Rocha, Rene R., Caroline J. Tolbert, Daniel C. Bowen, and Christopher J. Clark. 2010. "Race and Turnout: Does Descriptive Representation in State Legislatures Increase Minority Voting?" *Political Research Quarterly* 63: 890–907.

Rocha, Rene R., and Robert D. Wrinkle. 2011. "Gender, Ethnicity, and Support for Bilingual Education: Will Just Any Woman or Latino Do? A Contingent 'No.'" *Policy Studies Journal* 39(2): 309–28.

Rodriguez, Clara E. 2000. *Changing Race: Latinos, the Census, and the History of Ethnicity in the United States.* New York: New York University Press.

Ross, Loretta J. 2006. "The Color of Choice: White Supremacy and Reproductive Justice." In *Color of Violence: The INCITE! Anthology*, ed. INCITE! Women of Color Against Violence. Cambridge, MA: South End.

Rouse, Stella M. 2013. *Latinos in the Legislative Process: Interests and Influence.* New York: Cambridge University Press.

Rule, Wilma. 1992 "Multimember Legislative Districts: Minority and Anglo Women's and Men's Recruitment Opportunity." In *United States Electoral Systems: Their Impact on Women and Minorities*, ed. Wilma Rule and Joseph F. Zimmerman. New York: Greenwood Press.

Saint-Germain, Michelle A. 1989. "Does Their Difference Make a Difference? The Impact of Women on Public Policy in the Arizona Legislature." *Social Science Quarterly* 70: 956–68.

Sanbonmatsu, Kira. 2002. "Political Parties and the Recruitment of Women to State Legislatures." *Journal of Politics* 64(3): 791–809.

Sanbonmatsu, Kira. 2006. *Where Women Run: Gender and Party in the American States.* Ann Arbor: University of Michigan Press.

222 REFERENCES

Sanbonmatsu, Kira. 2015a. "Why Not a Woman of Color? The Candidacies of US Women of Color for Statewide Executive Office." *Oxford Handbooks Online*. https://www.oxfordhandbooks.com/view/10.1093/oxfordhb/9780199935307.001.0001/oxfordhb-9780199935307-e-43. Accessed 5 February 2020.

Sanbonmatsu, Kira. 2015b. "Electing Women of Color: The Role of Campaign Trainings." *Journal of Women, Politics & Policy* 36(2): 137–60.

Sanchez, Gabriel, and Jason L. Morin. 2011. "The Effect of Descriptive Representation on Latinos' Views of Government and of Themselves." *Social Science Quarterly* 92(2): 483–508.

Sarbaugh-Thompson, Marjorie. 2010. "Measuring 'Term Limitedness' in U.S. Multi-State Research." *State Politics & Policy Quarterly* 10(2): 199–217.

Schattschneider, E. E. 1960. *The Semisovereign People: A Realist's View of Democracy in America*. New York: Holt, Rinehart and Winston.

Schiller, Wendy. 1995. "Senators as Political Entrepreneurs: Using Bill Sponsorship to Shape Legislative Agendas." *American Journal of Political Science* 39: 186–203.

Schlesinger, Mark, and Caroline Heldman. 2001. "Gender Gap or Gender Gaps? New Perspectives on Support for Government Action and Policies." *Journal of Politics* 63(1): 59–92.

Scola, Becki. 2014. *Gender, Race, and Office Holding in the United States: Representation at the Intersections*. New York: Routledge.

Shah, Paru. 2014. "It Takes a Black Candidate: A Supply-Side Theory of Minority Representation." *Political Research Quarterly* 67(2): 266–79.

Shah, Paru, Jamil Scott, and Eric Gonzalez Juenke. 2019. "Women of Color Candidates: Examining Emergence and Success in State Legislative Elections." *Politics, Groups, and Identities* 7(2): 429–43.

Shapiro, Robert Y., and Harpreet Mahajan. 1986. "Gender Differences in Policy Preferences: A Summary of Trends from the 1960s to the 1980s." *Public Opinion Quarterly* 50(1): 42–61.

Shields, Stephanie A. 2008. "Gender: An Intersectionality Perspective." *Sex Roles* 59(5–6): 301–11.

Sigman, Rachel, and Staffan I. Lindberg. 2018. "Democracy for All: Conceptualizing and Measuring Egalitarian Democracy." *Political Science Research and Methods* 7(3): 595–612.

Silva, Andrea, and Carrie Skulley. 2019. "Always Running: Candidate Emergence among Women of Color over Time." *Political Research Quarterly* 72(2): 342–59.

Simien, Evelyn M. 2006. *Black Feminist Voices in Politics*. Albany: State University of New York Press.

Simien, Evelyn M. 2007. "Doing Intersectionality Research: From Conceptual Issues to Practical Examples." *Politics & Gender* 3(2): 264–71.

Simien, Evelyn M. 2015. *Historic Firsts: How Symbolic Empowerment Changes U.S. Politics*. New York: Oxford University Press.

Simien, Evelyn M., and Ange-Marie Hancock. 2011. "Mini–Symposium: Intersectionality Research." *Political Research Quarterly* 64(1): 185–86.

Smith, Anna Marie. 2007. *Welfare Reform and Sexual Regulation*. Cambridge: Cambridge University Press.

Smooth, Wendy G. 2006a. "African American Women and Electoral Politics: Journeying from the Shadows to the Spotlight." In *Gender and Elections: Shaping the Future of*

American Politics, ed. Susan J. Carroll and Richard L. Fox. New York: Cambridge University Press.

Smooth, Wendy. 2006b. "Intersectionality in Electoral Politics: A Mess Worth Making." *Politics & Gender* 2(3): 400–14.

Smooth, Wendy. 2008. "Gender, Race, and the Exercise of Power and Influence." In *Legislative Women: Getting Elected, Getting Ahead*, ed. Beth Reingold. Boulder, CO: Lynne Rienner, 175–96.

Smooth, Wendy. 2011. "Standing for Women? Which Women? The Substantive Representation of Women's Interests and the Research Imperative of Intersectionality." *Politics & Gender* 7(3): 436–41.

Squire, Peverill. 2007. "Measuring State Legislative Professionalism: The Squire Index Revisited." *State Politics & Policy Quarterly* 7(2): 211–27.

Soss, Joe, Meghan Condon, Matthew Holleque, and Amber Wichowsky. 2006. "The Illusion of Technique: How Method-Driven Research Leads Welfare Scholarship Astray." *Social Science Quarterly* 87(4): 798–807.

Soss, Joe, Sanford Schram, Thomas Vartanian, and Erin O'Brien. 2001. "Setting the Terms of Relief: Explaining State Policy Choices in the Devolution Revolution." *American Journal of Political Science* 45(2): 378–95.

Soss, Joe, Sanford Schram, Thomas Vartanian, and Erin O'Brien. 2003. "The Hard Line and the Color Line: Race, Welfare, and the Roots of Get-Tough Reform." In *Race and the Politics of Welfare Reform*, ed. Sanford F. Schram, Joe Soss, and Richard C. Fording. Ann Arbor: University of Michigan Press, 225–53.

Spade, Dean. 2013. "Intersectional Resistance and Law Reform." *Signs* 38(4): 1031–55.

Sparks, Holloway. 2003. "Queens, Teens, and Model Mothers." In *Race and the Politics of Welfare Reform*, ed. Sanford F. Schram, Joe Soss, and Richard C. Fording. Ann Arbor: University of Michigan Press, 171–95.

Spierings, Niels. 2012. "The Inclusion of Quantitative Techniques and Diversity in the Mainstream of Feminist Research." *European Journal of Women's Studies* 19(3): 331–47.

Stokes-Brown, Atiya Kai, and Kathleen Dolan. 2010. "Race, Gender, and Symbolic Representation: African American Female Candidates as Mobilizing Agents." *Journal of Elections, Public Opinion and Parties* 20(4): 473–94.

Strolovitch, Dara Z. 2007. *Affirmative Advocacy: Race, Class, and Gender in Interest Group Politics*. Chicago: University of Chicago Press.

Sulkin, Tracy. 2011. *The Legislative Legacy of Congressional Campaigns*. New York: Cambridge University Press.

Swain, Carol M. 1993. *Black Faces, Black Interests: The Representation of African Americans in Congress*. Cambridge, MA: Harvard University Press.

Swers, Michele L. 2002. *The Difference Women Make: The Policy Impact of Women in Congress*. Chicago: University of Chicago Press.

Swers, Michele L. 2013. *Women in the Club: Gender and Policy Making in the Senate*. Chicago: University of Chicago Press.

Swers, Michele L., and Carin Larson. 2005. "Women in Congress: Do They Act as Advocates for Women's Issues?" In *Women and Elective Office: Past, Present, and Future*. 2nd ed., ed. Sue Thomas and Clyde Wilcox. New York: Oxford University Press.

Swers, Michele L., and Stella M. Rouse. 2011. "Descriptive Representation: Understanding the Impact of Identity on Substantive Representation of Group Interests." In *The Oxford*

Handbook of the American Congress, ed. George C. Edwards III, Frances E. Lee, and Eric Schickler. Oxford: Oxford University Press.

Takash, Paule Cruz. 1997. "Breaking Barriers to Representation: Chicana/Latina Elected Officials in California." In *Women Transforming Politics: An Alternative Reader*, ed. Cathy J. Cohen, Kathleen B. Jones, and Joan C. Tronto. New York: New York University Press.

Tamerius, Karin L. 1995. "Sex, Gender, and Leadership in the Representation of Women." In *Gender Power, Leadership, and Governance*, ed. Georgia Duerst-Lahti and Rita Mae Kelly. Ann Arbor: University of Michigan Press.

Tate, Katherine. 2003. *Black Faces in the Mirror: African Americans and Their Representatives in the U.S. Congress*. Princeton, NJ: Princeton University Press.

Tausanovitch, Chris, and Christopher Warshaw. 2013. "Measuring Constituent Policy Preferences in Congress, State Legislatures, and Cities." *Journal of Politics* 75(2): 330–42.

Thomas, Sue. 1994. *How Women Legislate*. New York: Oxford University Press.

Tolbert, Caroline J., and Gertrude A. Steuernagel. 2001. "Women Lawmakers, State Mandates and Women's Health." *Women and Politics* 22(2): 1–39.

Trounstine, Jessica, and Melody E. Valdini. 2008. "The Context Matters: The Effects of Single-Member versus At-Large Districts on City Council Diversity." *American Journal of Political Science* 52(3): 554–69.

Uhlaner Carole Jean, and Becki Scola. 2015. "Collective Representation as a Mobilizer: Race/Ethnicity, Gender, and Their Intersections at the State Level." *State Politics & Policy Quarterly* 16(2): 227–63.

Verloo, Mieke. 2013. "Intersectional and Cross-Movement Politics & Policies: Reflections on Current Practices and Debates." *Signs* 38(4): 893–915.

Volden, Craig. 2002. "The Politics of Competitive Federalism: A Race to the Bottom in Welfare Benefits?" *American Journal of Political Science* 46(2): 352–63.

Volden, Craig, Alan E. Wiseman, and Dana E. Wittmer. 2013. "When Are Women More Effective Lawmakers Than Men?" *American Journal of Political Science* 57(2): 326–41.

Wallace, Sophia J. 2014. "Representing Latinos: Examining Descriptive and Substantive Representation in Congress." *Political Research Quarterly* 67(4): 917–29.

Ward, Orlanda. 2016. "Seeing Double: Race, Gender, and Coverage of Minority Women's Campaigns for the U.S. House of Representatives." *Politics & Gender* 12(2): 317–42.

Weaver, Vesla M., and Amy E. Lerman. 2010. "Political Consequences of the Carceral State." *American Political Science Review* 104(4): 817–33.

Webb, Gary. 2007. "Driving While Black: Tracking Unspoken Law-Enforcement Racism." *Esquire*, January 29. www.esquire.com/news-politics/a1223/driving-while-black0499. Accessed February 23, 2020. [Originally published as: DWB, *Esquire 131*(4) (April 1999): 118–27].

Welch, Susan, and Rebekah Herrick. 1992. "The Impact of At-Large Elections on the Representation of Minority Women." In *United States Electoral Systems: Their Impact on Women and Minorities*, ed. Wilma Rule and Joseph F. Zimmerman. New York: Greenwood Press.

Weldon, S. Laurel. 2002. *Protest, Policy, and the Problem of Violence against Women*. Pittsburgh, PA: University of Pittsburgh Press.

Weldon, S. Laurel. 2004. "The Dimensions and Policy Impact of Feminist Civil Society: Democratic Policymaking on Violence against Women in the Fifty U.S. States." *International Feminist Journal of Politics* 6(1): 1–28.

Weldon, S. Laurel. 2006. "Women's Movements, Identity Politics & Policy Impact: A Study of Policies on Violence against Women in the 50 U.S. States." *Political Research Quarterly* 58(1): 111–22.

Whitby, Kenny, and George Krause. 2001. "Race, Issue Heterogeneity, and Public Policy: The Republican Revolution in the 104th Congress and the Representation of African-American Policy Interests." *British Journal of Political Science* 31: 555–72.

Whittier, Nancy. 2016. "Carceral and Intersectional Feminism in Congress: The Violence Against Women Act, Discourse, and Policy." *Gender & Society* 30(5): 791–818.

Williams, Linda Faye. 2001. "The Civil Rights–Black Power Legacy: Black Women Elected Officials at the Local, State, and National Levels." In *Sisters in the Struggle: African American Women in the Civil Rights–Black Power Movement*, ed. Bettye Collier-Thomas and V.P. Franklin. New York: New York University Press.

Williams, Rhonda Y. 2004. *The Politics of Public Housing: Black Women's Struggles against Urban Inequality*. New York: Oxford University Press.

Williams, Melissa S. 1998. *Voice, Trust, and Memory: Marginalized Groups and the Failings of Liberal Representation*. Princeton, NJ: Princeton University Press.

Williams, Tonya M. 2016. "Why Are You Under the Skirts of Women?: Race, Gender, and Abortion Policy in the Georgia State Legislature." In *Distinct Identities: Minority Women in U.S. Politics*, ed. Nadia E. Brown and Sarah Allen Gershon. New York: Routledge.

Wilson, Walter Clark. 2010. "Descriptive Representation and Latino Interest Bill Sponsorship in Congress." *Social Science Quarterly* 91(4): 1043–62.

Wilson, Walter Clark. 2017. *From Inclusion to Influence: Latino Representation in Congress and Latino Political Incorporation in America*. Ann Arbor: University of Michigan Press.

Wolbrecht, Christina. 2002. "Female Legislators and the Women's Rights Agenda: From Feminine Mystique to Feminist Era." In *Women Transforming Congress*, ed. Cindy Simon Rosenthal. Norman: University of Oklahoma Press.

Wolff, Jonas. 2018. "Political Incorporation in Measures of Democracy: A Missing Dimension (and the Case of Bolivia)." *Democratization* 35(4): 692–708

Index

Gershon, Sarah Allen, 97, 100
Gill, Nia, 129, 131
Goldberg, Jackie, 139
Gonzales-Gutierrez, Serena, 33
Great Recession, 6, 150
group incorporation, 161, 165–66
group interests
  coding bill issue content, 71–74
  data for analysis, 68–76
  between descriptive and substantive
    representation, 16–17
  hypotheses, 64–68
  links between descriptive and
    substantive representation, 57–94
  single-axis approaches to, 60–63
group-specific issues
  bill issues, 77–82
  substantive representation and, 85–88

Hancock, Ange-Marie, 9
Hankivsky, Olena, 134
Hawkesworth, Mary, 154–55
Hawley, Judy, 139
Haynie, Kerry L., 62
hazardous waste, 135
HBCUs (Historically Black Colleges and
  Universities), 37
healthcare bills, 131–35, 137
  group interests, 61
  race-gender representation,
    65–68, 83–85
  sponsorship of, 88, 92–93
Higher Education Border Work Group, 88
Hispanics. See Latinx
Historically Black Colleges and
  Universities (HBCUs), 37
HIV/AIDS, 73, 91, 138, 176
House Research Organization (HRO), 123
human papillomavirus (HPV), 88

identities
  legislators, 98
  socially constructed and
    recognized, 38
identity politics, 12, 20
immigrants, 61, 73, 119, 132
inclusion, 2
intersectionality
  biases, 64–68

comparing single-axis approaches
  to, 147–72
intersectional models, 156, 167–70
overview, 9–14
theories of intersectional
  representation, 98–101
of welfare politics, 153
intersectional policymaking,
  18–19, 119–45
  analysis of, 123–44
  overview, 119–21
  proposals, 121–22

Joint Center for Political and Economic
  Studies, 37
Jones, Leroy, 142
Jordan-Zachery, Julia, 130

Kinder, Donald R., 61
Kinship Support Services Program, 131

Langbein, Laura, 152
Latinx, 4, 5, 140–41. See also race;
  race-gender
  citizenry, 40, 46
  in Congress advocating for women, 65
  defined, 8
  electoral ambitions of, 174
  geographic variation in descriptive
    representation, 27–30
  interest bills, 61
  intersectional proposals by, 128
  political leadership, 66
  as race-gender policy leaders, 175
  representation across gender at state
    level, 43–48
  sponsorship of bills, 93–94
  state and district population of, 40
  in state houses analysis, 41–43
  state legislators, 156
  strategic intersectionality, 99
  welfare benefits, 148
League of United Latin American Citizens
  (LULAC), 129
legislation, cross-sector, 134–35
Lexis-Nexis State Capital online
  database, 72
liberal electorates, 39
limited English proficiency (LEP), 61